I0797912

THE DEFINITIVE GUIDE TO
RIFLES, AMMO, AND OPTICS

Get the best [rifle] that you can, of course; but do not worship it. Bear in mind that, whatever its trajectory and smashing quality, it is only a gun, and can kill nothing that you miss with it.

—HORACE KEPHART, *Camping and Woodcraft*, 1917

THE DEFINITIVE GUIDE TO RIFLES, AMMO, AND OPTICS

FOR DEER AND OTHER BIG GAME

PETER J. FIDUCCIA

FOREWORD by JAY H. CASSELL

Skyhorse Publishing

Skyhorse Publishing books may be purchased in bulk at special discounts for sales promotion, corporate gifts, fund-raising, or educational purposes. Special editions can also be created to specifications. For details, contact the Special Sales Department, Skyhorse Publishing, 307 West 36th Street, 11th Floor, New York, NY 10018 or info@skyhorsepublishing.com.

Visit our website at www.skyhorsepublishing.com.
Please follow our publisher Tony Lyons on Instagram @tonylyonsisuncertain

10 9 8 7 6 5 4 3 2 1

Library of Congress Cataloging-in-Publication Data is available on file.

Cover design by David Ter-Avanesyan
Cover image credit: Winchester Ammunition

Print ISBN: 978–1–5107–5553–6
Ebook ISBN: 978–1–5107–8436–9

Printed in China

To all those who stalk white-tailed deer and other big game in the woods, fields, mountains, and deserts in an ardent search filled with heightened anticipation of a successful hunt.

May you locate the game you seek, press your cheek to your rifle stock with conviction, peer through your scope with calm assurance, and have your bullet find its mark with deadly accuracy.

Disclaimer

Please note that the information provided in chapter 3 about cartridge choices for hunting big game in North America and Africa is intended for educational and informational purposes only. The selection of a cartridge for hunting should be made based on individual preferences, experience, and the specific requirements of the hunting environment and game species targeted. It is important for hunters to familiarize themselves with and adhere to all local laws, regulations, and ethical guidelines governing hunting practices in their respective areas. Additionally, the effectiveness of a cartridge in the field may vary depending on factors such as shot placement, bullet and firearm performance, and environmental conditions. The author and publisher of this chapter accept no liability for any consequences arising from the use or misuse of the information provided herein. Always consult local authorities and seek professional guidance when making decisions related to hunting and firearm use.

Additionally, when it comes to hunting any large or especially dangerous game, the information provided in this compendium is for your consideration only. All rifle calibers, cartridges, actions, and other equipment should be selected based on personal preference and determined by each hunter after conducting careful research on potential options. The accuracy of heavy-duty rifle actions, cartridges, and bullet types depends on the hunter's ability to shoot larger cartridges accurately. In other words, the shooter must be able to manage felt recoil effectively to ensure precise shooting.

Contents

Foreword

If you picked up a copy of this new book by my long-time friend and colleague Peter J. Fiduccia, chances are you are a hunter, probably a deer hunter. After all, deer—and in particular, whitetails—are the most popular big game animals in North America. They inhabit, and are hunted in, every state in the union except for Hawaii and Alaska, where a distant relative, the blacktail deer, is hunted in such coastal islands as Kodiak and Afognak. Whitetails are also hunted in most Canadian provinces.

But think back to when you first started hunting. Were you introduced to the sport by a parent or grand-parent? A sibling? Or perhaps by a friend? No matter how you were introduced to hunting, the fact is that once you were exposed to it, it probably felt perfectly natural to you, a primal instinct that was always there coming to light. You were destined to find it.

Now think back to your first gun. Mine was a Daisy BB gun that my father bought for me and taught me how to use. Dad eventually got a Winchester .22 for me, which I would shoot at a local target range, all the while under his close guidance. In my early teens, my parents sent me to summer camp in New York's Adirondack Mountains, where I signed up for one of the riflery courses. There, under supervision of the camp counselors, I was able to shoot a Mossberg .22 at the rifle range, to my heart's content. I thrived on it, and eventually worked my way through the National Rifle Association (NRA)'s riflery program, earning a number of sharpshooter accolades in the process. I have always had a special feeling for the Mossberg .22, as I shot it so much that it almost became a part of me.

The first rifle I bought for big game hunting was a Browning .30–06 BBR. I got that in 1982, prior to a North Woods whitetail hunt. Jerry Robinson, the Gundogs editor at *Sports Afield* magazine, where I landed a job in 1979, suggested it to me, as a versatile gun that I could hunt with in a variety of situations, using a variety of cartridges. I started with 180-grain Winchester cartridge bullets, although I eventually switched to 165-grain cartridge bullets, which I felt were somewhat flatter shooting and just as lethal. I shot my first whitetail with that gun, a spike buck weighing more than 150 pounds, which I got with one shot while still-hunting down a trail in Maine's Allagash region. After gutting it out with the help of a fellow hunter who heard the shot and came to help me, I dragged that buck for a mile downhill, where I had stashed a canoe. Loading that buck into the canoe, and then paddling across the lake to our group's tent camp, was a euphoric experience. I was on cloud nine when I got back to camp and showed off my buck to the guys. I'll never forget that day. It was the first of what turned out to be a lifetime's worth of hunting memories.

That was a long time ago. Since then I have had a lot of unforgettable hunts, with rifles ranging in caliber from .223 Rems for prairie dogs to .338 Win Mags for elk in Wyoming. Hunting and firearms: Once they are in your blood, you're hooked. They become part of you.

Still, when Peter told me he was planning to write a book on rifles, ammunition, and optics for hunting whitetails and other big game, I was a bit skeptical. I knew that he certainly has the technical knowledge to write such a book; long known as a whitetail hunting authority, he has hunted big rack bucks all over the continent, from Texas to Anticosti Island in Quebec, from his beloved New York State to Montana and Wyoming. He has hunted not only whitetails, but also pronghorn antelope, mule deer, wild boars, black bear, moose, caribou, elk, and plains game in Africa. Over the years, by carefully studying the habits of the animals he hunts, he has accrued tremendous knowledge of all things hunting. Conversing with him, it's obvious he knows what he is talking about. He can talk about not only ammunition, ballistics, cartridges, and types of bullets, but also deer anatomy, hunting strategies, whitetail behavior, planting large and small food plots for deer, game preparation and cooking, and just about anything else on the subject.

But a book on rifles, ammo, and optics? Hasn't the topic already been covered by such hunting authorities as Jack O'Connor, Elmer Keith, John Wooters, Larry Koller, Jim Carmichel, David Petzal, and Grits Gresham, to name but a few? What more could Peter add to the vast storehouse of hunting knowledge? Hasn't it all been said?

As I discovered when I recently read his new book, *Rifles, Ammo, & Optics: For Deer and Other Big Game*, Peter has a lot to say. Chapter 2 is worth the price of admission all by itself. In this chapter, Peter names what he considers to be the 18 best calibers and actions a hunter might consider for whitetails, including the likes of such venerable calibers as the .243 Winchester, the .270 Win, the .280 Remington, the .30–30 (the original whitetail cartridge), the .30–06 (my personal favorite), and the .35 Whelen (perhaps overlooked by some, but more than suitable for any big game animal in North America). In discussing each of the 18, Peter covers the origins and evolution of each, its pros and cons, why it might be good for your personal hunting needs, plus why another caliber might also be considered. He also includes all of the pertinent information a hunter needs to know when deciding which rifle to take afield, including such important information as barrel lengths, bullet weights, muzzle velocity, muzzle energy, and common actions for each (bolt action vs. semi-auto and so on). Peter's knowledge on each cartridge is vast and makes you think about what you currently hunt with, and what you might consider switching to instead.

That, of course, is not all, as Peter drills down into important topics such as ammunition (what's available, in what calibers, why you should perhaps use a 150-grain cartridge in one situation and, say, a 180-grain cartridge in another), and whether you might want to use a jacketed bullet vs. a soft-point or a partition bullet. Helping the reader sort through the incredible array of what's available and make smart choices for certain calibers in certain situations is what this book is all about.

Other subjects covered in the book include actions, dealing with recoil, the importance of correctly zeroing sighting-in, shooting from the bench and in the field, taking the shot (what is too far, what is ethical, what is not), and much more.

Ultimately, as Peter stresses, when it comes to hunting, you should shoot with the gun that you are comfortable with—one that you can shoot accurately. In hunting, it's up to each hunter to know his or her firearm intimately, to practice to the point where he or she is confident when taking a shot at an animal, and to make a clean kill. Peter Fiduccia will help you achieve this goal. And, along the way, you will gain more knowledge about firearms than you ever thought possible.

I am glad I read this book. I like to think I know a fair amount about rifles and ammo, but I learned so much in my first reading that I know I'll learn even more the second time around. You can be sure it will find a home on the shelf of my hunting library, in the company of books by hunting legends such as O'Connor, Wooters, Koller, and all the others. I'm guessing it will find a comfortable home in your library as well.

—Jay H. Cassell

▲ Jay Cassell—The author's longtime friend, colleague, hunting buddy, and comrade in arms.

Preface

I like sporting guns because they are tools that help us fit into the natural puzzle;
and fine sporting guns because they are wonderful objects.
—STEPHEN BODIO, *Good Guns*, 1986

What inspired me to write this book began many decades ago when I first began reading numerous outdoor magazine articles about how big game hunting was a concoction of woodsmanship, marksmanship, the anatomy, biology, and behavior of game hunted, and the importance of owning reliable firearms equipment. The more I read, the more I realized deer hunting was not just about killing deer. It entailed much more. But first, I realized if I wanted to become a big game hunter, I had to start my journey by owning a big game rifle.

Regardless of one's age, owning your first rifle is an exhilarating and unforgettable milestone. It's a moment etched into memory incorporating the finest of details, fated for future recollection in the years to come. For me, that moment unfolded when I was seventeen years old, six decades past. It was my father, who oddly did not hunt, who ushered me into this rite of passage, guiding me to acquire my inaugural rifle—a Marlin 336 Gold Trigger lever-action .30–30 with a 20-inch barrel.

From the moment I took the rifle from its box at home, I was instantly captivated. I held it for what seemed like hours smelling its "newness," feeling its stoutness, and repeatedly working its lever action. It was a profound realization that this piece of steel and wood was now mine. I distinctly remember thinking, "This rifle is my gateway to the realm of deer hunting." A prophecy it soon fulfilled. Such is the significance of my first rifle purchase, seared into memory.

Before embarking on my first deer hunt, I outfitted my Marlin 336 with a riflescope and stocked up on Remington .30–30 130-grain Core-Lokt Round Nose cartridges. Over the next couple of deer seasons, my .30–30, nicknamed Deadeye Dan, and I pursued whitetails from the southern tip of Orange County, New York, to the most northern expanses of the Adirondack Mountains, all in an attempt to bag a whitetail buck. Deadeye Dan and I were inseparable, until a fateful afternoon unfolded.

Sitting at the base of a weathered oak tree on the vast multi-thousand-acre expanse of International Paper Company's woodlands near the tiny hamlet of Childwold, New York, bad luck found me. In a newly fallen light snowfall, I sat quietly at the base of the tree. My strategy was simplistic. I would wait quietly for an unsuspecting buck to pass by, and then I would shoot it.

The tranquil, snow-laden setting belied what was about to take place during my fourth deer hunt. Abruptly, a buck appeared. Its high, wide, four-point set of antlers sent a rush of excitement throughout my body. With bated breath, I took aim and fired at its lung area. The crack of the rifle shattered the stillness, causing the buck freeze in its tracks. Rather than instantly chambering another round and firing at the buck again, I stared dumbfounded at it as the buck indifferently looked around. I was fully expecting it to collapse to the ground. It did not! A mistake I would never make again.

My hesitation proved costly. Instead of swiftly chambering another round, I found myself locked in a gaze with the buck, its curiosity palpable. I worked the lever in an attempt to load another cartridge, but in my haste, I jammed the cartridge into the loading gate. I watched helplessly as the buck vanished into the Adirondack wilderness. After a diligent search over the new snow, I found no viable sign to indicate the bullet had hit the deer. Reluctantly, I concluded I missed it. I chalked up the entire incident to a case of the "heebie-jeebies."

The journey back to Brooklyn was laden with introspection. Recollections of Jack O'Connor's writings flooded my mind, his fervent advocacy for the *reliability* of a bolt-action rifle echoed in my thoughts. It was then that I resolved to acquire another of O'Connor's highly touted recommendations—a .270 Winchester Model 70 bolt-action rifle. I later christened her as Ol' Betsy. Thus commenced my pilgrimage into the intricacies of rifles, cartridges, and optics.

The early seventies beckoned me to Crawford, Colorado, where fate intertwined my path with Jim Curry. His friends called him "JC" A purveyor of hunting expeditions, JC guided four to six clients per week to hunt for elk or mule deer on one or the other of his two small wilderness camps. One was on Electric Mountain in the Gunnison National Forest; the other was on the West Elk Mountain range not far from the hamlet of Hotchkiss.

On occasion, I helped JC during the hunting season. I found myself immersed in the rituals of a wilderness hunt, from packing gear into panniers on horses and mules at the trailhead, to evening campfire conversations at wilderness camps at day's end. Around crackling flames, devoid of spirits (JC ran a dry camp) but rich in camaraderie, tales of the daily hunts unfolded. Amid discussions of game sightings and hunting tactics, conversations inevitably gravitated toward rifle calibers, cartridges, and optics. These nightly symposiums, though long-winded, yielded invaluable insights, complemented by the discussions of the articles of revered gun writers like Jack O'Connor and Peter Capstick.

My journey eventually culminated in a full-time career as a multimedia outdoor communicator (TV, radio, outdoor magazine articles, newspaper columns, and books). This career afforded me the privilege of field-testing a myriad of rifles, cartridges, and optics, enriching my understanding of and knowledge about of these subjects.

Over the years, I often thought about writing a book on rifles, ammunition, and optics aimed at novice and typical everyday hunters. Therefore, this tome intentionally avoids the highly specialized language and intricate information often found in texts aimed at seasoned firearm experts and those who delve deeply into these subjects. Instead, I will focus on practical, accessible information for novices, or typical Joe and Jane big game hunters.

In the realm of big game hunting, rifle actions, cartridges, and optics are indispensable allies, facilitating ethical and efficient kills. Every hunter should approach the selection of these tools with discernment and diligence, as they form the foundation of hunting success in the field.

Throughout this book, I share insights I have gathered over the past six decades. From the nuances of bullet selection to the recommendations of accurate shot placement, each chapter serves as a guide for both novice and average hunters that aspire to be more successful big game hunters.

In conclusion, I urge you to choose your big game hunting tools wisely and become intimately familiar with them. May this volume serve as a guiding light on your journey, illuminating the path to fulfillment and success in the timeless quest of stalking big game animals.

Introduction

We kill the game to eat it. Tasting it, we thank it. Thanking it, we remember it:
How we hunted it, how it tested us, how we overcame it, how it finally fell.
—CHARLES FURGUS, *A Rough Shooting Dog*, 1996

On a bone-chilling Wyoming morning, I posted myself with steadfast resolve, leaning against the sturdy frame of a wide Gambel oak tree at the edge of the woods. My vantage point overlooked a well-used deer trail a few hundred yards across a narrow ravine. The trail cut through a dense thicket of quaking aspens intermingled with deciduous trees. I'd discovered the trail two days earlier. It was heavily marked with the telltale signs of buck activity—rubs and scrapes. So on this morning, I implemented my ambush strategy well before dawn.

By late morning, I had no sightings of buck activity, but my confidence remained unshaken. I knew it was only a matter of time before a buck would pass along the trail. Around midafternoon, though, my limbs protested with gnawing cramps and my body shook badly from the bitter cold. My patience was weakening. I was in dire straits, because this day was certainly testing my mettle more than most. I had to constantly remind myself that enduring discomfort is an inherent part of the hunter's creed. So, with dogged determination, I refused to yield. I relied on my unwavering optimism to quell my discomfort and fleeting moments of doubt, resolute in my commitment to either see a buck or succumb to the frigid embrace of last legal light.

With only a couple of hours of the hunt remaining, a buck materialized from the shadowy recesses of the woods, approximately 350 yards away. With measured steps, it traversed the game trail, steadily closing the gap between us. At intervals, the buck paused to scrutinize the forest floor, likely in search of signs of a receptive doe. Seizing the opportune moment, I formulated my plan: I would wait for the buck to stop again, then take my shot as it stood broadside to me.

Despite my diminished hearing, the buck's grunts resonated clearly as it drew nearer, around 150 yards away. With practiced precision, I emitted a *low,* burp-like grunt—a ploy that lured the buck to a standstill as it glanced my way. But it was too late, I had already sent the .270 WSM 150-grain Winchester® Power Point® to the buck's shoulder blade. In an instant, it was over; the buck collapsed, its life extinguished before it knew what befell it. It wasn't a record-breaking trophy, but a respectable 10-pointer nonetheless—that gave testament to my perseverance.

As I reflected on the hunt, I couldn't help but marvel at the flawless performance of my gear: the rifle, action, cartridge, bullet design, and scope—all executed their roles with unparalleled precision. Yet, beyond the technicalities of gear, this experience underscored the profound significance of hunting, particularly the pursuit of whitetails and other big game. For hunters, the end of a big game hunting season heralds not closure, but renewed anticipation. It begins the endless countdown to the upcoming hunting season that sparks visions of taking our quarry.

As big game hunters, we immerse ourselves in the lore of the hunt, devouring every scrap of knowledge, exchanging tales with kin and comrades, all in fervent anticipation of the next adventure. This is the essence of the hunter's life—a sacred tradition, rich in camaraderie and reverence for the game and the forests. And in this pursuit, the rifle, its ammunition, and optics aren't only tools; they are extensions of a big game hunter's passion, integral to our quest for the ultimate reward, meat on the table and antlers on the wall.

▲ After a successful day afield, hunters become further gratified by preparing their own wild-game table fare. During the frigid days of winter, my favorite venison recipe is a zesty and aromatic moose or elk stew; either provides an exquisite culinary cuisine! Credit: Fiduccia Enterprises.

Chapter One

WE HUNT, WE KILL, WE EAT: The Moral Compass of the Hunter

I kill it, I grill it.
—TED NUGENT, *Kill It & Grill It*, 2002

When I am confronted by those who question my passion for hunting, whether they stand in opposition or not, I meet their gaze unflinchingly. I offer no apologies, no veiled explanations. Nor do I conform to societal norms to justify my pursuit of deer and other game. For me, hunting is not mere killing of game; it is a visceral connection to life itself. In the crisp, frost-laden dawn, I find sustenance for my soul, not discomfort. In the silence of the wild, I discover comfort, not apprehension. I confront the stark reality of mortality with each hunt, acknowledging that death is an inherent part of hunting. I am, in essence, a predator in the eyes of my prey. I hunt, I kill, and I eat. As a hunter, I embrace the primal act of the kill without reservation or excuses.

Some anthropologists theorize that six to eight million years ago a four-legged chimpanzee-like hominin, also known as a great ape, dropped from a tree. Once its feet were firmly planted on the ground, it carefully scanned the savanna from all fours looking for the presence of predators. Not being able to see over the high brush and prairie lands, it began to cautiously push through the tall grass in search of food. Without the slightest warning, a large feline predator pounced from the cover, and with a single deep bite to its prey's neck, the cat instantly snapped the small hominid's spine.

▲ Once early hominids were capable of standing on two legs and looking over the grasslands to avoid predators, their evolution as hunters began. Credit: ID 281377700 © Ianm35 | Dreamstime.com.

According to evolutionary biologists, about 4 million years ago in Africa, yet another similar primate jumped down from the canopy above. No one is sure how or why but some groups of apes, who were for the most part arboreal at that time, dropped out of the trees and began walking upright. A popular theory is that it first evolved to free the hands to carry food. Before leaving to forage for fruits and nuts, it, too, first vigilantly scrutinized the savanna grasslands in search of potential predators. By this time, however, the creature known as *Australopithecus afarensis* had evolved. Instead of looking *through* the grass on all four legs, this early hominin *stood up* on its hind legs and cast a wary eye both through and *over* the top of the grasslands. Only after she found no predators close by did *Australopithecus afarensis* have the chance to safely forage for her fruits and nuts. After gathering her bounty, she quickly walked upright back to the safety of the trees, climbed up into the canopy, and ate what she had collected.

Through the eons of time there are countless similar examples of evolutionary arms races between predators and their prey. That includes today's hunters and their prey as well, with a steady ebb and flow between hunters developing new successful hunting tactics and deer and other game eventually evolving defensive adaptations to counter them. These adaptations are often portrayed between hunter and prey as reciprocal, with prey and predator acting as two sides in a ceaseless evolutionary battle of war, a rule that science refers to as coevolution.

About 1.9 million years ago, a new, taller, longer-armed and longer-legged bipedal hominid with the body blueprint of modern humans came onto the evolutionary scene. This hominid was different from its predecessors in several ways. The crucial divergence, though, was *Homo erectus* had developed a larger brain—an engine that required more energy than just fruits and nuts could supply. So, *H. erectus* became *the* first hunter and consumer of a much heavier diet of meat.

But Mother Nature had not finished sculpting her hominid models yet. About 250,000 to 300,000 years ago (which is regarded by biologists, anthropologists, et al. as "a mere blink in evolutionary time"), Mother Nature evolved Homo erectus into the larger brained, fleet-footed, and stronger *Homo sapiens* (who were primarily hunter–gatherers). They were the hunters and

▼ During humankind's evolutionary periods, the rule of coevolution states that humans and their prey were kept in a constant state of development. Credit: ID 64241326 © Nicolas Fernandez | Dreamstime.com.

the gatherers during that era, and according to human evolutionary biologist at Harvard, Daniel Lieberman, "Our species [Homo sapiens, hunter-gatherer] was as fit as today's pro athletes." One of their most extraordinary behaviors was that they migrated from Africa around 60,000 to 90,000 years ago, and progressively and doggedly walked into every habitable crevice on planet earth.

About 10,000 years ago, during a time known as the Neolithic period, another evolutionary step forward took place. The sole hominids left on earth were *Homo sapiens* (farmer). As *H. sapiens* moved across the planet, where they could, they settled down and began to raise crops and domestic animals for food consumption to survive.

This period is the time frame I feel a genetic departure took place in our DNA makeup. A separation that I speculate defines why some of today's *Homo sapiens* hunt, and why some of them don't. A genetic marker is a gene or DNA sequence with a known location on a chromosome that can be used to identify individuals or species. It can also be described as a variation that may arise due to a mutation or alteration in the genomic loci that can be observed.

Therefore, my conjecture is that some of today's *H. sapiens* (industrial/post-industrial), a.k.a. the ultramodern "us," still harbor a functional genetic marker that keeps some of our brains strongly bonded to principally being meat-eating hunters and other *H. sapiens* bonded to simply being farmers and gatherers (nonhunters). **While there are no specific scientific facts about my supposition,** I strongly believe one exists.

For those of us who actively seek out the hunt, simply for the love of the hunt itself, must, in my mind's eye, have a hunting marker within our chromosomes. It encodes the genetic instructions responsible for why some people have a deep connection, or inherent

▼ Our earliest relatives were forced to hunt game in order to survive. Ten thousand years ago a departure took place and *Homo sapiens* transitioned from being solely hunters to hunter-gatherers. Credit: ID 45934995 © Hbcs0084 | Dreamstime.com.

desire, to hunt animals. It may well be a marker that is efficiently concealed deeply in our DNA and has not yet been identified by those in the scientific community. Realistically, biologists and other scientists are justifiably focused on identifying genome markers to help cure diseases rather than spending their valuable time trying to document a marker that compels some people to pursue the hunt, others not to, and still some to even loathe it.

Candidly, it is obvious that there is no doubt that today's hunters do not do so predominantly for food or survival anymore. As a species, we no longer have to work hard to acquire food, nor work diligently to survive. Instead, those who hunt do so instinctively to satisfy a genetic urge to hunt wild game.

In the end, this is why I believe some people are inexplicably drawn to, and have a deep connection to, the craving of the hunt. And why other people have equally confounded feelings and deep-seated aversions to hunting. To some degree, my theory about having an inherited hunting gene also explains why some people consistently excel as hunters and others have to work harder at being successful hunters. My theory is that this is all due to the coding variants in relation to hunting. Consequently, all hunters who have inherited the hunting chromosome possess an instinctive aptitude to pursue game. If you nurture the awareness, you will inevitably develop higher levels of hunting skills that are naturally coupled with more hunting success. Lastly, by embracing the hunt for what it realistically is—the killing of game—you will become a hunter to whom *the hunt* matters most.

The earliest hunters were compelled to hurl stones that were mostly ineffective at their intended quarries. The next evolution was the prehistoric human who used long spears at close distances to snuff out game like the woolly mammoth. In their urgency to hunt for food, they often lost their lives. Over time, bows and arrows were used to kill game more effectively than ever before. Today, hunters use a wide array of hunting weapons to kill their game. Without question, rifles and ammunition are *the* most effective implements ever used by hunters. Herein are numerous chapters that will help you select the right rifle, ammo, and optics to be a more highly successful and skilled hunter.

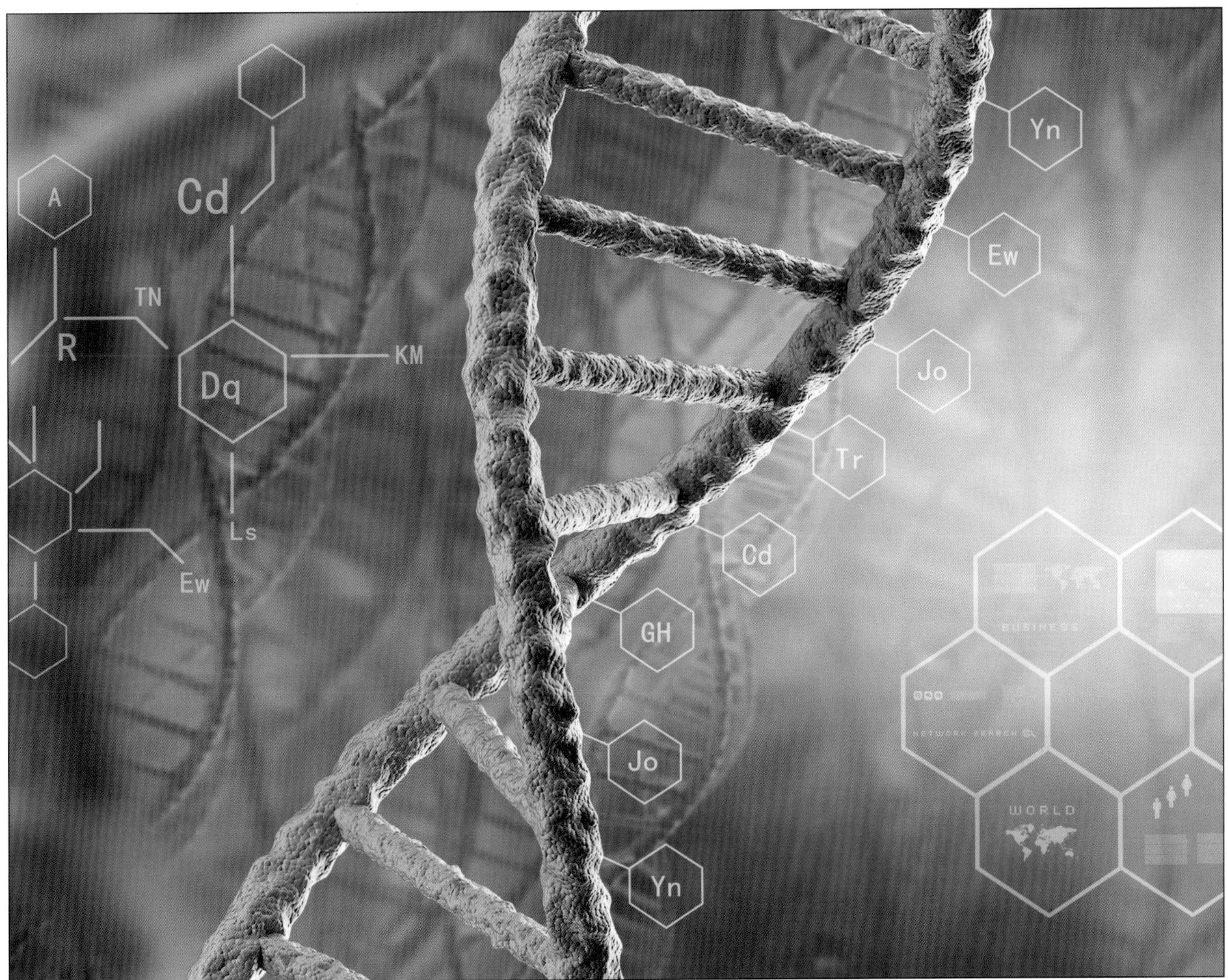

▲ I firmly believe people are drawn to hunting because of a variant in their DNA. Their desire to hunt is instinctive. Credit: ID 59808832 © Nexusplexus | Dreamstime.com

▼ The most essential elements when buying a rifle include its caliber, fit, action, bullet availability, shooting comfort, finish, and the type of game hunted with it. Credit: Browning

Chapter Two

TOP EIGHTEEN GUNS: Popular Calibers for Deer and Other Big Game

I like sporting guns because they are tools that help us fit into the natural puzzle; and fine sporting guns because they are wonderful objects.
—STEPHEN BODIO, *Good Guns,* 1986

Throughout this book when I refer to deer rifle calibers, and cartridges, I am talking about them mostly being used to hunt white-tailed deer. However, the recommendations also apply to hunting all other popular North American deer species and also include antelope, mountain goat, black bear,

▼ "Quality sporting goods stores, including big box and reliable independent retailers, have considerable choices of firearms from which to choose. Many local gun shops, like Mayhoods in Norwich, New York, provide customers with knowledgeable recommendations and advice." Credit: Fiduccia Ent.

bighorn sheep, and other big game. There is also a separate chapter on rifles and cartridges for hunting North American dangerous game such as razorback hogs, grizzly bears, Kodiak brown bears, polar bears, and other wild game that can cause serious injury or even death to a hunter.

At no time before has there been a better opportunity to buy a rifle for stalking whitetails and other big game animals. Why? Simply because many rifles today can qualify for exceeding a hunter's expectations. Mostly because over the last decade the latest designs, manufacturing, methods, and high-tech materials have set the bar of quality quite high. The choices can be mind-numbing. Selecting a caliber, action, weight, length, and stock type can leave even a gun writer bewildered. The following are some of the most popular calibers. The list, in no particular order, includes cartridges that have proven to be worthy choices beyond any doubt. The following 18 cartridges are considered the most validated big game rounds that can be trusted for hunting a wide array of big game animals throughout North America and other places in the world.

.223 REMINGTON

The .223 Rem. was created in the 1960s, and yes, it can bring down deer but only within its limitations. While some hunters claim it is an "excellent" whitetail round, an equal number claim the .223 is less than adequate for hunting deer. But that is a bit strong, and somewhat of a myth.

Factually, modern premium bullets penetrate deeper and expand more reliably than any other time in history. This has come to the forefront for small calibers like the .223 and the recent resurgence of popularity of the .243 Winchester. It's not about the laws of physics anymore, but rather that of the technological advancements of bullet technology that has developed more high-tech calibers that are better fitted for different types of hunted game animals. Therefore, such developments can be applied to the .223 as a suitable deer cartridge.

Hence, the .223 does garner a place as a deer cartridge, albeit limited to the size of the deer hunted. The cartridge depends on velocity to deliver deep penetration and considerable tissue damage. The key element though, is to make sure the impact velocities are high. Basically that means keeping shots at deer to about 150 yards. If that distance is surpassed, the velocity drops below the level needed for energetic bullet expansion.

What the .223 Remington is also revered for is its shootability. It is a small round that doesn't pack a noticeable punch. Hence, it delivers light recoil, which enhances accuracy. The .223 produces only 2- to 4-ft-lbs. of recoil energy (about a half dozen times less than a .270). Like a .243, it is best used by new or young hunters and even small-bodied adults.

Today, the .223 is touted as a *small* deer cartridge. Meaning it will kill smaller-bodied deer like Coues, Columbian, and South Texas whitetails. With that said, though, it is not a good choice for big-bodied whitetails and is not considered appropriate as a mule deer cartridge. Like any caliber cartridge, the .223 requires good shot placement in order to kill a deer quickly and humanely. Let it be known, though: because it is *not* legal to hunt deer with a .223 caliber rifle in all states, it is wise to check a state's game laws first. So, if anyone reading this wonders why I included the .223, it's because of the die-hard .223 aficionados.

BALLISTICS .223

Optimum Barrel Length: 20–24 inches
Average Bullet Weight: 64 grains (Rem)
Average Muzzle Velocity: 3,020 fps
Average Muzzle Energy: 1,296–1,300 ft-lbs.
Most Common Action: Bolt

▲ The .223 cartridge can be used to hunt light-bodied deer. An appropriate cartridge is Winchester's .223 64-grain extreme point® cartridges. However, if the .223 rifle has a slow barrel twist rate, consider using a bullet weight of 60 grains or less. Hunting with a .223 is not legal in every state; be sure to check the local game laws. Credit: Winchester Ammunition.

.243 WINCHESTER

The best place to start with the .243 is that it was created in 1955. The .243 Winchester is a sensible caliber. Because it isn't a large load, it does not pack much energy. But like any caliber, with accurate bullet placement, the .243 is quite capable of killing whitetails and smaller deer like Coues, Sitka, and South Texas deer. The .243 Winchester is also a good choice for mule deer hunting at what can be termed average midrange distances using a medium-grain expanding bullet and, of course, correct shot placement. Generally speaking, a .243 is most suited to lighter body-framed hunters, including young hunters or smaller-built men and women. But that is not to say it cannot, or should not, be used by anyone who chooses to do so.

The .243 became so popular because this caliber performs very well with light-recoiling bullets. It is also an excellent choice for hunting coyotes and other predators because of its extensive range. Its flat trajectory and accuracy allow it to shoot at various ranges. It is capable of reaching out and touching predators at 300 yards or more. The .243 is versatile in that it can kill anything from coyotes to white-tailed deer, reducing the need for hunters to have multiple rifles. The 80-grain loads are designed for varmint hunting. The 100-grain loads are designed for medium game. It should be noted that .243 cartridges, like the .223 cartridges, are not the best choice to hunt larger and heavier deer species. The .243 Winchester is an acceptable choice for mule deer hunting when (a) the game is within a midrange distance; (b) a medium-grain cartridge with an expanding bullet is used; and (c) good shot placement is executed.

The .243 cartridge is a lighter load when compared to other larger calibers. And it does not pack as much muzzle energy. A .243 cartridge can kill a whitetail effectively, yet it works most efficiently when a deer is closer than 150 yards. In my experiences with a .243, I have discovered that it does its best work on making reliable fast kills on deer at ranges within 100 to 125 yards, providing impact velocities are at or above 2,650 fps.

While it can be surprisingly accurate at 200 yards and more, the .243 cartridge cannot retain enough terminal energy to *reliably* kill a thicker-skinned, larger game animal efficiently, particularly at distances greater than 200 yards. The .243 is a good choice, though, to hunt *thin-skinned* big game, like antelope. Then its kill zone can effectively move out to 250 to 300 yards or so.

As an FYI, the .243 Winchester accommodates lightweight bullets (90 grains) that are optimized for hunting varmints at long ranges up to 300 yards. Another advantage of the .243 rifle is that it generally produces less meat damage compared to larger-caliber rifles. This can be advantageous for hunters who want to save as much meat as possible from excessive bullet damage. With the concerns of ammunition shortages these days, the .243 ammunition is widely available and tends to be more affordable compared to some larger hunting cartridges. Overall, a .243 is a practical choice for hunters who want a capable deer rifle and ammunition that will not break the piggy bank.

In the end, though, if a hunter's primary concern is knockdown power, the .243 Winchester may not be an excellent choice. Then the next logical step is to seek out a larger caliber and cartridge. As Mr. Spock from *Star Trek* might say, "Maybe the .25–06 Remington or the .257 Weatherby Magnum would be a more logical choice, Captain."

BALLISTICS .243

Optimum Barrel Length: 24 inches
Average Bullet Weight: 100 grains (Federal, BTSP)
Average Muzzle Velocity: 2,960 fps
Average Muzzle Energy: 1,945 ft-lbs.
Most Common Action: Bolt

▲ The .243 Winchester is regarded as a sensible caliber. Different types of loads are used to hunt deer and predators like coyotes and other varmints. Credit: Deposit Photos—081423

.25–06 REMINGTON

The .25–06 Remington gained popularity as a whitetail hunting rifle mostly because of its combination of high ballistic coefficient cartridges combined with high muzzle velocities. It has been said that the .25–06 may be one of the most versatile big game cartridges for North America. It is part of the family known as quarter bores, which include the .257 Roberts and the .257 Weatherby. It is by far the most popular quarter bore. Forgetting their popularity, the quarter bores do perform quite well on white-tailed deer.

The .25–06 Remington results in flat cartridge trajectory as well as retaining downrange kinetic energy. The cartridge also has long-distance abilities, availability of streamlined bullet designs, and high velocities. While the cartridge will get the job done when hunting whitetails, it is said that it can come up short, though, for larger, heavier-skinned deer such as mule deer, elk, barren-ground caribou, and eastern moose. It is also an excellent choice for hunting animals from prairie dogs to coyotes and feral hogs. For its size, it also tends to deliver a noticeable amount of recoil. The .25–06 demonstrates a lower ballistic coefficient and at longer ranges, making the bullet vulnerable to wind drift.

BALLISTICS .25–06 REMINGTON

Optimum Barrel Length: 24 inches
Average Bullet Weight: 100 grains (Core-Lokt Soft Point)
Average Muzzle Velocity: 3,200–3,400 fps
Average Muzzle Energy: 2,300–2,400 ft-lbs.
Most Common Action/s: Bolt, Semi-Auto

▼ The .25-06 has long-range capabilities due to its high velocity and flat trajectory. It can reach out and touch a whitetail in open agricultural fields or in vast open areas in the western states. What makes the .25-06 even more ideal is its light recoil, usually less than 15 ft-lbs. in an 8-pound rifle. Credit: Mossberg

.257 WEATHERBY MAGNUM

The .257 Weatherby Magnum (WBM) was developed in the early 1960s. It should not be confused with the .257 Roberts, as both are classic calibers. As famous Chef Emeril Lagasse said "Bam!" to express taking certain recipes to the next level, "Bam!" can also describe how the .257 Weatherby Magnum elevates the ballistics of the .257 Roberts. The .257 WBM can drive even the heaviest .25 caliber bullets to a muzzle velocity of about 3,300 to 2,400 fps depending on the rifle's barrel length. The .257 Weatherby Mag is known for having a very flat trajectory. How flat you ask? Well it is said you can hold it dead-on at an animal that is 300 yards away and hit it spot-on! It also has all kinds of kinetic energy. Furthermore, the .257 Weatherby Mag is renowned for its long-range capabilities. It was *specifically* designed for long-range shooting capable of delivering exceptional, spot-on accuracy, at extended ranges up to 500 yards.

Because of the cartridge's use of lighter bullets it is more prone to be used to hunt medium game species rather than heavy-skinned animals like the big dangerous bears (polar, brown, and grizzly). When this cartridge really shines is when it comes to shooting predators at extreme long distances of 500 yards. It also comes in handy when hunting pronghorn antelope at far distances.

But it is not limited to only small, thin-skinned game like pronghorns; it is also an excellent choice for hunting deer species like whitetails, mule deer, elk, and even Eastern and Shiras moose, albeit with heavier bullets ranging in weight from 100 to 115 grains. Although the .257 WBM has been used to hunt elk and moose with success in North America, some also say it is ill-advised for those deer species. Other hunters contest that statement, however, stating with accurate shot placement and the proper loads, the .257 Weatherby Magnum can hold its own for most big game in the continental United States.

Moreover, the cartridge has also had its success for those who hunt mountain sheep and goat in the Rocky Mountain States and Canadian provinces. Even where shooting distances for these two big game animals are typically extra-long, the .257 Weatherby Mag is

▲ The .257 Weatherby Magnum can be considered a cartridge that does it all. From taking a far-off western desert coyote or dropping a massive, swollen-necked northern whitetail at 250 yards, the .257 performs flawlessly. Credit: Weatherby.

quite capable of reaching those types of long ranges. Additionally, the .257 Weatherby is also an ideal cartridge for hunting plains game in Africa. The cartridge is effective when hunting impala, gemsbok, waterbuck, nyala, blesbok, and more.

For those hunters who like to get double work from their rifles, the .257 makes an ideal long-range caliber for shooting predators like coyotes, bobcat, fox, and even cougar and lynx. It is also perfect for hunting woodchucks or prairie dogs, all at long ranges. But be advised, the ammunition is not cheap, which makes using the .257 WBM as a varmint caliber, well, costly. There are, of course, better calibers for these small predators and varmints, such as the .223 or the .243, which have less-expensive ammo.

When it comes down to it, as a cartridge for deer and other big game, the .257 Weatherby Magnum has one more advantage: mild felt recoil. For this reason, and all the reasons already mentioned, the .257 WBM should not be ignored or underappreciated by big game hunters, especially those who enjoy shooting a magnum firearm. The .257 Weatherby Magnum is a near perfect choice for younger hunters or adults who are small-framed and do not enjoy dealing with the felt recoil of more traditional larger magnum calibers. One last thought about the .257 Weatherby Magnum is that if I were to compare it to other great flat-shooting, high-velocity cartridges, it would be the .25–06 Remington and one of my favorite calibers, the .264 Winchester Magnum. All of these calibers are well-suited for stalking a variety of big game animals. Hey, where are you going? Oh, I see, out to buy a .257 Weatherby Magnum, eh?

BALLISTICS .257 WEATHERBY MAGNUM

Optimum Barrel Length: 24–26 inches
Average Bullet Weight: 115 grains (Nosler Ballistic Tip)
Average Muzzle Velocity: 3,400 fps
Average Muzzle Energy: 2,950 ft-lb.
Most Common Action/s: Bolt

6.5 CREEDMOOR

The 6.5 Creedmoor was first designed by Hornady in 2007. Since then, many firearm companies have developed the 6.5 Creedmoor caliber including, but not limited to, Sig Sauer, Henry, Browning, Ruger, Mossberg, Winchester, Remington, and Savage. When at least a half dozen manufacturers produce a particular rifle caliber, you can bet it is, in fact, popular. The 6.5 Creedmoor is becoming a popular rifle caliber for hunting deer. It has a high ballistic coefficient, flat trajectory, long range, and reduced wind factor along with manageable recoil and a wide selection of bullet types.

The Creedmoor's overwhelming popularity was quickly noticed by ammunition manufacturers, and it triggered them (pun intended) to produce this load. Because of the competition between ammo companies, Creedmoor deer ammunition is very affordable—as far as ammunition prices go today.

Most, if not all, of the 6.5 Creedmoor's family of cartridges will deliver excellent accuracy and reliable expansion. Some loads, though, are designed as "more than capable" ammunition to hunt antelope, all species of deer, and even black bear. The 6.5 Creedmoor is rated as an exceptional choice for taking bighorn sheep or mountain goats as well. Here is an essential element to remember when buying ammunition for the 6.5 Creedmoor. It is wise to always select 6.5 ammo specifically designed for hunting rather than target shooting. For target shooters, it is hard to find a more accurate factory load available today. The round stays accelerated out to about 1,000 yards or more. For long-distance hunting, consider the 6.5 Creedmoor. (Note: I'm not suggesting nor endorsing shooting big game at these distances.)

There are several different brand cartridges available for the 6.5 Creedmoor. Their weights range from 120 to 143 grains. The 140 grain was specifically developed for the die-hard whitetail hunter. Hornady's Heat Shield tip, EDLX bullets come in the Precision Hunter line and deliver "match-grade accuracy out to serious range." Bullets in 140-grain weight work superbly on whitetails. The 120-grain load is a viable choice for the 6.5 Creedmoor ammo for deer, pronghorn, feral hogs, javelina, and even black bear. This ammunition uses a slightly more aerodynamic bullet than the comparable 120-grain factory load in the Barnes VOR-TX line.

BALLISTICS 6.5 CREEDMOOR

Optimum Barrel Length: 24 inches
Average Bullet Weight: 140 grains (Nosler RDF)
Average Muzzle Velocity: 2,962 fps
Average Muzzle Energy: 2,315–2,347 ft-lbs.
Most Common Action: Bolt, Semi-Auto

▲ The 6.5 Creedmoor has become a very popular cartridge for hunting big game, particularly whitetail deer. It is accurate, has mild recoil, and it is versatile. It's a good choice for shooters with small frames or those who are supersensitive to recoil. Credit: Mossberg.

6.5–284 NORMA

The 6.5–284 Norma (6.5–284 N) does everything the 6.5 Creedmoor does in the field. Some say it even performs better than the 6.5 Creedmoor. I have included it here mostly for those who like to shoot at sensible longer distances. The 6.5–284 Norma has proven to be one of the most capable rifles for long-range hunting. If you detest long-range hunting practices, don't bite my head off just yet. I do too. I discuss the morality of long-range hunting in the chapter called "How Far Is Too Far?" That being said, this cartridge can shoot far—as far as 1,200 yards! The 6.5–284 outclasses most of the other popular hunting cartridges in terms of retained weight and minimal wind drift at extreme distances. However, no sensible hunter should ever consider shooting at game at such extended distances no matter how talented of a shooter they are.

As with the 6.5 Creedmoor, bullets in the 120- to 140-grain weight range work extremely well on deer-size game. However, when hunting larger game animals, a 140-grain bullet designed for excellent controlled expansion and deep penetration will prove to be a significantly better choice.

While this cartridge has the ability to kill game at 1,000 yards and more, again, I have to ask how far is too far? Even if you are Chuck Conners from the TV show *The Rifleman*, capable of placing your first shot into a vital zone time and again, it is still an unreasonable distance to shoot wild game at, out of respect for the animals being hunted. I would bet 99.9 percent of you reading this, like me, are absolutely not capable of shooting animals at 1,000 yards or more. No offense meant here, but that is simply the truth. Hunters with a pinpoint accurate 6.5–284 Norma should use their judgment and keep their shooting distances within ethical limits.

However, with all that said, a 6.5–284 Norma is an excellent choice when hunting open-country antelope, mule deer, and mountain goat. With sturdy tri-legged shooting sticks, ranges can be achieved ethically at 300 to 400 yards without the 6.5–284 Norma even breaking a sweat! It is also an awesome cartridge for shooting coyotes at slightly longer ranges. Heck, if you must shoot game at distances longer than mentioned, at least keep it to hunting prairie dogs. These highly destructive critters can cause havoc with western terrain. So, shooting them accurately at 500 yards or more with a 6.5–284 Norma is acceptable. Finally this cartridge will also be a top-shelf selection for shooting eastern woodchucks at extended distances. For the record, the 6.5–284 Norma is dimensionally almost identical with its parent the .284 Winchester.

BALLISTICS 6.5–284 NORMA

Optimum Barrel Length: 24 inches
Average Bullet Weight: 129 grains
Average Muzzle Velocity: 2,965 fps
Average Muzzle Energy: 2,518 ft-lbs.
Most Common Action: Bolt

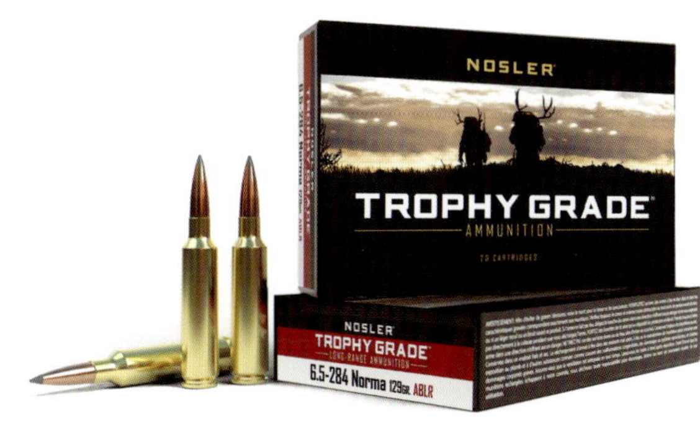

▲ The 6.5-284 Norma is rated as being an extremely accurate long-range round for hunters who shoot game at practical and ethical extended-range distances. For 1,000-yard target shooters the 6.5-284 Norma is a top choice. An improved version of the 6.5-284 was used to set a 1,000-yard world record with a 1.564-inch group. Credit: Nosler

.264 WINCHESTER MAGNUM

The .264 Winchester Magnum was introduced in 1958 and is based on the .338 Winchester Magnum case. This cartridge is a .338 Win Mag case necked down to a .264 caliber bullet. The cartridge has a reputation for being a flat-shooting, long-range cartridge that is suitable for hunting big game animals such as elk, moose, and bear. The .264 Win Mag is often overshadowed in discussions of hunting rifles in North America. However, the .264 rifle stands out as a true powerhouse within the realm of standard-length magnums, outpacing even the renowned .257 Weatherby in terms of speed and trajectory. Its undeniable punch should not be underestimated, making it a standout choice for any hunter who stalks prey from whitetails to moose. Regrettably, despite its merits, the .264 Win Mag has faded somewhat into obscurity in terms of popularity, a fate akin to that of the dinosaurs. Yet, skipping over this caliber would be a missed opportunity, as the .264 offers a wealth of benefits to hunters.

I can personally vouch for its exceptional impact, having taken down numerous mule deer, some at considerable distances, with a .264 Win Mag in hand. Like its counterpart, the .270, the .264 Win Mag reliably caters to the needs of far-shooting hunters pursuing the game mentioned above. However, it's crucial to note that to fully harness its velocity potential, a barrel length of 26 inches is recommended.

Moreover, the .264 Win Mag achieves remarkable speeds, propelling 85-grain hollow points at about 3,650 fps and 100-grain projectiles at about 3,500 fps. Opting for these lighter bullets significantly mitigates recoil, earning the caliber a reputation for being light, particularly when firing 140-grain bullets. Investing in premium ammunition is advisable, as it ensures optimal performance, especially at close ranges where high-impact velocity is paramount.

Speaking from experience, the .264 Winchester Magnum, akin to the 6.5 cartridge, boasts exceptional accuracy, effortlessly yielding Minute of Angle (MOA) groups with bullet options ranging from 129 to 140 grains. I favor the 140-grain loads that are known for reliable expansion and swift, decisive wound channels.

However, hunters must exercise caution when selecting the appropriate bullet weight for their intended game. Ultimately, the .264 Win Mag emerges as a formidable and highly efficient medium cartridge, swiftly dispatching game even at distances exceeding 250 yards. Whether targeting whitetails, mule deer, elk, caribou, or even eastern moose under typical conditions from moderate distances, the .264 Win Mag, especially when paired with a medium-grain expanding bullet and precise shot placement, proves to be a stellar choice. The .264 Win Mag pushes a 140-grain bullet at about 150 fps faster than a 6.5 Creedmoor can propel a 120-grain projectile. The added velocity, with the correct bullet, allows the .264 to maintain supersonic velocities as far out as 1,350 yards. So the .264 Winchester Magnum is an ideal choice for taking large game at ethical distances.

BALLISTICS .264 WIN MAG.

Optimum Barrel Length: 26 inches
Average Bullet Weight: 140 grains (Winchester Power Point)
Average Muzzle Velocity: 3,030 fps
Average Muzzle Energy: 2,854 ft-lbs.
Most Common Action: Bolt

▲ The .264 is an extremely accurate caliber for hunting whitetails and other deer species. The current crop of .264 hunting ammo make this a notable cartridge. I shot this buck with a .264 Winchester Model 70 XTR Sporter Win Mag. Credit: Fiduccia Ent.

.270 WINCHESTER

In 1925 the Winchester Company necked down the .30–06 to a .277 and—poof—the .270 Winchester was created. At the time, it was a flat-shooting sporting cartridge specifically designed for medium-sized and larger deer species. Its recoil was less than the .30–06 Springfield, thus helping to make it a more popular caliber back then.

My kinship with the .270 began around 1967. The Model 70 .270 Win's fame was largely due to the renowned gun writer of the time, Jack O'Connor. O'Connor's writing career started in the 1930s and he became one of the most influential gun writers of his era, contributing extensively to the "big three" magazines—*Outdoor Life*, *Sports Afield*, and *Field & Stream*—as well as other outdoor publications. During his writing career, O'Connor puffed the praises of the .270 (albeit justifiably) in nearly all of his writings. As you may have read in this or any other of my books, my relationship with the .270 Win. began after I missed an opportunity to shoot a buck when I clumsily jammed a cartridge in my Marlin lever-action .336. The next day, I took O'Connor's advice and bought 'Ol Betsey—my .270 Win. The rifle and I were inseparable for decades. I hunted throughout the Northeast and Western states with 'Ol Betsey. In fact, 'Ol Betsey is the rifle most of my son's friends used on their first deer hunts on our farm. She has performed flawlessly for more than sixty years. It would be hard for me to deny my admiration for this classic caliber.

▲ Jack O'Connor (January 22, 1902–January 20, 1978) was the shooting editor for *Outdoor Life* for thirty-one years. His extensive knowledge of cartridges made him a celebrity outdoorsman. O'Connor's zealous articles were saturated with his expert advice about cartridges, particularly the .270 Winchester, which he hunted with almost exclusively. O'Connor took a wide variety of North American big game, including giant Alaskan moose, with the .270 Win. He single-handedly influenced countless big game hunters, including me, to buy his absolute favorite caliber that he unashamedly wrote about endlessly. O'Connor's numerous writings made the .270 Winchester caliber a highly sought after caliber. Credit: Jack O'Connor

One would think the .270's popularity would have generated a myriad of cartridges—but it did not. The .270 is very similar to the .280. However, its bullets are superfast. A 130-grain bullet can reach speeds of 2,500 fps to about 3,200 fps. The average factory stock load is touted to reach 2,900 fps. Precisely loaded hand loads can push those numbers even higher.

Anyone who has hunted whitetails or other larger deer species like mule deer or elk with a .270 would almost certainly agree it performs especially well on these game animals. It has immeasurable qualities that make it a nearly perfect caliber—at least for me. Over the decades, I have witnessed countless game animals drop like they were hit by an immensely powerful single left hook to the head by the heavyweight Gerry Cooney. Additionally, for shooting game at long ranges, the .270 can compete with most any other long-range cartridge (other than the super magnums).

Today the .270 Winchester has an average bullet weight between 130 and 180 grains. For whitetail deer, an excellent cartridge choice would be a 130-grain Winchester XP. When hunting a larger deer species with a .270, then a larger cartridge like the Federal Vital-Shok 150 grain would be better. This flat shooting son of a gun (pun intended) will reach out and touch them. The following stats are for the 150-grain cartridge. The 130 grain has some impressive numbers as well with an average muzzle velocity of 3,050 fps, and an average muzzle energy of 1,500 ft-lbs.

BALLISTICS .270 WINCHESTER

Optimum Barrel Length: 22–24 inches
Average Bullet Weight: 150 grains
Average Muzzle Velocity: 2,850 fps
Average Muzzle Energy: 2,705 ft-lbs.
Most Common Action: Bolt

▲ The venerable .270 Winchester rifle cartridge, developed in 1923, is considered by many to be one of the flattest shooting cartridges then—and now. It's also known for its ability to retain energy, maintaining up to 1,500 ft-lbs. of energy at around 300-plus yards. It has taken more than its fair share of big game since its inception. It is also considered an accurate cartridge, particularly when a hunter equips the rifle with a high-quality scope such as the one seen here. Credit: TRACT Optics.

.270 WINCHESTER SHORT MAGNUM (WSM)

The .270 WSM holds a special place in my arsenal as one of my top absolute favorite calibers. It made its debut in 2002 courtesy of Winchester, and since then, I, along with many fellow hunters, have come to appreciate its compact yet potent nature. This cartridge shines in lightweight short-action rifles, delivering a remarkable combination of power and effectiveness. Capable of delivering high shock and ensuring quick kills at distances of 300 yards and beyond, the .270 WSM stands as a versatile choice for whitetails, elk, and even moose.

Compared to its predecessor, the old .270 caliber, the .270 WSM boasts superior ballistics—a fact that even causes me to apologize to my trusty "Ol' Betsey." Take, for instance, the Winchester .270 WSM 150-gr. XP3 bullet, which clocks in at 3,136 fps and approximately 3,276 ft-lbs. of muzzle energy.

My personal .270 WSM, a Kimber 8400 Classic, has seen action against a range of game, including whitetails, mule deer, caribou, elk, and numerous moose. Loaded with Winchester's Supreme Elite 150-grain XP3 cartridges, it has proven time and again its ability to handle everything from white-tailed deer to larger species without hesitation. With its consistent knockdown power, there's no doubt in my mind about its reliability.

The .270 WSM, coupled with its array of available cartridges, truly earns its reputation as a one-punch knockout specialist, provided the hunter executes accurate shot placement. I've even witnessed instances where less-than-ideal shots still resulted in a successful takedown of a bull moose or elk, underscoring the caliber's impressive stopping power.

It's worth noting that for deer, a classic grain cartridge like the 130-grain Winchester's Deer Season XP, engineered specifically for deer hunters, offers excellent performance. The Extreme Point bullet's oversize impact diameter translates to enhanced impact trauma, better energy transfer, and larger wound cavities for faster knockdown. For me, knockdown power has always been an important element. Similarly, Federal Vital-Shok 140- to 150-grain bullets serve well for whitetail, elk, and moose. However, my personal preference lies with Winchester and/or Federal 150-grain bullets, which have consistently delivered outstanding results in the field. I am entirely devoted to this cartridge. It has *never* failed to perform on any big game I have hunted with it.

▲ I have taken many big game animals using my .270 WSM with cartridges that range from 130 to 150 grains. The felt recoil is manageable, if not comfortable. It's accurate and hard-hitting. With accurate bullet placement in the shoulder, it will drop whitetails to moose in their tracks. Credit: Winchester Ammunition.

BALLISTICS .270 WSM

Optimum Barrel Length: 24 inches
Average Bullet Weight: 150 grains (Federal Vital Shok)
Average Muzzle Velocity: 3,120 fps
Average Muzzle Energy: 3,284 ft-lbs.
Most Common Action: Bolt

7MM-08 REMINGTON

The 7mm-08 Remington was created in the 1980s. It offers light recoil, which believe it or not, is often compared to a .243 or a .25–06. Its bullet diameter is similar to a .280, providing ample entry and exit wounds. It also has plenty of powder behind the bullet, which increases energy transfer loads at impact.

The 7mm-08 is a flat-shooting rifle but not a long-distance rifle. It is quite capable, though, of reaching out to 200 to 300 yards, making it another fine caliber for all deer species. Its advantage over the .243 is that it shoots heavier bullets. Its advantage over the .308 is that when the bullets are a similar weight, the 7mm-08 bullets are longer and slightly more slender, which enables them to carry their velocity and energy somewhat farther downrange than the .308. My good friend Wayne van Zwoll, PhD, of *Petersen's Hunting Magazine* wrote this about the 7mm-08, "With an efficient case design and bullet weight range suitable for most North American big game, the 7mm-08 a fine choice for all-around hunting."

Moreover, its civil recoil is a perfect match for lightweight, short-action rifles. The benefits of the 7mm-08 Remington, like the .308 Winchester, include flat trajectory, minimum recoil, terrific balance, and effective killing power for medium-bodied and larger whitetails and other deer species in North America. This holds especially true when the cartridges are matched carefully to the game hunted and good shot placement is delivered. By the way, the 7mm-08 will deliver less felt recoil than it cousin the 7mm-Rem Mag.

BALLISTICS 7MM-08 REMINGTON

Optimum Barrel Length: 20–24 inches
Average Bullet Weight: 140 grains (soft-point Core Lokt)
Average Muzzle Velocity: 2,700–2,800 fps
Average Muzzle Energy: 2,400–2,500 ft-lb.
Most Common Action: Bolt

▲ The 7mm-08 is another flat-shooting rifle with a range of about 300 yards. It is a terrific caliber for hunting whitetails and all other deer species. Its light recoil helps hunters retain their accuracy. Credit: Savage Arms.

.280 REMINGTON

The .280 Remington was introduced in 1957, making it the younger brother (or sister) of the old .270 warhorse that was released in 1925. But it never achieved the spotlight that shined on its sibling. That was mainly due to, yup, you may have guessed it already, the unwavering champion of the .270 Win., famed gun writer Jack O'Connor. He never passed up an opportunity to sing the praises of the .270 Win.

When I lived in Colorado, I first hunted big game strictly with a .270 Win. bolt-action rifle using 130-grain cartridges. As I recall, they were advertised at 3,100 fps. I never knew if that was exaggerated back then, but I was sold on buying the ammunition. In the late 1970s, I increased my growing gun collection with the addition of a .280 Remington bolt action. Like its brethren before it (the .270 Win.), it, too, was touted as a fast-shooting, relatively flat-flying, round.

In 2006, P. O. Ackley made a case modification to increase the powder and add the cartridge to Ackley's line of "Ackley Improved" cartridges—renaming the cartridge the .280 AI (Ackley Improved). Today, the .280 AI has gained more recognition than its predecessor, the outstanding .280 Remington. If you have an older .280 Remington, you can easily have a gunsmith convert the chamber to a .280 AI. Or, like I have done, keep it as it was first intended to be, an excellent rifle that utilizes many superb cartridges.

Additionally, it is capable of developing energy almost identical to the .30–06. But its lighter bullets provide a better ballistic coefficient. A .280 produces ideal performance with 140- to 150-grain bullets. It will deliver deep penetration, especially when using other bullets like the Sierra 170 grain, the Pro-Hunter 160 grain, the 175-grain GameKing bullets, 150-grain Scirocco, 154-grain Interbond, or 160-grain Nosler Partition. All of these cartridges provide excellent results when hunting medium- to tough-skinned game, even at extended ranges up to 300 yards.

I have had consistent success hunting with the .280. I took a dandy 7x7 bull elk at Northern Wildlife Ventures in Debden, Saskatchewan at just under 300 yards with my .280. While this was an unusually long shot for me, the bull was broadside and standing still. I fired a single 140-grain bullet that hit the bull's scapula. The bullet penetrated deeply through the one shoulder and made a sizeable bone-crushing impact on the opposite shoulder, shattering both scapulas.

BALLISTICS .280 REMINGTON

Optimum Barrel Length: 24–26 inches
Average Bullet Weight: 140 grains
Average Muzzle Velocity: 3,040 fps
Average Muzzle Energy: 2,872 ft-lbs.
Most Common Action: Bolt

▲ The .280 Remington never attained the popularity that the .270 Winchester enjoyed, mostly due to dismal marketing. It is little known though that the .280 Rem beats the performance of the .270 Win, 7mm-08 Rem, .30-06 Springfield, and other calibers. The .280 Rem is quite capable of taking even the largest of deer species like the bull elk seen here. In my view, it is a terrific cartridge. Credit: Fiduccia Ent.

7MM REMINGTON MAGNUM

The 7mm Remington Magnum (7mm Rem Mag) rifle cartridge was introduced as a commercially available round in 1962. This cartridge couldn't be excluded from this roundup as it is one of the most popular big game cartridges. I hold great esteem for it. With cartridges in the 140- to 150-grain range, it doesn't perform greater than ordinary cartridges including the .30–06 or .270, using comparable-weight bullets. However, when the projectiles become heavier, that's when the 7mm Rem Mag comes to the forefront.

The 7mm (.284) diameter bullets are inherently more aerodynamic, at least in common weights, than their somewhat fatter colleagues. The magnum versions of those fatter cousins hit harder, due to a larger frontal diameter and increased bullet weight. But for most hunters, including seasoned veteran hunters, the 7mm Rem. Mag is easier to shoot mostly due to its less recoil.

The 7mm Remington Magnum is a resourceful hunting cartridge used to hunt big game throughout North America, including whitetail deer and all other deer species. It's also a good choice in open-country hunting when stalking mule deer, sheep, and goat. It can even be used to hunt all African plains game.

The 7mm Rem Mag is widely known as a do-it-all type cartridge for big game hunting. It can be loaded light with smaller 140- to 150-grain bullets pushing 3,200 fps muzzle velocity for thinner-skinned animals like whitetail deer or pronghorns. Or it can be loaded with heavier bullets up to 175 grains, where it can reach about 2,800 fps out of the muzzle. Again, this makes the 7mm Rem Mag a great choice for larger deer species like moose or elk and even tough African game.

When considering the 7mm Remington Mag's felt recoil, it offers a nice combination of delivered energy, flat shooting characteristics, and manageable recoil. I own a 7mm Rem Mag and, having shot it on many hunts, I can attest to its recoil as being very manageable. All in all, the 7mm Remington Magnum is a powerful, versatile cartridge that is popular among hunters and long-range shooters. There is no denying that its flat trajectory, high velocity, and energy transfer make it an excellent choice.

▲ While hunting moose in Newfoundland, I spotted this giant black bear walking across a bog several hundred yards away. I used a moose calf alarm-distress call that brought the bear in to about a hundred yards. I was hunting with Hornady 150-grain CX cartridges, and my shot dropped the bear in its tracks. The bear missed Boone & Crockett by 3/8 of an inch. Credit: Jay Cassell.

BALLISTICS .7MM REM MAG.

Optimum Barrel Length: 26–28 inches
Average Bullet Weight: 140 to 175 grains
Average Muzzle Velocity: An impressive 3,150 fps
Average Muzzle Energy: 2,997 ft-lbs.
Most Common Action: Bolt

.30–30 WINCHESTER

The .30–30 Win. has been around for 125 years. It is, without a doubt, the original whitetail cartridge—bar none. No other known cartridge can claim that it has stood up to the test of time as well as the .30–30 has in its lifespan. It has been claimed to be the most famous and popular hunting rifle. It has been touted to have killed more whitetail deer than any other rifle—ever. I am not sure if this claim is true or not, but it was my sole reason for buying my first .30–30 rifle more than 60 years ago.

Since its inception, the .30–30 has continued to be produced and remains a popular choice today. Undoubtedly, countless hunters, me included, began their hunting journeys with a .30–30 lever-action rifle. Even now, it stands out as an exceptionally reliable caliber.

It is quite dependable for killing whitetails and other deer species up to 200 yards away, but only when it is paired with an appropriate quality cartridge. It is not designed to be a solid choice at distances more than that, however. The .30–30 is known for having moderate recoil. Ammo is abundant and affordable.

Henry Repeating Arms, Winchester Repeating Arms, Marlin Firearms, Browning Firearms, and others manufacture lever-action .30–30 rifles. Some gun writers are not big fans of the .30–30's ballistics. One way or the other, for me, the .30–30 is a fine deer rifle.

BALLISTICS .30–30 WINCHESTER

Optimum Barrel Length: 24–26 inches
Average Bullet Weight: 150 grains (Barnes Pioneer)
Average Muzzle Velocity: 2,335 fps
Average Muzzle Energy: 1,800–1,816 ft-lbs.
Most Common Action: Lever

▲ The esteemed .30-30 Winchester outperforms the .30-06 and .308 at 100 yards. It can be used to hunt all species of deer at short to moderate ranges including whitetails, mule deer, elk, caribou, moose, black bear, cougar, and feral hogs. It is claimed almost all hunters own or have owned a .30-30 rifle. Credit: Fiduccia Ent.

.308 WINCHESTER

This venerable 70-year-old caliber stands as a perennial favorite across a spectrum of hunting scenarios. The .308 Winchester cartridge boasts exceptional versatility, proving itself capable against all deer species and even certain larger game animals. Despite exhibiting more bullet-drop and marginally less energy compared to the .270 or the .30–06, the .308 Win demands respect with its formidable knockdown power—a force akin to the blow of Thor's hammer.

While some calibers may offer reduced recoil, the .308 Winchester maintains a reputation for manageable kick, particularly when contrasted with larger calibers. My wife and I can personally attest to its effectiveness in bringing down a variety of large game species, relying on quality 150-grain cartridges. Whether targeting eastern moose, elk, caribou, mule deer, or black bear, each animal succumbed swiftly to the .308 Winchester, underscoring its undeniable knockdown prowess with each well-placed shot.

In terms of ammunition availability, the .308 stands among the most accessible, alongside the venerable .30–06. Renowned for its deadly accuracy, the .308 holds the distinction of being regarded as the most precise among commercially manufactured .30 caliber cartridges. In sum, the .308 Winchester caliber rifle offers a harmonious blend of power, accuracy, versatility, and widespread ammunition availability, cementing its status as a perennially popular choice for a wide range of big game hunting situations. My wife Kate claims she would be hard-pressed to hunt with any other caliber for big game.

BALLISTICS .308 WINCHESTER

Optimum Barrel Length: 20–22 inches
Average Bullet Weight: 150 grains
Average Muzzle Velocity: 2,700–2,800 fps
Average Muzzle Energy: 2,700–2,800 ft-lbs.
Most Common Action: Bolt, Semi-Auto

▲ A .308 Winchester is a versatile big game cartridge. Its primary advantages are increased effective range, kinetic energy, and reliable penetration. With the proper loads it can be used to hunt almost any game in North America. Credit: PCFImages.

.30–06 SPRINGFIELD

The .30–06 has surpassed being a century old. But its old age has not dampened its popularity nor its ability as a terrific all-around big game rifle caliber. In fact, it can be justifiably claimed that the .30–06 Springfield is *the* quintessential rifle caliber. It is also often referred to as the "all-American *general use* big game cartridge." By all indications, its popularity should not change any time soon. While some hunters are died-in-the-wool fans of the .30–06, others prefer similar but larger cartridge options. The reason for that is the .30–06 has lower velocities than other cartridges slightly larger than it.

However, the .30–06 is more than likely better and definitely more versatile than ever before. With a quality 150-grain bullet, it will shoot flat enough to kill any whitetail or mule deer. With a 180-grain bullet, it is spot-on for killing elk, black bear, and moose quickly and effectively. The one thing the .30–06 can undeniably lay claim to, though, is its wide array of various types of solid ammunition. The .30–06 round provides the best performance with loads ranging between 150 and 180 grains. Although it would be at its limits, the .30–06 can provide adequate results when loaded with 220-grain soft-point cartridges. Lastly, the .30–06 cartridge has a flat trajectory and excellent long-range performance, allowing hunters to take shots accurately at extended distances. With appropriate bullet selection and shot placement, it can effectively harvest game at distances of 300 yards and more.

When it comes to stopping power, the .30–06 cartridge delivers significant kinetic energy, making it capable of quickly and ethically taking down game animals with well-placed shots. Its power makes it suitable for hunting larger game species where deep penetration and expansion are necessary. When a whitetail or any of the other larger deer species is hit with a .30–06 bullet, it is pretty much a knockout blow.

BALLISTICS .30–06 SPRINGFIELD

Optimum Barrel Length: 24 inches
Average Bullet Weight: 150 grains
Average Muzzle Velocity: 2,910 fps (Federal)
Average Muzzle Energy: 2,820 ft-lbs.
Most Common Action: Bolt
Free Recoil: 17.6 ft-lbs.

▲ The .30-06 can be used to take any big game critter using 150- to 220-grain cartridges. For dangerous game, nothing less than a 220-grain load is recommended. The vast selection of ammunition accounts for the .30-06's versatility as an all-around workhorse of a big game cartridge. Credit: Leupold.

.300 WINCHESTER MAGNUM

The .300 Win Mag is considered to be one of the finest long-range whitetail and other deer species cartridges of all time. It can fire a 180-grain bullet at nearly 3,000 fps and retains 1,760 ft-lbs. of energy at a whopping distance of 350 to 500 yards. Look as you may, but it would be hard to find a better long-range performer.

The downside is that there is a price to pay for that kind of performance and power. It is called (ouch) *felt* recoil punishment. There, I said it. Its recoil and muzzle blast are noticeably harsh. There are few hunters who can withstand that kind of punishment and still shoot the rifle without flinching. I am counting myself among them. Unfortunately, we all know where flinching leads—either to missing the game or, worse yet, making a poor shot and wounding it. Therefore, when hunting with a .300 Win Mag, it is highly recommended to mitigate the heavy recoil by using a quality suppressor, muzzle brake, or blast shield (where it is legal), and include a high-end butt stock recoil pad. In doing so, you will be able to eliminate flinching and increase accuracy.

If you enjoy long-range shooting and don't mind spending a bit more money to buy this caliber, the .300 Winchester Magnum is a top choice. It has some notable advantages. It is a versatile caliber where a hunter can use the same rifle and cartridge for a variety of big game hunting trips without compromising performance. In fact, the .300 Win Mag's high velocity and energy retention make it less subject to wind drift and bullet drop compared to lighter calibers. In so doing, it makes it an excellent choice for hunting deer in windy or adverse weather conditions. It delivers an incredible amount of energy transfer at the point of impact, resulting in the UFC/MMA round-kick to the head knockdown-and-out power of heavyweight MMA fighter Francis Ngannou.

The .300 Win Mag is also well known as a lethal elk dropper and a fatal moose crusher. Moreover, it can take down even larger big game like grizzly and brown bear. However, you'll want to use a properly constructed bullet like Barnes TSX, TTSX, LRX, Nosler partition, Accubond, Swift a-frame, or Scirocco II. This caliber may not always achieve a pass-through, but it delivers substantial energy upon impact, providing significant knockdown power. Although the most popular action for this caliber is a bolt action, the semi-auto actions are popular as well.

One of the newest bolt-action additions to the .300 Win Mag manufactured is Browning's X-Bolt 2 Speed SPR (also available in other calibers). It is a honey of a rifle that big game hunters will prize owning. Consequently, you may not want to overlook Browning's X-Bolt.

▲ The Winchester .300 Mag's claim to fame is its deadly speed and knockdown power. It is one of the most versatile calibers for big game hunting, as it's more than capable of taking whitetails and mule deer, and also quite proficient at taking down the larger big game like elk, moose, and the great bears. Credit: Fiduccia Ent.

If knockdown power is high on your preference list, though, rush out and buy a .300 Win Mag. Keep in mind that when the .300 Win Mag is used to hunt whitetails, it is certainly more gun than is needed to drop one in its tracks. And, when shooting whitetails at short ranges, depending upon bullet placement, it can create a lot of meat tissue damage. But for larger deer species and other big game the .300 Win Mag is an excellent choice.

BALLISTICS .300 WIN MAG

Optimum Barrel Length: 26–28 inches
Average Bullet Weight: 150 grains (Winchester Mag)
Average Muzzle Velocity: 3,260 fps
Average Muzzle Energy: 3,900–4,000 ft-lbs. (you read that correctly)
Most Common Action: Bolt
Free Recoil: About 30-ft lbs.

▲ The 190-grain 300 Winchester Magnum is considered effective for large game like elk, moose, bear, etc., at long distances. This load is specifically designed for big game hunting and features a Nosler Accubond long range bullet known for its deep penetration and controlled expansion. Credit: Winchester Ammunition.

.338 FEDERAL

I hold the .338 Federal in high esteem. Why? Because its cartridges have bullets that range from light to heavy. The lighter bullets can be used very successfully for deer and the heavier bullets will do the job nicely on Cape buffalo. The lighter bullets are faster and more versatile; the heavier bullets smack game harder and penetrate more deeply. The .338 also can be used for long-distance ranges that most hunters would generally shy away from.

The Federal .338 is a rifle cartridge founded on the parent case of the .308 Winchester case necked up to .33 caliber. It was developed in a joint effort between Federal Cartridge and Sako Rifle Company in 2006. Heed this: the .338 Federal can ultimately be one of the smartest choices made by a big game hunter, especially if one likes or requires a lightweight, pleasant-to-shoot, short-action rifle. For instance, my Kimber Model 84M .338 Federal Montana weighs just over five pounds.

The .338 Federal performs well using bullets that weigh between 180 and 225 grains. It is these lighter bullets in this caliber that have a muzzle velocity of 2,750 and 2,650 fps, respectively, that perform exceptionally well. In the aforementioned grains it is a remarkably effective choice as an all-around big game rifle and cartridge. However, the heavier the cartridge, the harder the recoil. Again, it is highly recommended to mitigate the heavy recoil by using a quality suppressor, muzzle brake, or blast shield, and include a high-end butt stock recoil pad. In doing so, you will be able to eliminate flinching and increase accuracy.

When shooting lighter load groups, though, the .338 Federal has much more manageable recoil and dead-on accuracy. It is a reliable, lightweight hunting rifle that can achieve a range of about 300 yards. It is unquestionably among the best deer and other big game rifle and cartridge combinations available.

When using heavier loads such as 200 to 250 grains, the .338 Federal offers "heavyweight Tyson Fury" knockout power that is, as mentioned, sufficient enough to put down a Cape buffalo. The heavier bullets will deeply penetrate, breaking even the hardest of bones. But that is not to say its 180- to 195-grain bullets are any less effective on all species of deer. If a hunter can shoot the .338 well (i.e. no flinching), he or she can even use it to make a deadly mark on a

▲ A .338 Federal shoots flatter and hits game harder than a .30-06. It's a highly efficient short-action cartridge that flattens all big game (like the hammer of Thor) including deer species, black bear, and feral hogs—and does so with less felt recoil. Credit: Fiduccia Ent.

grizzly or brown bear. But again—*only* if the right grain cartridge is used and the hunter can handle shooting the .338 Federal well.

Consider this surprising fact about the .338 Federal: it does not kick all that hard and recoils less than a .30–06 firing 180-grain bullets, making it less unkind on the shoulder. It also produces more muzzle energy than a 7mm Remington magnum pushing 160-grain bullets. Many of the .338 Federal's factory loads create more than 3,000 ft-lbs. of muzzle energy. It provides pinpoint accuracy.

The .338 Federal has an array of bullet types and weights, giving hunters more choices to tailor a type of round to a specific type of game animal. The cartridge has potent knockdown striking power for a light, short-action rifle. The Federal factory loads feature a good selection of cartridges that are competitive with other popular and effective cartridges. All of this should impress the many big game hunters who prefer the mid-caliber deer rounds, like the .35 Remington. Unfortunately, even with all those attributes the .338 Fed simply does not get the respect it deserves. The .338 Federal is a terrific cartridge, providing performance far exceeding what its looks might suggest.

Although the .338 is a highly versatile cartridge, its marketing has not effectively conveyed this to reach a broader audience. Consequently, it is not frequently sought after as a whitetail deer rifle and cartridge. That's too bad. I regard my sweet-shooting Kimber 84M .338 Federal as a quality deer rifle and cartridge. Moreover, I regard it as the ideal moose caliber. The .338 Federal checks off more boxes as an all-around big game cartridge and rifle than many other cartridges and rifles do, but not a lot of hunters recognize that. Go figure.

BALLISTICS .338 FEDERAL

Optimum Barrel Length: 22 inches
Average Bullet Weight: 160 grains
Average Muzzle Velocity: 2,900 fps
Average Muzzle Energy: 3,000 ft-lbs.
Most Common Action: Bolt

▼ The .338 Federal does not get the kudos it deserves as a whitetail deer cartridge. If you asked a hundred hunters if they agreed with that statement, most would not have an answer. That's because a majority of deer hunters have never used a .338 Federal. Credit: 34933728 © Bruce Macqueen | Dreamstime.com

.375 HOLLAND & HOLLAND MAGNUM

The .375 H&H Magnum (.375 H&H Mag) is a medium-bore rifle cartridge that was introduced in 1912 by Holland & Holland. My favorite outdoor writer, yup, you probably guessed who that would be by now, Jack O'Connor, referred to the .375 Holland & Holland Magnum as the "Queen of the Medium Bores." Since then it has become one of the top 10 most popular calibers worldwide. It is mostly used for hunting dangerous game. For more than 100 years the cartridge has boasted an indisputable record for bringing down XXXL animals. Many hunters state the .375 H&H Magnum delivers an impeccable balance of power, effectiveness, and less recoil. In fact, the recoil from this cartridge is rated as "relatively mild" when compared to larger big-bore cartridges. It is also a flat shooting cartridge capable of a trajectory up to 300 yards.

The .375 H&H Mag is an all-round cartridge when loaded with 300 to 350 grains, which is more than adequate for killing heavy, thick-skinned dangerous game. This includes the largest of Africa's Big 5: elephant, Cape buffalo, rhino, lion, and leopard. Most recently, Africa now claims a new Big 7, which adds crocodiles and the very nasty hippo.

It is said by some African professional hunters (PHs) though, that the .375 H&H Mag is considered being "under-gunned" (underpowered) for what is known in Africa as "class 4 game" like elephant, rhino, and Cape buffalo. Of course, there are larger loads from which to choose, including the .416 Rem. Mag, .458 Lott, .500 Nitro, and the game-changing, nose-bleeding, .700 Nitro Express. But the .375 H&H Mag cannot be topped for its versatility. This cartridge is a flat-shooting son of a gun (pun intended) that also delivers power, penetration, and considerably less recoil than the other cartridges mentioned.

Another terrific quality of the .375 H&H Mag is its shootability. Other faster .375s may shoot flatter and hit harder, but they also deliver much heavier recoil, which makes them all more difficult for some hunters to shoot accurately. Therefore, those who claim the .375 H&H Mag can be under-gunned would have a hard argument to make against the countless hunters who have used the .375 H&H Mag consistently to dispatch large, dangerous game animals for over a century.

Additionally, the .375 H&H Mag can do the job of knocking down life-threatening game animals of North

▼ Not even a charging Cape buffalo can frighten a .375 H&H Mag. Credit: ID 150530552 © Patrice Correia | Dreamstime.com

America. This includes the great bears: polar, extra-large Kodiak brown bears, unpredictable grizzly bears, and the hard-to-stop, ferocious wild boar. It will also put down bad tempered, volatile bison, musk ox, and giant Alaskan moose, most often in their tracks. In fact, many hunters who pursue dangerous game wherever they roam would literally not be caught dead without using a .375 H&H Mag because of these points.

Where the .375 H&H Mag also stands out, however, is with lighter loads. It is versatile enough to be used to hunt black bear, whitetails, mule deer, elk, caribou, and other game. However, it can be more gun than needed when hunting thinner-skinned game like south Texas whitetail deer. There are two different weights of bullets for the cartridge; one is 230 to 265 grains, which makes it ideal for small to medium types of wild game. The other bullet is heavier, weighing about 300 grains. It can penetrate effortlessly through any wild game considered to be thick-skinned.

Even matching up with the most high-tech cartridges designed today, the venerable .375 H&H Magnum ranks near the top of the best-known cartridges for thick-skinned dangerous game, no matter where such dangerous game roams (Africa, North America, India, etc.). The types of ammunition for the .375 H&H Mag include a 300-grain bonded or expanding monolithic bullet, a Nosler Partition, Trophy Bonded Bear claw, or a Barnes TSX.

So, is the .375 H&H Mag good for you? That's hard for me to say because there are too many variables. Hunters must do their homework to make that choice. As a wrap up, however, what I can say about the .375 H&H Mag is this: it is a terrific caliber with better-than-average performance—particularly for dangerous game. Its bone-crunching ballistics will result most often in one-shot kills. They will be the norm no matter what game is being hunted.

BALLISTICS .375 H&H MAGNUM

Optimum Barrel Length: 24 inches
Average Bullet Weight: 300 grains
Average Muzzle Velocity: 2,450–2,550 fps
Average Muzzle Energy: 2,960 ft-lbs.
Most Common Action: Bolt, single shot, double shot
Free Recoil Energy: 38 ft-lbs.

▲ The beauty of a .375 H&H Mag is only surpassed by its flawless performance afield. Credit: theexplora.com.

CONCLUSION

There are no easy answers when it comes to selecting a rifle caliber and its accompanying ammunition. While I have listed some of my favorite calibers and cartridges, there are others to choose from. All that is needed is for you to do your due diligence before making a final choice.

Remember, though, in the end, accurate shot placement is more important by leaps and bounds than the type of rifle caliber, action, cartridge, and bullet chosen. It is not required to shoot a bull moose with a powerful firearm and load such as a .300 Win Mag with a 220-grain cartridge and a designer bullet, or even a .375 H&H Mag with a 300-grain cartridge, in order to kill it. Not by a long shot. One well-placed shot from a .270, .308, or a .30–06 with a 150-grain cartridge is quite capable of killing a moose. Excellent shot placement is the name of the game in big game hunting. Therefore, it is vital for hunters to become intimately familiar with big game anatomy. We will speak more about shot placement in chapter 13.

▲ There is no doubt that straight wall cartridges provide accuracy and stopping power, albeit within their effective range. Credit: Hornady.

Chapter Three

STRAIGHT WALLS: The Benefits of Short, Fat, Powerful Cartridges

When a bullet from a straight-wall cartridge hits big game animals accurately, it causes a swift and decisive end.
—P. CODY FIDUCCIA, *Woods N' Water* (TV series), 2022

When it comes to all the terms associated with rifles and cartridges or, for that matter, anything else about hunting firearms, the jargon is nearly infinite. This includes straight-walled cartridges (SWCs or straight walls). For novices and even some experienced hunters, firearm terminology is sometimes difficult to keep up with. At times it can also be downright confusing and frustrating, too. For instance, the terminology, *mathematics,* and other related topics revolving around just the subject of ballistics can sizzle anyone's brain. In this chapter, the endgame is to simply clarify what straight-walled cartridges are and what wild game can be hunted with them.

Essentially, SWCs can be effective ammunition for hunting whitetails, other deer species, and even some robust, thick-skinned game animals like grizzly bears and other large, dangerous game, provided they are used with the proper loads and within the distance limitations of a straight-walled cartridge. However, SWCs have recently become the cat's meow for hunting white-tailed deer in states that restrict bottleneck ammunition, and even in states that do not. The key fact about *most* straight-walled cartridges is their ideal ranges are 100 to 200 yards. At those distances, their velocity holds up and provides accuracy and power. Over that distance things can get dicey because SWCs are large and heavy—making them prone to drop rapidly. With that said, though, SWCs have recently been developed to push their accuracy to 300 yards or slightly more. But there is more to the narrative about straight-walled cartridges.

▲ All straight-walled cartridges are loaded to be big bad brutes. They are capable of taking a wide range of game from whitetails to Kodiak brown bears. The caution here is such game all has to be within a straight-walled cartridge's distance limitations. Credit: Fiduccia Ent.

THE CARTRIDGE DESIGN

Within the overall distinct types of cartridges, the two primary varieties of cartridge case designs include bottleneck and straight-walled cases. What makes SWCs *distinctive* is that they do not taper or have a shoulder on the case. Instead, a straight-walled cartridge has the same diameter throughout the entire length of its case, while bottleneck ammunition is tapered toward the bullet's neck. Bottleneck ammunition is also called "necked down"; this design essentially means that the base and rim diameters are significantly wider than the neck of the cartridge. Technically speaking, the cartridge diameter will always be slightly narrower. Since there is more available volume in the case behind the bullet, this design allows for more velocity and energy than straight-walled cartridges. Therefore, SWCs were given their moniker because of the specific shape of the cartridge itself.

Here is an example of this: a bottleneck .308 Winchester cartridge has a base diameter of .4709 inches and a neck diameter of .3433 inches. A .444 Marlin straight-walled cartridge has a base of .4706 inches and a neck diameter of .453 inches. It becomes obvious that the .308 Winchester significantly narrows at the neck while the .444 Marlin hardly narrows at all.

WHERE THEY ARE USED

For many years, some states had game laws that required shotgun-only regulations for hunting deer. The use of shotguns in these states was due mostly, if not entirely, to safety concerns of shooting typical bottleneck ammunition at much longer distances, particularly when hunting in open, flatter landscapes. Some of these states included Iowa, Ohio, Michigan, and Illinois. Today, many states have reformed the shotgun-only law and have embraced centerfire, straight-walled rifle cartridges for deer hunting. That escalated SWCs popularity tenfold. Furthermore, straight-walled cartridges have provided a significant alternative to hard-kicking shotguns, even when shotguns are loaded with quality slugs and sabots.

Straight wall regulations can vary from state to state. For example, Minnesota may allow straight-walled cartridges in certain hunting areas, but not throughout the entire state's hunting zones. Some states allow SWCs for hunting on private land, but not on public property. In Iowa, straight-walled cartridges can only be used when deer hunting during the special youth and disabled hunting seasons, and the first and second shotgun seasons. In Ohio, deer hunters can use straight-walled cartridges with bullets measuring from .357 to .50 inches in diameter and hunters cannot carry firearms loaded with more than three rounds.

There are also some states that only regulate the length and caliber of straight-walled cartridges. For instance, in Michigan, a straight-walled cartridge case excluding the bullet, must be between 1.16 and 1.8 inches and .35 caliber or larger. There are even regulations about what types of rifle actions are allowed when shooting straight-walled cartridges that vary from state to state.

Furthermore, as if this all wasn't enough, each state may have different designations for straight-walled cartridges. Such standards include velocity, bullet diameter, case sizes, and other factors. Consequently, it is absolutely vital and wise to check each state's straight-walled regulations *thoroughly* prior to hunting.

POPULARITY

Straight-walled cartridges were once regarded as a novelty (or afterthought) by most hunters. However, as noted, straight-walled cartridges have become *significantly* more popular. One reason can be attributed to the fact that straight-walled cartridges include, but are not limited to, a variety of cartridges, including the .360 Buckhammer, .350 Legend, .444 Marlin, .45–70 Government, .400 Legend, and the .50 Beowulf.

Another point that lends itself to the popularity of straight-walled cartridges is that there are now many AR-platform rifles being manufactured specifically for these rounds. Hence, if straight-walled cartridges are legal for use in your area, you are now presented with the option of using any of the dozen or more SWCs instead of your trusty shotgun for hunting deer and other game animals. The main advantage of a straight-walled round compared to a slug fired from a shotgun is the SWC's deadly accuracy. Gun writers and hunters have come to accept that straight-walled rounds are more reliable, powerful, and accurate, offering greater range than shotgun slugs. Compared to the plastic-hulled shotshell slugs or one-shot muzzleloaders,

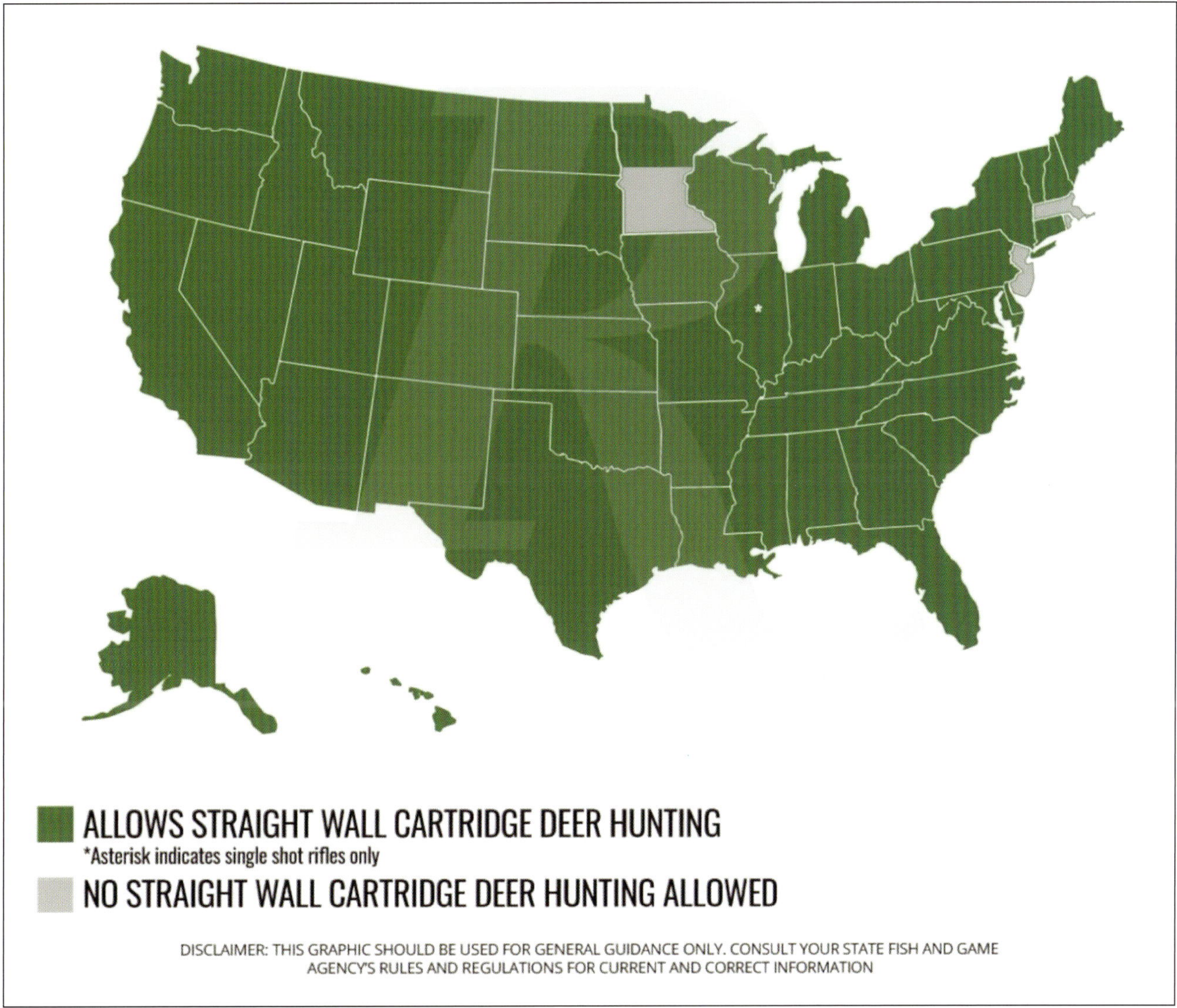

▲ This map shows the states in which hunting with straight-wall cartridges is permitted. It is always wise to check state game laws for new or updated regulations. Credit: Remington Arms.

SWCs are a huge benefit to hunters who are limited by state rules in their firearm options.

It's not only these accolades that contributed to a resurgence in straight-walled rifles and cartridges that made them more popular, but rather the changes of some hunting laws in certain states.

VELOCITY

Here's where straight-walled cartridges might meet Mr. Drawback for some hunters. When compared to bottleneck cartridges, SWC's main disadvantage is that they were specifically not designed for long-distance shooting. SWCs are designed to negatively impact their ballistics, inhibiting the bullets from traveling the usual types of further distances reached by traditional bottleneck (tapered) rifle cartridges. What limits a straight-walled cartridge from achieving longer distances is its straight-walled design, which does not allow the type of greater pressure that tapered cartridges accomplish. So, the lower pressure directly reduces the bullet's overall velocity and, thus, prevents the longer distances that traditional bullets are capable of traveling.

▲ If shooting long distances is a primary component to your hunting conditions, then hunting with SWCs might not be appropriate for you—due to their limited distances. Credit: Fiduccia Ent.

▲ The .400 Win Legend is a hard-hitting cartridge with what is referred to as "mild" recoil. It has enough downrange energy to kill medium-sized game within 300 yards. Credit: Winchester.

AVERAGE BULLET RANGE

Because there is less room for propellant *behind* the bullet compared to the bullet *diameter*, straight-walled cartridges tend to be slower and hence have a shorter range than standard bottle-necked ammunition. Most gun writers write about the fact that straight-walled cartridges have limited range capabilities. However, I do not consider the 200-yard distance to be a drawback. Think about it: how many whitetails or other deer species are actually shot at distances greater than 200 yards? In my opinion, not enough to be concerned about. Anyone hunting with SWCs can expect dependable kills out to 200 yards. With some newer SWC rounds, this distance is farther.

Because of a recent surge in the use of SWCs by hunters, many manufacturers have increased the development of straight-walled cartridges. The fact is today's straight-walled rounds have better distance capabilities than most rifled shotguns. Generally, some SWCs have a range of 200 to 300 yards or so.

So, straight-walled cartridges offer a tremendous amount of functionality in a number of firearm types. They produce enough terminal velocity, generally around 2,000–2,500 fps within their ranges. The SWCs will dependably kill deer, elk, caribou, moose, and even larger and thicker-skinned big game animals like the great bears, wild hogs, and bison.

As far as the states that require straight-walled cartridges, remember it's this reduced range that, at least in theory, makes them safer for hunting purposes in densely populated areas. But as mentioned, they are *highly* effective loads to kill deer and other big game.

ACCURACY

Straight-walled cartridges produce tighter, more consistent groups compared to even the most modern shotgun slugs or sabot loads. Even highly accurate

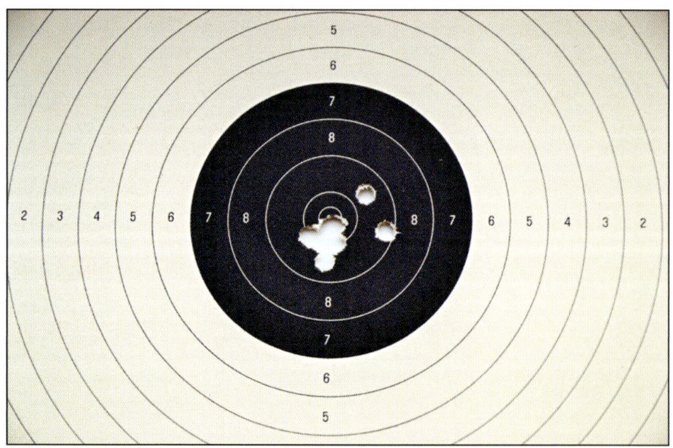

▲ With proper zeroing techniques, straight-wall cartridges can deliver tighter, more consistent groups than more modern shotgun or sabot loads. Credit: ID 42275416 © Martina Vaculikova|Dreamstime.

slug guns are known to occasionally throw inexplicable fliers more often than hunters care to admit. Straight-walled rifles, being rifles, rarely have this issue. Cartridges like the .360 Buckhammer, .450 Bushmaster, .45–70 Govt., and .400 Legend provide enough accuracy (and their bullets retain enough energy) to confidently reach out across a cut cornfield and make an accurate 200-yard-plus kill-shot.

BALLISTICS

Straight-walled loads produce average muzzle velocities of 2,000 to 2,500 fps, a few hundred feet per second faster than most shotgun loads. Some bullets have better ballistic coefficients than slugs, too. One example of a straight-walled load having better ballistics is Hornady's 265-grain FTX Lever Evolution for the .444 Marlin. With a 100-yard zero, the .444 Marlin FTX bullet drops 7.5 inches at 200 yards and drifts 8.6 inches in a 10 mph wind. Conversely, Hornady's 300-grain FTX SST 12-gauge slug zeroed at 100-yard drops and drifts about 12 inches at 200 yards.

GUIDE TO RECOIL ENERGY

1. Greater than 30 ft-lbs. is considered massive felt recoil that can be difficult for even seasoned veteran hunters to shoot accurately.
2. Greater than 25 ft-lbs., shot from a lightweight rifle: even practiced shooters can have issues to shoot more than a dozen or so rounds without developing a serious flinch as well as a bruised shoulder.
3. Greater than 15 ft-lbs., even at this reduced figure, it becomes considerably more difficult to see the bullet's impact on a target or animal through a scope due to the recoil involved.
4. Less than 10 ft-lbs., felt recoil is considered to be light. It is an ideal range for young shooters, small-framed men and women, etc.
5. Less than 4 ft-lbs. is noted to be almost undetectable as recoil and more like vibration from a shove.

FELT RECOIL

Strong felt recoil is a boogeyman that must be considered when shooting some of the more powerful straight-walled cartridge loads. Other SWCs have diminished recoil concerns, and there are even some that have manageable recoil. For instance, a .444 Marlin has the same mild recoil that is associated with the .35 Whelan at about 12.16 ft-lbs. of felt recoil. For a SWC that is pretty light. The .400 Legend SWC offers 100 percent more energy than a 12-gauge slug with an amazing 55 percent less felt recoil! It brings the same amount of energy as the .450 Bushmaster, with a significant reduction in felt recoil of 20 percent. The .400 Legend also offers 25 percent more energy than the .350 Legend for more penetration and improved terminal ballistics. So it's easy to see that not all SWCs deliver shoulder-bruising, heavy, felt recoil.

In fact, the .450 Bushmaster, .360 Buckhammer, and .350 Legend are also SWCs that generate *less felt* recoil than a 12-gauge slug (25.01 ft-lbs.). Get this, the .350 Legend produces about 8.5 pounds of felt recoil (or less) in a 7-pound rifle—less recoil than a .243 Win. This type of recoil is pretty easy to tolerate for most hunters, especially small-framed men and women.

▲ The .350 Legend delivers less felt recoil than most straight-walled cartridges. It produces about 8.5 lbs. (or less) of felt recoil from a 7 lb. rifle, delivering less recoil than a .243 Win. Credit: Winchester.

▲ Straight-walled cartridges are often associated with hunting whitetails and other deer species. However, they are quite capable of taking thicker-skinned game equally as well. Credit: 75912352 © Vorasate Ariyarattanahirun | Dreamstime.com

On the other hand, the .400 Legend with a 215-grain Power Point cartridge produces 16.26 ft-lbs. of recoil, almost roughly double that of the .243 but still quite manageable. This recoil is nearly the same as that delivered from a .308 Winchester. Being able to have a choice of SWCs that don't knock a hunter down before the bullet knocks down the prey is a true benefit. It also helps make straight-walled cartridges a superior choice for hunters who are sensitive to the dreads of superstrong recoil from shotguns.

.35 WHELEN

The .35 Whelen was developed in 1922. In 1998, Remington Arms Company standardized the cartridge as a conventional commercial round. The parent of this cartridge is the .30–06 Springfield. I believe that is why, unlike the .338 Federal, the .35 Whelen has a solid following among big game hunters. And why not? The long and the short of the .35 Whelen is that it is rated as an "excellent" rifle choice for hunting deer and other game. Do not confuse the .35 Whelen with the .35 Remington. The .35 Remington is a smaller cartridge than the .308 Winchester. They will not work in the same rifle.

The .35 Whelen is available in several factory rounds and factory chambered in several different rifles. It has accumulated a remarkable record all over the world, rivaling the .375 Holland & Holland in its effectiveness. The Whelen's biggest asset is that its maximum point-blank range (MPBR) is 300 yards with a 225-grain bullet. The .35 Whelen, when using a 225-grain Accubond, is quite capable of bringing down a grizzly bear. The .35 Whelen is a characteristically accurate round. It will reliably drop game ranging in size from a white-tailed deer to an Alaskan/Yukon bull moose. In fact, it is also commonly referred to as an ideal elk cartridge. Furthermore, it has a felt recoil that most hunters can tolerate. For larger, and more potentially dangerous, game, like a red-eyed, Kodiak brown bear at full charge, heavier cartridges are a must. Therefore the .35 Whelen is more than suitable for any North American big game animal.

The .35 Whelen is a tremendously versatile cartridge due to its ability to produce excellent hydrostatic shock that results in quick kills on light- to relatively large-bodied game as well as producing deep and broad channel wounding. No need for anything more to be said about the .35 Whelen.

BALLISTICS .35 WHELEN

Optimum Barrel Length: 22–24 inches
Average Bullet Weight: 200–225 grains
Average Muzzle Velocity: 2,798–2,613 fps
Average Muzzle Energy: 3,478–3,412 ft.-lbs.
Most Common Action: Bolt, semi-auto, single shot

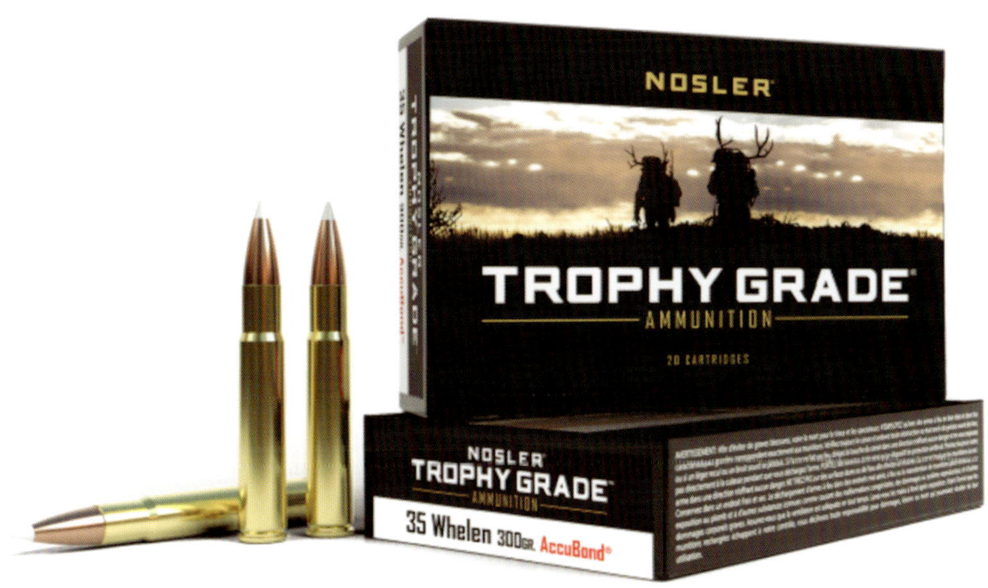

▲ The Nosler AccuBond® is designed for accuracy for shooting over long or short distances. It is recognized for its undeniable reliability. Credit: Nosler

.360 BUCKHAMMER

In 2023, Remington released the .360 Buckhammer (BHMR). It is a modern, rimmed, straight-walled cartridge optimized for lever-action rifles and even revolvers. It is now creeping into the hearts and minds of many whitetail hunters. One reason for that is because of its moniker—Buckhammer. Just by reading the label on the box, you realize the .360 Buckhammer is going to *"hammer"* deer and other big game. So the selection of this cartridge is somewhat of a no-brainer. It is a .30–30 case straightened to hold a .35-caliber bullet. What spurred the .360 into production was the success of the .350 Legend. The .350 Legend became a highly popular straight-walled caliber and cartridge choice almost overnight. That did not escape the attention of Remington, which realized they were missing some notable market action. Hence, they released the .360 BHMR.

After many gun authorities field-tested the .360 BHMR, it was proclaimed as the "new sheriff in town." Remington states the .360 BHMR is "the straight-walled cartridge that flattens them all. The .360 BHMR delivers flat trajectories and more bone-busting energy and velocity out to 200 yards and more than the rest." That's quite a claim. But it should not be doubted. The .360 BHMR is a faster version of the .30–30 Winchester.

This .360 BHMR cartridge gives hunters the capability to use brush-busting .358 diameter bullets (either supersonic or subsonic). Remington also offers a 200-grain Core-Lokt ammo in the .360 Buckhammer.

The Buckhammer's combination of shootability, accuracy, and velocity offers advantages over similar SWCs in its class—like a .350 Legend or .30–30 Winchester—without the heavy recoil so often noted on .45–70 Gov. or .450 Bushmaster. This has made BHMR a popular choice among deer hunters.

The .360 BHMR is optimized for lever-action rifles. The case measures 1.80 inches with a cartridge length of 2.50 inches, which meets the regulations of many of the Midwestern states. A Remington Core-Lokt 180-grain bullet departs the muzzle at 2,400 fps with an accompanying energy of 2,303 ft-lbs. If it is zeroed at 150 yards, the 180-grain Core Lokt would be 1.65 inches high at 100 yards and 4.50 inches low at 200 yards. What does that all amount to? A terrific 200-yard deer-hammering cartridge. Again, these numbers better the performance of the .30–30 Winchester, with a bullet with better frontal diameter.

▲ The .360 Buckhammer was recently acclaimed by many as the new straight-walled cartridge of the deer woods. Remington has two loads for the 360 Buckhammer ammunition: one is 180 grain and the other is 200 grain. Noted for their lever-action rifles, Henry manufactures an excellent Buckhammer. Credits: Remington Ammunition and Henry Firearms.

BALLISTICS .360 BUCKHAMMER

Optimum Barrel Length: 28–32 inches
Average Bullet Weight: 180 grains (Core-Lokt).
Average Muzzle Velocity: 2,400 fps
Average Muzzle Energy: 2,300 ft-lbs.
Free Recoil: 14.1 ft-lbs.
Most Common Action: Lever

.400 LEGEND

The .400 Legend (.400 LGND) was created by Winchester Repeating Arms. It also made its debut in 2023. At that time, it was one of the newest of the straight-walled cartridges. In the reviews of many gun writers, it was claimed the .400 Legend "checks off every box."

The .400 Legend is a straight-walled cartridge that offers superior ballistics, deep penetration, and excellent accuracy. This cartridge provides greater accuracy with less felt-recoil punishment. Additionally the .400 LGND has the capability to be used in a modern sporting rifle. Its cartridge's overall length also fits within a standard AR-style rifle receiver. These are two reasons to please modern rifle fans.

The .400 LGND features a bullet diameter of .4005 inches. Available loads are a 215-grain bullet, Power Point and a 300-grain SuperSuppressed. As noted earlier, the .400 LGND offers deep penetration, excellent accuracy, and quick knockdown power all with less felt recoil. It effectively connects the gap between the .350 Legend and the .450 Bushmaster. It strikes with more power than the .350, but with a lot less Baba Yaga felt recoil than the .450 Bushmaster. It is well on its way to being the top selection of the straight-walled cartridges—overtaking both the .350 Legend and the .360 Buckhammer. What more can a deer hunter ask for in a straight-walled cartridge?

BALLISTICS .400 LEGEND

Optimum Barrel Length: 20 inches
Average Bullet Weight: 215 grains (Power Point)
Average Muzzle Velocity: 2,250–2,300 fps
Average Muzzle Energy: 2,416 ft-lbs.
Free Recoil: 16.26 ft-lbs.
Most Common Action: Lever

▼ The .400 Legend is quite capable of taking whitetails at distances up to 300 yards. For larger deer species, the distances should be kept to 200 yards. It is also used for taking feral hogs and black bear. Credit: Winchester Ammunition.

.350 LEGEND

Before touting anything else about the .350 Legend, let me say it is known as one of the most mild-mannered centerfire rounds of the SWCs. I have shot it several times, and I can say the felt recoil comes across my shoulder as little more than a slight thrust. It also provides an advantage in trajectory. Realistically, the .350 shares many characteristics with the .223 Remington. Moreover, it is both equally comfortable in a bolt-action rifle as it is in an AR platform. It uses bullets of .358-inch diameter and a case length of 2.71 inches with a cartridge length of 2.25 inches. The cartridge delivers enough energy to achieve lethal terminal effects on large deer species out to 200 yards (in the hands of a good shooter), and it kills whitetails with "surgical precision" at distances to 250 yards. However, be advised it quickly starts dropping significantly once it has reached its maximum distance. The .350 Legend is also a terrific woodland cartridge for any state in the Northeast or New England.

Finally, the .350 Legend is a cartridge engineered for deer hunters to deliver massive downrange energy transfer along with improved penetration. It has a lower cost—that's a good one—scant recoil—that is even better—and large-caliber effectiveness on medium-sized game—better yet! It is certainly more gun than any whitetail hunter can ask for.

All that in one caliber makes the .350 Legend an all-around excellent deer hunting choice among the lineup of straight-walled cartridges. Winchester primarily developed the .350 Legend for hunting white-tailed deer, but it also serves well on some larger deer species like mule deer, feral boars, and black bear. It can be marginal as an elk killer and is definitely not recommended to hunt Alaskan or even eastern moose.

The ammunition is widely available, and it is priced more affordably than most other medium- to large-caliber cartridges. For .350 Legend ammunition choices look to Winchester, Hornady, Federal, Barnes, Browning, Nosler, and others.

BALLISTICS .350 LEGEND

Optimum Barrel Length: 18–24 inches
Average Bullet Weight: 180 grains
Average Muzzle Velocity: 2,325–2,400 fps
Average Muzzle Energy: 1,800–1,900 ft-lbs.
Free Recoil: 8.52 meager pounds (in a 7-pound rifle)
Most Common Action: Bolt, lever, and standard AR-15

◀ There is no doubt that the .350 Legend is a top straight-walled cartridge choice for hunting white-tailed deer—no matter where they are found. Credit: brm1949 | Deposit Photos.

.444 MARLIN

The .444 Marlin was created in 1964. It was designed to replace the .45–70 Government. It is known for being a powerful cartridge that can take down whitetails, elk, moose, and black bears. However, with the right load and bullet type, it can be used to kill any of the large great bears. Hence, it is capable of dropping most any large game animal in North America.

The stout .444 has some incredibly serious knock-down-and-out power. Furthermore, at 150 yards, the .444 Marlin's knockout power is said to even overshadow a .300 H&H Mag. That's some scary power. With all that power you would expect an equally strong felt recoil. However, you would be wrong. The .444 comes with mild recoil. Ballistic figures demonstrate the .444 Marlin with a 240-grain bullet loaded to 2,400 feet per second (in a 7.5-pound rifle) has a recoil of 23.3 pounds. Some would call that a little more than mild.

The .444 Marlin is an excellent straight-walled, big-bore hunting cartridge for a lever-action rifle. After hearing that, some might say the .444 is overkill for hunting white-tailed deer. However, it is also a top-notch brush cartridge and will perform at its apex in that environment. When hunting with the .444 Marlin, a well-placed shot results in dead—*absolutely* dead.

▲ The. 444 is a terrific choice as a brush gun that is ideal for whitetails, albeit somewhat over gunned. Where it shines is when hunting larger deer species like elk, Alaskan moose, and bears . . . all while delivering very manageable felt recoil. Credit: Marlin Firearms.

BALLISTICS .444 MARLIN

Optimum Barrel Length: 22–24 inches
Average Bullet Weight: 265 grain flex-tip bullet
Average Muzzle Velocity: 2,025–2,350 fps
Average Muzzle Energy: 3,180–3,200 ft-lbs.
Free Recoil: 22.99 ft-lbs.
Most Common Action: Lever

.450 BUSHMASTER

The .450 Bushmaster is recognized as one of the most well-known cartridges in the United States. The case is based on the .284 Winchester, which is the same diameter as the .30–06 Springfield. It was primarily designed for whitetail hunters and AR platforms, but it is also available in bolt-action platforms. The .450 Bushmaster is among other straight-walled cartridges that can be termed a BAL (big-ass load). The result is a handy, lightweight brush gun that packs plenty of punch. The .450 Bushmaster is basically in the exact same boat as the .50 Beowulf and the .458. The .450 Bushmaster is noted for its flat trajectory and accuracy out to 200 yards. If it is zeroed at 150 yards expect it to drop about 4.9 inches at200. After 200 yards, the drop rate notably increases. Therefore, the .450 cannot be considered a long-range gun.

If knock down power is a critical preference for a hunter, the .450 comes to the rescue as a thumper round. It consistently delivers hard-hitting performance. Alas, though, the .450 is known for its stout recoil. However, there are ways to mitigate the recoil by using a high-end recoil pad or a suppressor. The .450 Bushmaster remains a terrific choice even for much larger game like grizzly or Alaskan/Yukon moose. But it will only be accurate as long as the hunter can tame down or tolerate its recoil.

Of late, though, the .450 Bushmaster has been demoted as a top-choice straight-walled caliber. That is due to the more popular and newer straight-walled cartridges including the .400 Legend, .350 Legend, and the .360 Buckhammer. But for those who want knockdown power over all else, particularly when hunting bears and other larger, potentially risky game, it is a cartridge that checks most other boxes. That's not an issue when hunting whitetails, but it is especially important to keep in mind when hunting larger, more threatening game such as a cantankerous moose or bad-tempered grizzly bear.

BALLISTICS .450 BUSHMASTER

Optimum Barrel Length: 16 inches
Average Bullet Weight: 250 grains
Average Muzzle Velocity: 2,200–2,300 fps
Average Muzzle Energy: 2,448 ft-lbs.
Free Recoil: 27 ft-lbs.
Most Common Action: Lever and semi-auto

▲ One way to mitigate the heavy recoil of the .450 Bushmaster is with a recoil-reducing muzzle device. Prior to purchasing a larger-bore rifle, check to see if it has threads to receive a muzzle brake or suppressor; it'll make adding one of these devices go much quicker when the time comes. Credit: Griffin Armament.

.45–70 GOVERNMENT

The .45–70 Government was introduced in 1873. As an owner of a Marlin 1895 XLR caliber .45–70 Government, I can verify that a big advantage of this cartridge is related to its massive downrange retained velocity. The .45–70 delivers energy in a big way. It also produces a large entry and exit cavity and carries significant knock down-and-out power matched to the knockout power seen on the TV show *Robot Wars*. But you would not expect that kind of power to come for free, would you? Of course not. The price that the .45–70 gets for these accolades is that it delivers some heavy-duty felt recoil. It delivers a lot of bleepin' recoil! I know. I own a .45–70. The ammo is pricey, and there is a decreased ammunition availability issue at the time of this writing. Still, for the hardcore devotees that crave pure, unadulterated, knockdown power, the .45–70 is far and away a terrific choice.

The .45–70 Government is exceptionally effective to kill game ranging from whitetail deer and elk to Alaskan moose. It also can be used to hunt much larger, tougher, and more dangerous species like the great bears, bison, and musk ox. When hunting great bears, careful consideration must be given to the choice of cartridges. Factors such as downrange distance, bullet type, grain weight, wind and weather conditions, as well as the size and temperament of the grizzly, all play a role. Most critically, it is essential for the hunter to accurately place the first shot in a precise and deadly manner.

The .45–70 is also an applicable choice for hunting some African dangerous game, including Cape buffalo, but only with the proper load and bullet type. All African plains game species can be hunted with the .45–70.

Even a cursory examination of the .45–70 will reveal its extraordinary attribute: its *massive* bullet, which can weigh as much as 500 grains. One last comment, and it is an important one. The .45–70's accuracy is *totally* based on how well a hunter can handle its curb-stomping, head-smashing, felt recoil. It produces an average 32 ft-lbs. of felt recoil energy, depending on the exact cartridge load fired from a 7–7.5 lb. rifle. It would be wise for any owner of a .45–70 to reduce the recoil with a combination of a recoil-reducing muzzle brake, a quality buttstock pad, and other muzzle-reducing tool options.

BALLISTICS .45–70 GOVERNMENT

Optimum Barrel Length: 22–26 inches
Average Bullet Weight: 300 grains (strong) (JHP)
Average Muzzle Velocity: 2,275 fps
Average Muzzle Energy: 2,280 ft-lb.
Average Free Recoil: 30.81 ft-lbs.
Most Common Action: Lever

◀ The .45-70 is a versatile rifle for hunting almost anything that walks. The downside is its heavy-duty recoil, which can affect the shooter's accuracy. Therefore, recoil-reducing accessories are highly recommended. Credit: Fiduccia Ent.

POWERHOUSE STRAIGHT-WALLED OPTIONS

While the previously discussed straight-walled cartridges are more well-known and popular, there are still several other enormously powerful SWCs. Yet, they are often overlooked. Consequently, I condensed their information into brief overviews next.

.50 BEOWULF

So what the fuzzy is the .50 Beowulf? Well, if scary things frighten you, stop reading this. The .50 Beowulf is the largest, most menacing, bad-boy cartridge around. To get that tough-boy reputation it might have been raised in Brooklyn, New York. Nothing exceeds this round for putting a "hurt" on things. The round measures 2.26 inches, which is about the size of a small hot-dog cocktail wiener. However, it fits comfortably into an AR-15 platform.

The **.50 Beowulf** is a tremendously specialized .50 caliber straight-walled cartridge with exceptional power and penetration at close to medium range. The .50 Beowulf cartridge crashes through obstacles like a Trident II class cruise missile. Mass multiplied by velocity equals force. This SWC has bullet weights from 200 grains through 600 grains with 335-, 350- and 400-grain weights the most commonly used. The .50 Beowulf generates tons of energy: 300- to 400-grain bullets at 1,800 to 1,900 fps produce 2,300 to 2,800 ft-lbs. of energy. One might ask: what's the point of such a heavy-hitting cartridge? The answer is power—unadulterated power.

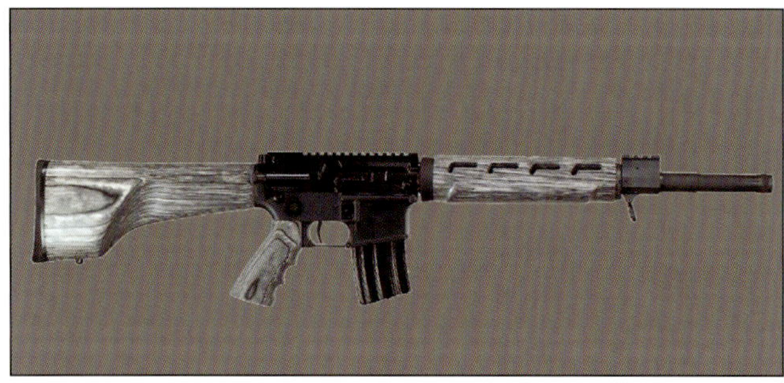

▲ You never have to be afraid of the big bad wolf or any other huntable big game animal in the world—the .50 Beowulf is your rifle caliber and cartridge Get this, although the .50-caliber cartridge produces a whopping 2,400 foot-pounds of muzzle energy, its felt recoil is comparable to a 12-gauge shotgun with 2-¾-inch bird shot. Credit: Alexander Arms

The best hunting bullets for the .50 Beowulf are typically heavy soft-point or hollow-point bullets designed for maximum expansion and stopping power on large-bodied game. Soft-point bullets retain energy longer and penetrate deeper. Hollow points use up most of their energy upon impacting the animal. These types of bullets ensure sufficient energy transfer for clean kills as long as the hunter makes a precise hit to the vitals. But if putting down a Kodiak brown bear like it was hit by a freight train is what you want, a .50 Beowulf will do the job. Here's the kicker: there is no kicker. A substantial difference is that the .50 Beowulf has *very* mild recoil compared to comparable cartridges like the .50 Browning (97 ft-lbs. of felt recoil). It also performs in short barrels. Oh, and it can reach out to touch stuff, too. It has a precise range of about 260 yards. While the most common barrel length is 16 inches, there are smaller barrels available.

Exceptional as it may be, the Alexander Arms .50 Beowulf Hunter AR-15 provides oodles of practicality. It is chambered for .50 Beowulf with its intimidating big brute of a cartridge. There is no question that the .50 Beowulf can put down every big game animal in North America including all the largest and most dangerous game animals North America, Africa, and India have to offer. According to Alexander Arms, "The heavy bullets from the Beowulf are quite capable of breaking both shoulders of a moose." So, if you're looking for a unique hunting rifle that can knock the snot out of any big game animal on Earth, the .50 Beowulf may be right up your alley.

BALLISTICS .50 BEOWULF

Optimum Barrel Length: 16 inches
Average Bullet Weight: 300–400 grains
Average Muzzle Velocity: 1,878–2,002 fps
Average Muzzle Energy: 2,800 ft-lbs.
Free Recoil Energy: 9.8–9.9 ft-lbs. (more of a shove than a kick)
Most Common Action: AR 15 semi-auto

.500 SMITH & WESSON MAGNUM

The .500 Smith & Wesson Magnum (S&W Mag) is available in both rifle and carbine models. It is equivalent to the heavyweight boxing champions of the world like Mike Tyson, the late George Foreman, or Evander Holyfield at their career peaks. The comparison is that the cartridge and the boxers both have enormous one-punch knockout power. If there ever was a cartridge that deserves distinction, the .500 S&W Mag rifle is it. Bullet weights range from 265 to 700 and several loads push a 500-plus-grain bullet to supersonic speed. The .500 S&W Magnum is said to be quite capable of dropping "any and every large game animal on the North American continent!" It pushes deep into an animal's body cavity, creating large wound channels. Therefore, the .500 S&W has excellent potential as a big game cartridge. I mean ***really*** big game like the great bears.

Big Horn Armory (BHA) developed the Model 89 lever action. There are two versions: a rifle and a carbine. A rifle with a barrel shorter than 20 inches is called a carbine. Practically speaking, while the .500 Smith & Wesson Magnum can be used to hunt whitetails, mule deer, and other deer species, some say it can be deemed as overkill for those animals.

Big Horn Armory developed the rifle cartridge with the intent of it delivering a crushing punch on thick-skinned, heavy-boned big game including Alaskan/Yukon moose, bison, grizzly, Kodiak brown bear, and polar bear. It is also not afraid to take on any of Africa's Big Five within its preferred range of 200 yards. However, with well-placed accuracy, that distance could be increased to 300 yards.

Oh, by the way, the .500 S&W Magnum SWC has a memorable kick! Of course that can be tamed with a substantial recoil pad, a muzzle brake, or a suppressor. They will help alleviate a nasty-looking hematoma.

BALLISTICS .500 SMITH & WESSON MAGNUM

Optimum Barrel Length: 22 inches (rifle)—18 inches (carbine).
Selected Bullet Weight: 400 grains (Double Tap)
Average Muzzle Velocity: 1,800–2,240 fps.
Average Muzzle Energy: 3,000–4,100 ft-lbs.
Free Recoil Energy: (Jurassic!) About 54 ft-lbs.
Most Common Action: Lever

▼ The Bighorn Armory Model 89 .500 S&W rifle can be used for hunting any of the deer species. Where it shines is for hunting thick-skinned, heavy-boned big game animals. Credit: Bighorn Armory

.44 REMINGTON MAGNUM

I know there will be a few reading this who may be thinking, "Are there really .44 magnum long-guns (rifles)?!" Yes. There are. Rifles that are chambered in .44 magnum are currently manufactured by Sturm, Ruger & Co., Marlin, Rossi, Winchester, CVA, and Henry Repeating Arms. Action choices include single-shot, bolt, semi-auto, and lever actions.

The .44 Remington Magnum rifle is a terrific deer cartridge. For hunters who enjoy tracking or still-hunting deer, a compact lever- or semi-auto .44 Rem Mag is an excellent choice. Because of its light weight and compact size it is also excellent for those who hunt steep ridges through the Northeast. I know because in my earlier hunting days I stalked whitetails throughout the Northeast and New England in big woods and brushy areas with a .44 semi-automatic rifle. The .44 Rem Mag delivers greater accuracy than most any slug shotgun. In addition, there are a wide variety of factory loads from which to choose.

▲ The .44 Rem Mag is the quintessential whitetail deer rifle. It is lightweight, compact, and easy to carry all day in the field. For whitetail hunters, Ruger's .44 Rem Mag is an ideal choice. Credit: Ruger.

In my earlier years of deer hunting, I hunted exclusively throughout several different Northeast and New England states. Most areas had heavily treed woodlots and thick, overgrown brush country. I found the .44 Rem Mag to be practical when I needed to quickly snap up my rifle and get on game in tough terrain. Another asset for a rifle that has decent knockdown power is that it has ultralight felt recoil. A bolt- or lever-action platform is an excellent choice for novice hunters—particularly because it is fun to shoot. For safety reasons with novice hunters, semi-auto actions may not be the right choice. For adults of light body stature, it is also a terrific choice in any of the offered platforms, which include bolt, lever, and semi-automatic actions.

I included this SW cartridge here because it is a terrific choice for hunting whitetails and other deer-sized game at short to medium ranges (up to 150 yards or so). It should be noted that the .44 Rem Mag is not meant for hunting large, thick-skinned game even within its recommended ranges.

The .44 Magnum's rimmed case measures a small 1.285 inches with a cartridge length of 1.61 inches. Factory ammunition choices feature bullets ranging from 200 grains to 340 grains, with a wide variety of bullet constructions. The ammunition is generally inexpensive and widely available. One last word: Because the recoil is so light, particularly when shooting a semi-auto, the .44 is a fun rifle to take to the range for a day of shooting.

BALLISTICS .44 REM MAG

Optimum Barrel Length: 16–18 inches
Average Bullet Weight: 248 grains
Average Muzzle Velocity: 1,688 fps
Average Muzzle Energy: 1,751 ft-lbs.
Free Recoil Energy: 9.8–11 ft-lbs.
Most Common Action: Lever, bolt, single shot, lever, and semi-automatic

.700 HOLLAND & HOLLAND NITRO EXPRESS

I'll wrap this chapter up with the Holland & Holland .700 Nitro Express. It is an extremely powerful and large-caliber cartridge, similar to the .375 H&H, primarily used for hunting dangerous game. It will kill anything that walks, flies, skips, jumps, hops, swims, or crawls on land or water. Therefore, it is best suited for experienced hunters seeking the ultimate challenge and hunting experience.

When it comes to drop-dead stopping power, the .700 Nitro Express delivers an immense amount of energy upon impact. It is fully capable of quickly incapacitating even the largest and most dangerous of all animals. Its massive bullet diameter and weight result in devastating terminal ballistics, making it highly effective for any game animal foolish enough to charge a hunter carrying a .700 Nitro.

The .700 Nitro excels when it comes to executing deep penetration. With its heavy bullets and high muzzle energy, the .700 Nitro Express is capable of penetrating deeply into the thickest-skinned game animals, including elephants, hippos, rhinos, bison, and alligators, all the while ensuring vital organ penetration and delivering cavernous lethal wound channels. Remember, due to its extreme power and bullet weight, the .700 Nitro Express has a limited effective range compared to smaller and faster straight-walled cartridges. It is typically used for close-range shooting, where its stopping power and penetration capabilities are most effective.

There is no doubt that among dangerous game aficionado hunters, the .700 Nitro Express has a well-established reputation for reliability and effectiveness in the field. Its performance has been proven time and time again by professional hunters and common Joe/Jane sportsmen/women throughout the world.

▲ Owning a H&H .700 Nitro is the epitome of a status symbol of gun ownership. It comes with a hefty price tag of no less than $400,000. You've heard the catchphrase, "Got Milk?" Well, the catchphrase for this beautiful firearm is "Got Expendable Cash?" Credit: Holland & Holland

Driving an $18 million Bugatti, owning a Malibu home, or having a Learjet 75 Liberty is highly impressive to many. However, among firearms enthusiasts and dangerous game hunters, carrying a .700 Nitro Express is the ultimate status symbol. A custom-built order for an H&H .700 Nitro Express can range as high as $400,000. Now you know why it's a status symbol—if we bought one, our better halves would probably kill us with it.

With all that said, the inimitable .700 Nitro does come with some drawbacks. The devil made me say it. The .700 Nitro Express generates extreme, shoulder-dislocating recoil, which can be punishing even for experienced hunters. Proper technique and a well-designed rifle with effective recoil mitigation features are absolutely essential to manage the recoil of this cartridge (managing recoil will be discussed in a later chapter). Then, of course, like fueling a Lear jet, the ammunition is crazy expensive. Don't believe that? Typically, a box of .700 Nitro Express ammo with five to ten rounds can cost several hundred dollars or more. Because there are very few .700 H&H Nitros made, they are extremely rare and costly.

BALLISTICS .700 NITRO EXPRESS

Optimum Barrel Length: 24–26 inches
Average Bullet Weight: 1,000 grains
Average Muzzle Velocity: 2,000 fps
Average Muzzle Energy: 8,900 ft-lb.
Free Recoil Energy: Shoulder-dislocating—have an orthopedic surgeon handy
Most Common Action: Double-barrel break-action, bolt, single

SUMMARY

So, what is the best straight-walled cartridge to use? Well, realistically, that should be left up to each hunter's needs and budget. Consequently, straight-walled cartridges are an ideal option when hunting in states that allow SWCs for deer hunting. However, nowadays all but a few states allow straight-walled cartridges, albeit with special SWC regulations, for hunting whitetail deer or other big game.

There are no simple answers when it comes to selecting a straight-walled rifle caliber, action, and accompanying ammunition. While I have listed a majority of the straight-wall cartridges, there are more straight-walled brand choices from which to choose. These include the .32–40 Win, .405 Win., .450 Nitro, .454 Casull, and .458 SOCOM. A hunter needs to do his or her due diligence before making a final choice. Remember, though, in the end, how accurately you shoot is far more important by leaps and bounds than the type of straight-walled rifle caliber, cartridge, and action you choose.

▲ Straight wall cartridges are powerful and provide excellent penetration on even the largest game. Credit: Winchester Ammunition.

▲ Whether hunting a giant Yukon/Alaskan moose or a smaller eastern moose, like the one here, a straight wall cartridge is a good choice, albeit within its range. Credit: Fiduccia Enterprises.

▲ When hunting life-threatening game, the caliber, cartridge, and riflescope play a vital role in bringing down a charging grizzly or Cape buffalo before it reaches a hunter. Credit: 6117736 (c) Alexander Sukonin | Dreamstime

Chapter Four

DEADLY GAME GEAR: Equipment Designed to Drop Life-Threatening Game

I don't know what there is about buffalo that frightens me so. Lions and leopards and rhinos excite me but don't frighten me. But the buff is so big and mean, and ugly, and hard to stop, and vindictive, and cruel, and surly, and ornery. He looks like he hates you personally. He looks like you owe him money. He looks like he is hunting you.
—ROBERT RUARK, *Horn of the Hunter*, 1954

While this book focuses mainly on gear for hunting typical big game, there's a special breed of hunter that deserves attention—those who pursue the world's most dangerous animals. These are creatures not only massive in size but also armed with unpredictable tempers and the power to turn the tables in an instant. In this chapter, we'll take a close look at the specialized equipment required to face these apex predators, the kind of game where, at any moment, the hunter can become the hunted.

▲ Hunting apex predators is part and parcel of human's earliest hunting beginnings. Credit: ID 371120708 (c) Vasyl Pashkovskiy | Dreamstime

Hunting dangerous game dates back to the days when our spear-wielding ancestors faced off against saber-toothed cats, towering bears, massive predatory kangaroos, and woolly mammoths. Today's adrenaline-driven hunters pursue equally formidable beasts, armed with rifles, ammunition, and optics powerful enough to halt a 14,000-pound bull elephant in its tracks—with a single, well-placed shot.

EQUIPMENT MATTERS

When pursuing dangerous game, your equipment must be top-tier—your life may depend on it. Rifles must perform flawlessly, cartridges must deliver unquestionable stopping power, and riflescopes must be built to the highest standards. That means crystal-clear clarity, resistance to fogging even in harsh weather, the ability to gather light in those crucial low-light hours of dawn and dusk, and the durability to withstand brutal terrain. Simply put, quality gear isn't just a preference—it's a safeguard that allows hunters to track lethal game with a greater margin of safety.

While riflescopes play a vital role in any dangerous game setup, this chapter focuses solely on rifle calibers and cartridges. For a detailed breakdown of scope selection, refer to chapter 16.

For each of these animals, several big-bore rifle calibers offer solid performance. But rather than muddy the waters with every possible option, I'll highlight the most recommended choice for each species. I'll also explain exactly why these animals have earned their fearsome reputations. All references will focus on adult males.

AFRICAN BULL ELEPHANT

The African bull elephant is a behemoth animal. At shoulder height it can reach 14 feet, weigh 14,000 pounds, and have massive 10-foot-long tusks. Older and younger bulls are particularly dangerous. When threatened or surprised, bull elephants will charge a hunter, creating a mind-bending threatening situation for the hunter to stop the charge before getting trampled! When a bull is in musth (a condition associated with mating) is when this animal is most hazardous.

When pursuing elephants, the choice of rifle caliber and cartridge is crucial. Together, they must deliver dependable stopping power, deep penetration, and top-notch bullet performance capable of penetrating thick skin, dense muscle, and heavy bones. Therefore, savvy elephant hunters know to use powerful calibers and cartridges that they can shoot comfortably and accurately. A popular choice is the .458 Win Mag. Modern solid bullets are the most recommended and reliable choice when stalking bull elephants.

.458 WINCHESTER MAGNUM

Optimum Barrel Length: 24 inches
Average Bullet Weight: 450 grains
Average Muzzle Velocity: 2,200–2,300 fps
Average Muzzle Energy: About 5,740 ft-lbs.

▲ Stopping the charge of a massive bull elephant is akin to stopping a heavy-duty bulldozer. Therefore, using the proper calibers and associated cartridges are crucial elements for a hunter's safety and success. Credit: ID 216612400 © Anna C. Nagel | Dreamstime.com

Most Common Action: Bolt Action
Recoil Energy: 62.3 ft lbs. with a 9-lb. rifle

CAPE BUFFALO

Never doubt that the African Cape buffalo is one murderous, surly, ill-tempered, sneaky son of a bitch. Buffalo kill over 200 people a year—including hunters. Thus, it has earned its moniker as one of Africa's most perilous Big Five animals.

Cape buffalo are massive animals; they weigh up to 2,000 pounds, stand 5 feet at the shoulder, reach up to 11 feet long, and have a thick hide. When threatened, it will quickly charge a hunter, and it will be completely immersed in killing its target as hurtfully as possible (Its horns can disembowel you before you can say "Ouch."). Cape buffalo are extremely aggressive, hazardous, and devious when they are wounded. They will often wait in ambush and then attack their pursuer. They are moody, unpredictable, belligerent, and extremely short-tempered animals, even when they are not disturbed or threatened. Death by Cape buffalo is a dreadful way to meet your Maker.

The .416 Rigby Magnum (or Remington) is the most popular caliber used to hunt Cape buffalo. The .416 Rigby holds a slight edge over the .375 calibers because it is exclusively loaded with 400-grain bullets providing better stopping power and penetration. Both solid and soft-point bullets can be used.

.416 RIGBY MAGNUM

Optimum Barrel Length: 20–22 inches
Average Bullet Weight: 400 grains
Average Muzzle Velocity: 2,350–2,500 fps
Average Muzzle Energy: 5,100–5,115 ft-lbs.
Most Common Action: Bolt-Action Platform
Recoil Energy: About 58.1 ft-lbs. with a 9-lb. rifle

AFRICAN LION

When hunting lions, expect danger at every turn. Lions are incredibly strong and exceptionally dangerous when provoked or wounded. An adult male can weigh up to 450 pounds, stand 3.5 feet at the shoulder, and be about 8 feet long. It has razor-sharp 3-inch canines

▲ A wounded buffalo is crazy hazardous. It will hide in cover waiting to charge and assassinate the hunter that injured it. At the last second, it will drop its head and charge. But by then—it's way too late for a hunter to respond. Credit: ID 24638163 © Jonathan Pledger | Dreamstime.com

and 2- to 3-inch sharp claws. A male lion has a staggering bite force of about 1,050 PSI!

Lion hunting can be extremely exciting and equally hazardous, particularly if the hunter is under-gunned. A recommended caliber is the venerable .375 H&H Magnum. Some say it is a bit overpowered for lion, but because its recoil is manageable, it shoots more accurately than other heavier big-bore calibers.

▲ With a well-placed shot, a hunt for a male lion can go smoothly. When wounded, though, it can go horribly bad. Credit: Deposit Photos

.375 H&H MAGNUM

Optimum Barrel Length: 20–24 inches
Average Bullet Weight: 300 grains
Average Muzzle Velocity: 2,530 fps
Average Muzzle Energy: 4,800 ft-lbs.
Most Common Action: Bolt-Action Platform
Recoil Energy: very manageable 37.3 with a 9 lb. rifle.

AFRICAN HIPPOPOTAMUS

Adult hippopotami are colossal animals that can weigh over 7,000 pounds. They are highly fierce, very territorial, and totally unpredictable. Hippos will attack anything foolish enough to enter their territory. They are the number one deadliest land animal on the planet and are responsible for killing 500 or more people annually. Their sharp canine teeth can reach 20 inches in length and can bite an adult crocodile (or a human) in half with a single bite!

Their huge size, strong skeleton, thick skin, and solid muscles make it vital for hunters to choose big-bore calibers to hunt them. With proper bullet choices and pinpoint shot placement, single-shot kills can be achieved. But, if a hunter makes a poor first hit, hippos can react amazingly fast with deadly vengeance.

▲ A hunter would never want to get between the jaws of a hippopotamus. The survival rate is next to nil. Credit: 7026027 © Isselee | Dreamstime.com

A recommended choice is the .404 Jeffery Magnum (.404 Nitro Express). It provides increased bullet diameter, overall power, and superior penetration and stopping power. Especially against the thick skin of a hippo. You do *not* want to wound a hippo, particularly on land, where the worst encounters take place. Otherwise, you will pay a very steep price for doing so.

.404 JEFFERY MAGNUM

Barrel Length: About 24–26 inches
Average Bullet Weight: 450 grains (w/jacketed bullet)
Average Muzzle Velocity: 2,200–2,400 fps
Average Muzzle Energy: 4,500–5,000 ft-lbs.
Most Common Action: Bolt Action
Recoil Energy: A manageable 41.0 ft lbs., with a 10.25 lb. rifle

AMERICAN BISON

Free-ranging North American bison are a huntable species in five states and a few Canadian provinces. Bison are heavier and substantially larger than the African Cape buffalo. They are known to charge from the slightest provocation. They charge with surprising speed and with the full intent to permanently disable the threat. Bison try to hook antagonists with their horns to gore an adversary. They also use their heads to violently throw antagonists high into the air and when the enemy lands, they use their heavy heads to crush the foe to death. Bison often stand nearby the attack, waiting patiently to further neutralize its assailant if need be. A full-blown attack almost guarantees a critical injury. It is rare for a hunter to survive such a pounding by an angered bison.

A good big-bore rifle caliber to hunt bison is the .338 Winchester Magnum. Gun writers often claim it is one of the most useful cartridges ever made, and it is very effective to hunt bison with. The .338 Win Mag is renowned for its power, deep penetration, and ability to handle the size and strength of dangerous-game animals. Use a heavy bullet such as Barnes 250-grain TSX or Swift 250- or 275-grain A-Frame.

.338 WINCHESTER MAGNUM

Barrel Length: About 26 inches
Average Bullet Weight: 220 grains
Average Muzzle Velocity: 2,660 fps
Average Muzzle Energy: 3,927 ft-lbs.
Most Common Action: Bolt Action
Recoil Energy: A manageable 33.1 ft lbs. with a 9 lb., rifle.

▲ Never trust the temperament of an ornery, unpredictable bull bison. Death by bison can be a crunching experience. These bovines can dismantle a hunter lickety-split. Credit: ID 75912352 © Vorasate Ariyarattanahirun | Dreamstime.com

KODIAK BROWN BEAR

A Kodiak brown bear is 5 feet at the shoulder and 10 feet tall when standing, weighs about 1,300 pounds, and has a mouth full of daggerlike teeth, 6-inch razor-sharp claws, and a bite force of 1,100 PSI that can easily crush a bowling ball! Imagine what it can do to a human head.

▲ Getting charged by this bear is so frightening a hunter could die of a heart attack. That would be the best result of the attack. Credit: ID 4272018 (c) JohnBell | Dreamstime

It is well-known that Kodiak brown bears exhibit little to no fear of humans. They can be highly aggressive and explosive, making them especially dangerous game. Death by a Kodiak brown bear is an absolutely unthinkable way to get to Valhalla.

A .300 Winchester Magnum is highly touted as a viable choice to hunt Kodiak brown bear under average conditions, from a midrange using an expanding bullet, and with correct good shot placement. It delivers stopping power and the ability to penetrate thick hides, dense muscles, and heavy bones. Slower powders are ideal for a .300 Win Mag. It is an accurate, hard-hitting cartridge capable of taking down an angry Kodiak brown bear. I make this decision based on a quote by Robert Ruark—"To hunt dangerous game you need to be scared enough to be cautious and brave enough to control your fear . . . and to use enough gun!" The .300 Win Mag is "enough gun." Period, end of discussion.

▲ A grizzly's disposition is so bad it would bite itself. These bears win the Oscar for being drama queens. Credit: © Howard Nevitt, Jr. | Dreamstime

.300 WINCHESTER MAGNUM

Barrel Length: 24-inches
Average Bullet Weight: 200 to 250 grains
Average Muzzle Velocity: 2,810 fps
Average Muzzle Energy: 3,600 to 4,100 ft-lbs.
Most Common Action: Bolt Action
Recoil Energy: 23.5 with a 8.5 lb., rifle.

.30–378 WEATHERBY MAGNUM

Barrel Length: 24 inches
Average Bullet Weight: 250 grains
Average Muzzle Velocity: 2,500 fps
Average Muzzle Energy: 3,470. ft-lbs.
Most Common Action: Bolt Action
Recoil Energy: About 71.1 ft-lbs. with a 10.25 lb. rifle

GRIZZLY BEAR

To understand why this bear exhibits mental and emotional instabilities and uncontrollable belligerence, just repeat its name, grizzly. It can weigh up to 800 pounds, stand 5 feet tall at the shoulder, and reach heights of almost 9 feet when they rear up on their hind legs. Grizzly bears have sharp teeth to go along with their extremely sharp six-inch claws. I can go on and on about how unstable this bear can be once it attacks a hunter but let me just say a grizzly bear is an unimaginably psychotic, sadistic, murderous bear. Hunters need a big-bore caliber to penetrate the thick hide of this bear. Only then might a grizzly take its medicine. The .30–378 Weatherby Magnum is a good choice, particularly when using tough, heavy bullets like 250-grain Hawk bullets. (It can double on the largest and most belligerent Alaskan Bull Moose during the rut too.)

POLAR BEAR

Under specific conditions, polar bear hunting is legal for US citizens in both Canada and Greenland; however, it is strictly controlled and requires quotas and permits for certain areas. Polar bears do not exhibit any fear of humans. They are the most carnivorous of all bear species. They will take full advantage of any food that carelessly presents itself, including hunters, creating the enigma of hunters becoming the hunted. That's no bull crap—no exaggeration—just a hardcore fact.

A polar bear can stand more than 11 feet tall and 8 feet in length, weigh more than 1,700 pounds, and have a bite force of about 1,200 PSI. Its instinct to purposely stalk and consume humans is a specific characteristic to this bear. Polar bears are far more hazardous than any other bear species. When threatened, wounded, or simply in a foul mood, their aggression becomes beyond description. Consequently, if you hunt polar bears with an improper caliber, cartridge, and bullet type make sure you have all your affairs in order and your life insurance policy is paid up.

To kill a polar bear safely, it should be 100 to 150 yards away and the rifle must provide heavy-duty stopping power. A large-caliber rifle such as an 8mm Magnum with 220 grains and sectional density (SD) .301 bullets is ideal. This recommendation will provide a quick and ethical kill. Because of the extraordinary danger of this bear, here are some other choices. Other common calibers include .375 H&H Magnum, .416 Remington Magnum, and the .458 Winchester Magnum. These calibers are known for their power, stopping ability, and capability to penetrate a polar bear's thick hide, heavy bones, and dense muscles.

8MM REMINGTON MAGNUM

Barrel Length: 26 inches
Average Bullet Weight: 220 grains
Average Muzzle Velocity: 2,965 fps
Average Muzzle Energy: 4,290 ft-lbs.
Most Common Action: Bolt Action
Recoil Energy: About 71.1 ft-lbs. with a 8.5-lb. rifle

A CAUTIONARY ENDING NOTE

Never—*never*—trust that a downed dangerous game animal is truly dead after just one shot. As you approach, be fully prepared to punch a second hole in its hide. Don't worry about the extra damage—a good taxidermist can fix it. On the other hand, if that animal jumps up and decides to settle the score, a doctor may not be able to fix *your* holes. And at that point, it'll be the undertaker doing the patchwork.

Whether you're new to the pursuit or a seasoned hunter, take this advice to heart. It just might save your life.

▲ Polar bears see humans as a potential food item. Therefore, really large calibers, cartridges, and bullet types are like chocolate cake to hunters: they provide a level of comfort. Credit: ID 15246 © Anthony Hathaway | Dreamstime.com

▲ No matter what type of big game is hunted, a cartridge must provide top-notch stopping power in order to provide a quick and ethical kill. Credit: 647668 © Chris Fourie | Dreamstime.com

Chapter Five

STOPPING POWER: How Caliber, Weight, and Velocity Combine to Bring Game Down Fast

"More than most American game animals, the pronghorn, by virtue of the terrain he inhabits, is genuinely the rifleman's choice."
—Thomas McIntyre, *Dreaming the Lion, 1993*

The preceding chapter covered the type of gear used to hunt the world's most *deadly and sizeable*, animals. This chapter is different in that it covers what type of stopping power is needed when hunting the more customary big game animals (elk, moose, black bear, etc.). At this point, it is important to differentiate game animals' size categories, they are divided into four dissimilar groups that include small (Coues deer) medium white-tailed mule deer etc.), large (moose, elk, etc.), and the massive dangerous game (elephant, Cape buffalo, Kodiak brown bear, etc.) body dimensions.

The animals discussed here, like all other big game, have comparable anatomy and skeletal features. The only differences arise in bone thickness, hair depth, body fat, and toughness of the hide that a bullet must penetrate differs from a mountain lion to an Alaskan bull moose. So, thought must be given to each of those factors, and equally important, the animal's ability to tolerate bullet punishment.

Consequently, before hunters select a rifle and cartridge, they should do their homework about the animals they plan to hunt and the equipment they intend to use. Even the type of terrain should be calculated into the equation. For instance, will the hunter be stalking a pronghorn antelope arid terrain desert of Arizona or a bull moose in the dense cover of Alaska.

A higher-velocity cartridge allows a hunter to increase the range at which a particular bullet will perform, making it an ideal choice for shooting antelope. A magnum cartridge provides a noticeable edge with penetration and knockdown power, for stalking a large

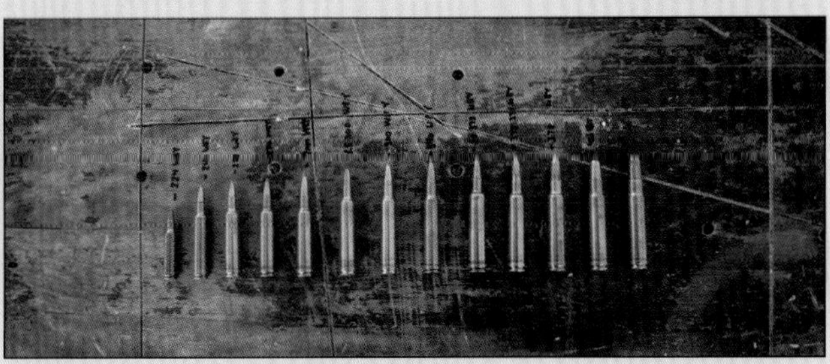

▲ Before selecting a particular cartridge for hunting a specific big game animal, do your due diligence. It requires careful thought to the elements of a hunt including distance, penetration, knockdown power, terrain, etc. Credit: Weatherby

Alaskan bull moose at a closer range. Consequently, cartridge loads and bullet types and a rifle's action must address those issues.

THE WAY BULLETS KILL

A rifle bullet works by transferring kinetic energy (to an animal) that causes a rippling shock wave through its tissue as the bullet careens through the animal's body destroying more and more tissue. It also disrupts the function of vital organs or the central nervous system. In turn, this causes blood loss and often shocks the animal's system. The more damage a bullet causes, the more likely it is to produce a quick kill. Sometimes all of this can cause shock to an animal's system, which can be *almost* instantly fatal, but not always reliably so.

POWER OF THE BULLET

Kinetic energy, the ability to cause damage, is the most common cause of killing power for rifle bullets, and it is a reasonable marker. But it is by no means the only factor or the most crucial factor. Energy gives an idea of how much power there is to initiate things like bullet expansion and penetration but does not guarantee that either of them will occur.

SECTIONAL DENSITY

Sectional density, bullet construction, and impact velocity are important factors affecting a bullet's penetration, if not the most important. Penetration is critical because the bullet must reach deep inside the animal in order to put its vital organs and nervous system out of commission. As mentioned previously, a bullet that fails to penetrate an animal properly is unlikely to knock down and dispatch the animal quickly and humanely.

Sectional density (SD) is the ratio of bullet weight to bore diameter (caliber). Higher sectional density means more mass is concentrated in a smaller frontal area, leading to better penetration because the projectile can better maintain its momentum as it encounters resistance from the target medium (a.k.a. hide, flesh, and bone).

BULLET WEIGHT AND DIAMETER

As the diameter of the bullet increases, so does its frontal area, resulting in a larger wound channel when it impacts an animal's body. There is a direct relationship

▲ There are many factors to consider when selecting a cartridge. Careful thought is needed to select the proper cartridge for the type of game hunted. Credit: Winchester Ammunition

between bullet frontal area and its effectiveness in causing damage, often referred to as killing power.

EXPANSION AND PENETRATION

More critical than the initial diameter of the bullet is its expanded diameter. A bullet that fails to expand typically inflicts minimal shock to an animal's internal system and disrupts less tissue. The structure of the bullet plays a crucial role in its killing power, facilitating both rapid expansion and the necessary penetration to reach vital organs in large animals, such as large game animals like elk, moose, bighorn sheep, etc.

Bullet manufacturers employ various strategies to achieve the desired terminal performance, usually aiming for a balance between expansion and penetration. Ideally, the front portion of the bullet should expand rapidly to nearly double its original diameter, maximizing tissue damage as it traverses through the animal. Meanwhile, the rear section of the bullet should remain intact to retain as much weight as possible, aiding in penetration. When the design works effectively, the bullet passes through the animal's vital organs fully expanded.

▲ Velocity significantly influences expansion, generally leading to more aggressive enlargement. Credit: ID 28978371 © Anton Zhuravkov | Dreamstime.com

Velocity significantly influences expansion, with higher velocities generally leading to more aggressive expansion. Bullet designs are tailored to specific impact velocity ranges. Conventional soft-point, hollow-point, and plastic-tip bullets typically perform optimally in standard calibers. However, for big-case magnum cartridges ranging from .300 WSM and above, tougher bullets are necessary to control expansion and prevent premature breakup at velocities exceeding 3,000 fps, particularly with lighter bullets of any caliber. These magnum cartridges should be given careful consideration when planning to hunt a musk ox, bighorn sheep, large black bear, or wild razorback.

An ideal bullet for large, heavy-skinned game should exhibit rapid expansion, creating a wide wound channel that maximizes tissue destruction as it careens through the animal's lungs. It's preferable for the bullet to retain some of its core to aid penetration. Nevertheless, a bullet that penetrates to the vital organs and then fragments, dispersing lead and jacket material throughout the animal's heart and lung area, will typically result in a quicker kill compared to one that creates a long, narrow wound channel through the lungs and exits the far side.

BULLETS FOR POWERFUL GAME

Other controlled expansion bullets are primarily intended for high velocity and/or large animals such as the Alaskan moose. These bullets require extra toughness to penetrate heavy fur, thick skin, and substantial bone structures before reaching the animal's vital organs. Premium controlled-expansion bullets, featuring dual cores, partitioned cores, special jackets, or bonded cores like the Remington Core-Lokt Ultra, Federal Fusion, Winchester Power Max, A-Frame Dead Tough, Speer African Grand Slam, CT Fail Safe, and Woodleigh Weldcore are essential for this purpose. These bullets are engineered to retain a significant portion (75 percent or more) of their core to ensure adequate penetration. They represent an excellent choice for use in high-velocity and big-bore cartridges designed for such game.

Manufacturing such bullets is more complex and costly compared to conventional bullets. Examples include the Barnes X-Bullet, CT Partition Gold, Nosler Partition, Speer Trophy Bonded, and Swift A-Frame, which are also suitable for larger game at magnum velocities, albeit at premium prices.

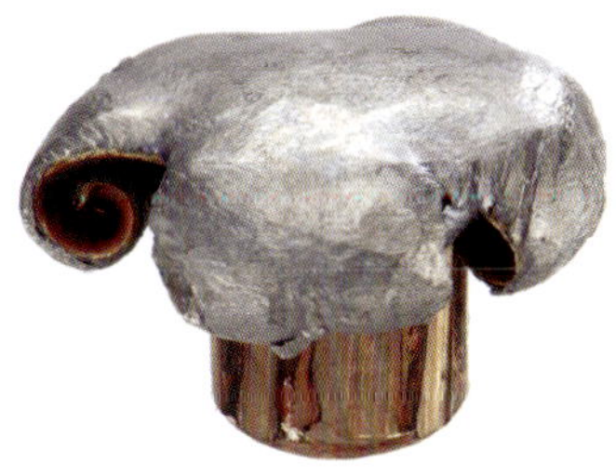

▲ Winchester's POWER MAX BONDED uses a proprietary bonding process to deliver massive expansion and long-range accuracy for maximum knockdown power. When hunting large, 700-pound bull elk, maximum knockdown power is a key element. Credit (for both images): Winchester Ammunition.

SHOT PLACEMENT

Bullet placement stands as the pivotal factor in determining killing effectiveness. Directing any adequate bullet into a vital area guarantees a swift demise for the animal. If a bullet disrupts the function of the animal's lungs or heart, its survival prospects diminish rapidly. This underscores why most experts advocate aiming for the scapula, or the lung area. These regions ensure swift and humane kills while minimizing the wastage of meat prized by hunters. The lung area, often referred to as the boiler room or breadbasket, presents the largest and most accessible vital area of the animal to target. The objective should be to hit one of these two areas. For more detailed insights into this topic, refer to chapter 13.

CHOOSE THE RIGHT BULLET DESIGN

Different bullets are needed for optimal terminal performance when hunting medium-sized animals like a 150-pound white-tailed deer versus a 1,200- to 1,600-pound Alaskan bull moose. As I reiterate throughout this book, always prioritize bullet placement as the foremost factor in achieving prompt and effective kills. Ensuring an adequate bullet reaches a vital area guarantees a swift kill. It also lessens the possibilities of having to track a wounded animal for long distances, or perhaps never finding a wounded game animal.

RELIABILITY OF THE RIFLE ACTION

Another equally important factor, particularly when hunting large game animals, is the action of the rifle. For instance, I would not chance being in the frigid backcountry of Alaska hunting a cranky bull moose

▲ This bull elk represents the best options for targeting the shoulder blade or lung area. Either of the two locations will deliver a quick and humane kill. Credit: ID 28193710 © Thomas Barrat | Dreamstime.com

▲ There are many rifle actions from which to choose. However, an overwhelming number of gun writers and hunters rate the venerable bolt action as the most reliable hunting firearm action. Credit: TRACTOptics

with an action that is prone to jamming up in cold freezing rain. The bolt action rates at the top for having very dependable action performance—bar none. While a semi-automatic rifle can deliver more firepower at greater speeds toward a charging bull moose, a single jam could be fatal, leaving you with no further need to worry about choosing the best type of rifle action.

RATE OF FIRE

The rate of fire is another important element to consider when stalking any type of big game animal. Bolt-action rifles not only achieve rapid firing, but they also offer rock solid dependability and have fewer parts that can break or, worse yet, are prone to jam up. Even the most experienced hunters can get nervous when they place the crosshairs on a charging wild hog, bull moose, or even an angry black bear. That stress alone may cause a shot to miss its exact aimpoint. That's enough to shift the odds from killing a black bear at a comfortable 100 yards away to worrying about killing it before it reaches you. Using a dependable action that can achieve a high rate of fire will increase your odds of stopping the animal and preventing it from running away or directly toward you. With proper range practice, a bolt-action rifle can indeed have a high enough rate of fire to accomplish that goal.

With all that said, another action that provides a dependable and a fast rate of fire is the revered lever action. The lever action delivers a host of benefits. They include fast and reliable action, more ammunition capacity, is lightweight and suitable for hunting various game animals, it also has accurate and impressive sights. A lever action is also ideal to slip into a gun-carrying case for carrying a rifle by horseback into remote areas.

CAPACITY

Using a rifle that has ample magazine capacity is another insurance policy when hunting big game animals. If you miss the first shot, or make a poor follow-up shot, having extra cartridges in the magazine can increase your chances of putting down a cantankerous Alaskan bull moose before it discovers who is shooting.

"SHOOTABILITY"

Shootability—being an outstanding shooter. All I have previously discussed will not mean anything if a hunter cannot accurately hit his or her big game animal. Hence, if you are going to use a big-bore magnum rifle like a .300 Win Mag or larger, be absolutely sure you can manage the felt recoil enough to perform good shot placement without flinching. Flinching decreases any hunter's shootability. It is highly recommended to practice with a big-bore rifle long before the hunt,

▲ To quickly drop any typical large game such as a grizzly bear, a well-placed shot is crucial. Credit: ID 23511700 © Dennis Donohue | Dreamstime.com

in order to determine if its felt recoil is tolerable. The best way to decrease or eliminate flinching is to equip the firearm with devices that are designed to suppress heavy felt recoil. As mentioned in other chapters, they include, but are not limited to, a quality recoil pad, muzzle brake, or a suppressor.

The end goal of any big game hunt is to place a single bullet in a vital spot to kill the animal as quickly as possible. But it also requires a hunter to be ready mentally and to have the proper gear to deliver an additional shot (or shots if the need arises) as accurately and quickly as possible. .

CONCLUSION

These large game animals range from the fearless menacing razorback hog, the cantankerous and unpredictable Alaskan/Yukon bull moose, to the ill-tempered black bear. Anyone hunting such large game would be well served not to take any of them lightly—ever.

A NOTE

When it comes to hunting any large or especially dangerous game, the information provided in this compendium is for your consideration only. All rifle calibers, cartridges, actions, and other equipment should be selected based on personal preference and determined by each hunter after conducting careful research on potential options. The accuracy of heavy-duty rifle actions, cartridges, and bullet types depends on the hunter's ability to shoot larger cartridges accurately. In other words, the shooter must be able to manage felt recoil effectively to ensure precise shooting.

▲ Wild razorback boars are not domestic pigs. They are considered among the most life-threatening traditional sized animals to hunt. Most hunters who are attacked by wild boars can end up with a nicked or severed artery. Stay alert when hunting wild boar. Credit: ID 18676878 © Wkruck | Dreamstime.com

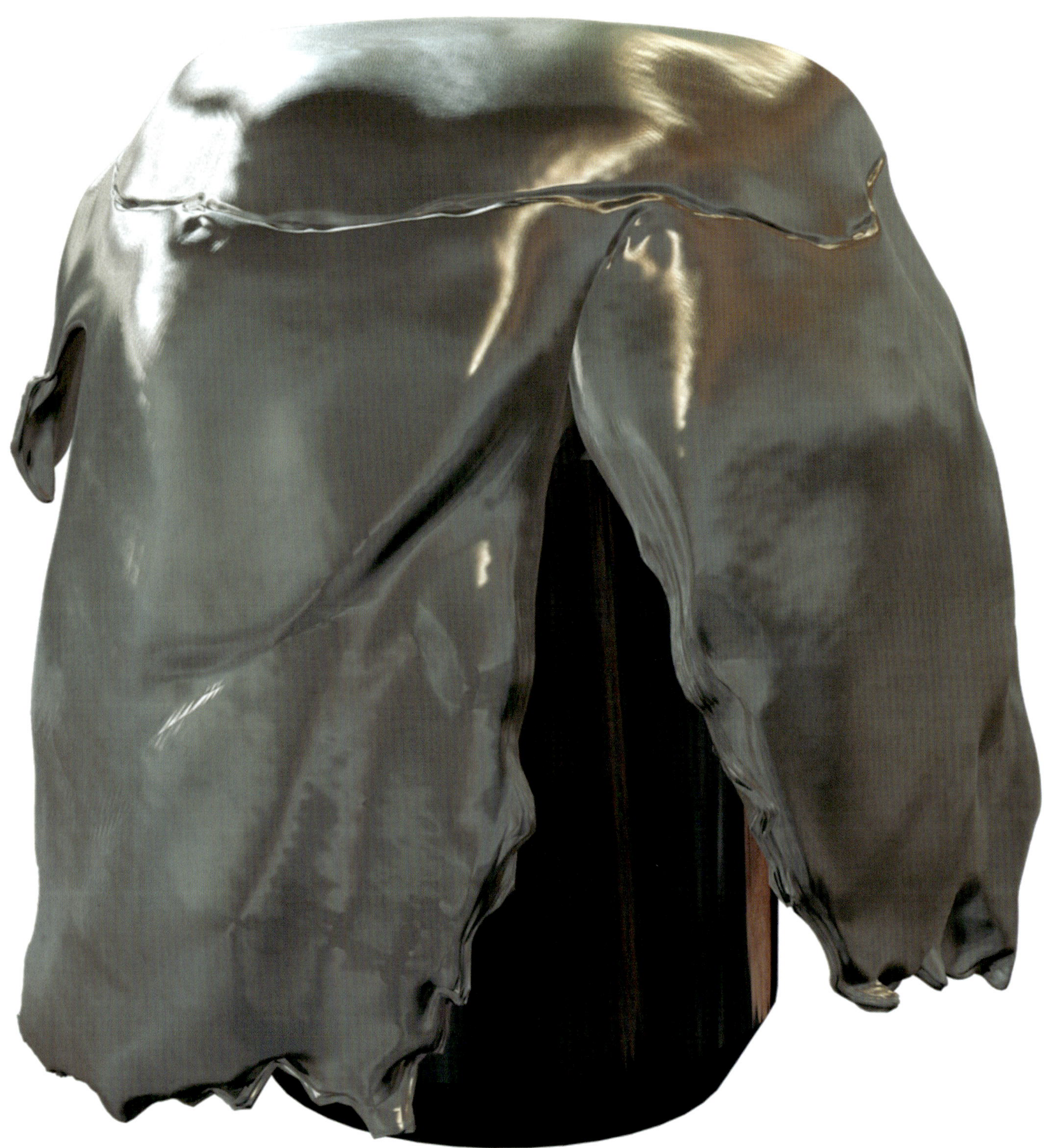

▲ All things considered; nothing is more important than selecting the right type of bullet for the type of game hunted. Credit: Winchester Ammunition

Chapter Six

ANATOMY OF A BULLET: Bullet Types, Shapes, and Their Intended Uses

The placing of the bullet is everything.
—COL. TOWNSEND WHELEN, *Mr. Rifleman* (with Bradford Angier), 1965

This chapter is about different types of bullets. They are literally the meat and potatoes of any hunt. While a rifle, scope, and cartridge load are important, they are nothing more than a missile to deliver the all-important bullet. Bullets are the most critical element for big game hunters. After all, it is this small chunk of lead and copper that kills the animal. But not all bullets are manufactured equally.

Unfortunately, bullet selection is often an overlooked tactic and can often be the component of a cartridge least paid attention to by hunters. Yet, understanding what to look for in bullets can help hunters to recognize what elements to consider when buying them. Hunters should seek bullets that are engineered to expand and penetrate game swiftly upon impact, creating deep wound channels that ensure a rapid and reliable kill.

▲ While all the elements of a cartridge are important, none is as critical as the bullet type. It is the bullet that can make or break a hunt. Credit: Hornady

Although manufacturers diligently produce a plethora of innovative bullet types, there is no one bullet design that can be called the "perfect bullet." No one bullet can guarantee a fast knockdown and humane one-shot kill. However, the correct bullet for the type of game and terrain being hunted will dramatically increase a hunter's odds of a quick, clean, and humane kill.

Differently designed bullets achieve different tasks. When buying cartridges with specific types of bullets, the ammunition can be more expensive than some other hunting ammo. There is little doubt that expensive ammunition contains superior elements, a result of higher manufacturing costs. Higher-priced ammunition is targeted to perform at higher standards. That, in itself, is well worth the cost. As Kurt Vonnegut's famous quote from *Cat's Cradle* states, "In this world, you get what you pay for." Those words fittingly apply here.

HUNTING BULLETS

The three types of bullets that are designed to hunt big game include cup and draw, impact extruded (premium), and homogeneous (one-piece). Cup and draw and impact extruded are made of a lead core enclosed by a copper jacket. Homogeneous bullets are constructed from a single piece of copper or copper alloy with no lead, making it legal in states that require no lead in bullets. Of the three types of bullets, impact extruded and homogenous are the best types of bullets suited for hunting big game.

▲ Cup and Draw are the most commonly used bullets with thin jackets that expand rapidly at the point of impact. It is said that at higher velocities they can over expand, resulting in too much mushrooming of the bullet, which can limit penetration. Credit: Winchester Ammunition

CUP AND DRAW

Cup and draw are the most used bullets. They generally have thin jackets that mushroom (expand) rapidly at the point of impacting soft tissue. At higher velocities, they can expand too much, and the larger frontal surface limits penetration. That results in not always penetrating deeply enough to efficiently damage vital areas. Some examples of cup and draw bullets include Winchester Power Point, Hornady SST, Federal Soft Point, Sierra GameKing, Remington Core-Lokt, Speer Hot-Core, and Berger VLC Hunting. All bullets of this type generally work well at slower impact velocities on deer-size game.

IMPACT EXTRUDED (PREMIUM)

Impact extruded (premium) bullets are made of a lead core bounded by copper. Because of their tough construction, impact extruded (premium) bullets expand consistently and penetrate deeply due to their thicker jackets that provide higher weight retention, resulting in better overall performance. The fact is Impact Extruded bullets are the most effective bullets for hunting large northern whitetails and other big game. Because they are heavy-duty, they are renowned for their bullet performance and reliability. A couple of examples of impact extruded (premium) hunting bullets are the Nosler Partition® and Ballistic Tip®.

HOMOGENEOUS

Homogeneous bullets, like the extruded bullets, have a tough construction. These bullets are known for their consistent expansion and deep penetration abilities. Homogeneous bullets are made from a single piece of copper, or copper alloy with no lead, and have a polymer tip that expands the second it contacts an animal. They are known for their superior accuracy and are regularly used for hunting big game. One example of a homogeneous hunting bullet is the Nosler E-Tip.®

Selecting the best types of bullets requires an understanding of the different bullet designs and how they will perform. Some of the bullets mentioned in this chapter are within the category of "controlled expansion" bullets.

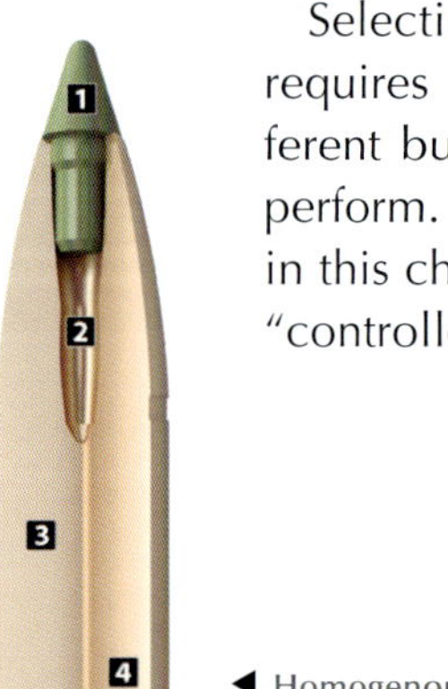

◀ Homogenous bullets are made from a single piece of copper or copper alloy with no lead. They are known for their superior accuracy. Credit: Nosler

TERMINAL PERFORMANCE

The way a bullet acts when it impacts an animal is referred to as terminal performance. This is what the bullet does as it passes through the hide, skin, fat, muscle, bone, and vital organs of an animal. For a bullet to be its most effective, it must expand enough to make a large wound channel while also retaining enough weight to penetrate deeply enough to reach the vital organs such as the heart and lungs. If a bullet expands too much upon impact, though, it won't penetrate as deeply, and if a bullet doesn't expand enough, it will penetrate deeply without causing the needed damage to effectively kill the animal. Controlled expansion bullets are a popular type of bullet that can perform differently depending on the range and impact velocity. An example of a controlled expansion bullet is a Ballistic Tip® with design features that balance expansion and penetration to create a good wound channel that penetrates deeply enough to damage internal organs. It also provides accuracy and reduces drag.

Bullet diameter and weight also have an impact on how well a bullet will perform on whitetails, larger deer species, and even other bigger game animals like bison, bear, etc. Usually, the larger animals require heavier bullets. Be cautious not to use too large a cartridge, as it will significantly increase felt recoil.

Enter stage right, accuracy; the most important factor when selecting a hunting bullet. This is where range practice plays a dramatic role. As noted in another chapter, always test for the types of cartridges your rifle likes to shoot best and which cartridges it does not. As mentioned in chapter 9, about zeroing a rifle, every rifle barrel is different. Some are really picky about what cartridges they like and do not like to shoot. The barrel will not be bashful about showing its preferences regarding different types of weights of bullets. The only way to discover this is to experiment with shooting different loads and bullet types at the range. As I have said throughout this book and in many of my other books and writings, accuracy promotes confidence, and confidence increases accuracy.

No single bullet is perfect for all hunters. Some prioritize long-range ballistics, while others focus on terminal performance or knockdown power. Some prefer bullets that fully expand and remain inside the game, while others look for entry and exit wounds. Preferences also vary between lead tips and polymer tips. Lead tips expand quickly but are less aerodynamic, whereas polymer tips offer better aerodynamics and resist deformation more effectively. As you can see, there are many factors to consider when selecting a bullet type.

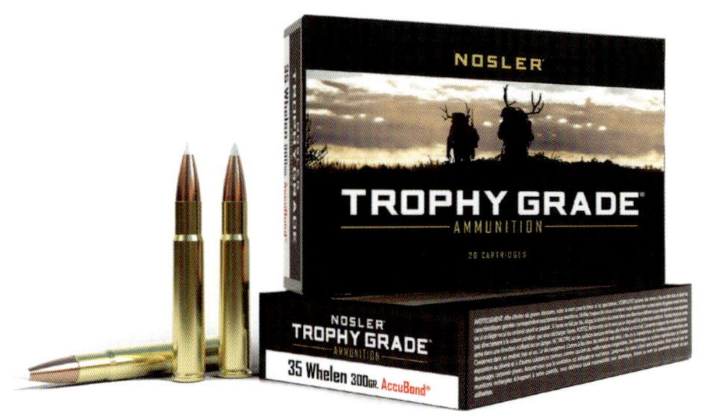

▲ Lead-tip bullets generally expand rapidly. However, they are not known to be as aerodynamic as a polymer tip. Credit: Nosler.

Below is bullet information for hunters to make up their own minds regarding what bullet type serves them best for hunting whitetails and other big game species. Keep in mind, when buying cartridges and bullet types it is once again wise to remember Kurt Vonnegut's quote, "In this world, you get what you pay for." There is no question that premium hunting bullets and ammunition will cost more, but their performance is well worth the money spent.

BULLET LINGO

Soft Point (SP): For deer and other big game with standard rifle calibers, soft-point bullets are hard to beat. A soft-point bullet is almost completely jacketed; however, the jacket stops short of covering the nose of the bullet, thereby exposing the soft lead that includes the bullet's core at its tip. Thus, the moniker "soft point." Big game hunters regularly choose SP bullets because of their excellent expansion on impact with an animal's hide and soft tissue. SP bullets are designed to increase their forward diameter while remaining intact in order to penetrate deeply enough to damage internal organs. SP bullets also make a wound channel with a diameter that is larger than the bullet itself. This is why they are often chosen for hunting large dangerous game, thick-skinned animals, and large game where hollow points are illegal. Soft-point bullets are constructed with a softer lead than other bullets, which deforms the bullet's nose, resulting in slower type expansion and greater penetration than a hollow point of the same caliber. Moreover, SP bullets transfer more mass into an animal before they open up and dump energy. Soft points of 130 grains and heavier out of your classic calibers work beautifully on whitetails.

▲ Soft Tip: A soft tip on the Power Point allows the bullet to preserve its reliability in flight. On impact, it expands very rapidly, which helps to create a large wound channel. Accurate shot placement with the expanded soft tip almost guarantees the takedown of mid- to large-size game. Credit: Winchester Ammunition.

During the years I lived in Colorado, soft-point bullets were immensely popular among big game hunters. I took elk, mule deer, and bear using either 130-grain or 150-grain SP bullets. Soft-point bullets also offer more expansion than a full metal jacket bullet and better penetration than a hollow point. That makes them an ideal choice for hunting large, dangerous, and tough game. One of the biggest advantages of SP bullets is that they are generally legal in places where hollow-point bullets are illegal to use. Steer clear of standard soft points for small-caliber rifles, though, since they can expand too rapidly, causing the bullet to shed too much material and weight to penetrate adequately.

Ballistic Tip: A ballistic tip is a trademark name for Nosler's line of hunting ammo, which is a hollow point with the front cavity filled with a hard plastic polymer. Hence, a ballistic-tip bullet is a jacketed hollow-point bullet with a plastic tip. Ballistic-tip bullets are within the cup and core category. The design creates an extremely aerodynamic bullet shape. The tip enhances the bullet's ballistics, allowing it to retain greater velocity and energy over longer distances. The bullet stays airborne longer by decreasing the effects of gravity and wind deflection. The advantages of using ballistic-tip ammo include accuracy, reduced drag, and reliable controlled expansion upon impact. Ballistic tips are more aerodynamic than traditional cup and core bullets, making them more accurate and applicable to hunting deer and other game. Their reduced drag and other improved ballistic properties also make them well-suited for long-range shooting. Manufacturers have experimented with the bullet's shape and jacket thickness to create different types of bullets for different hunting scenarios.

Boattail (BT): A boattail raises the bullet's ballistic coefficient. It is a type of spitzer bullet that has an angled, tapered base. The tapered base reduces drag and improves the bullet's ballistic coefficient. This means the bullet has less wind resistance and it flies straighter, with less arc; therefore it hits an animal harder. Because of their aerodynamic design, the bullet is a little more accurate at long ranges. Another way of saying this is that boattails were engineered for long-range velocity retention. This makes a boattail good for hunters who shoot game at long distances. It is often asked, though, which is better? Boattails or flat-based projectiles? With comparable profiles, a flat-based bullet has rapid expansion, which might give a hunter better accuracy in less-than-perfect shooting conditions. Also, flat-based bullets can provide more cartridge case capacity. That said, though, boattail bullets are almost always the choice when dealing with long-distance shooting. Their higher ballistic coefficient means they manage the air better than flat-based bullets. Therefore, boattails are somewhat better regarding weight retention and physical reliability. With all that said, there are some gun writer bullet pros who warn that not all rifles shoot boattails well. Should you encounter a similar issue, try a flat-based bullet. Your rifle may end up shooting better groups.

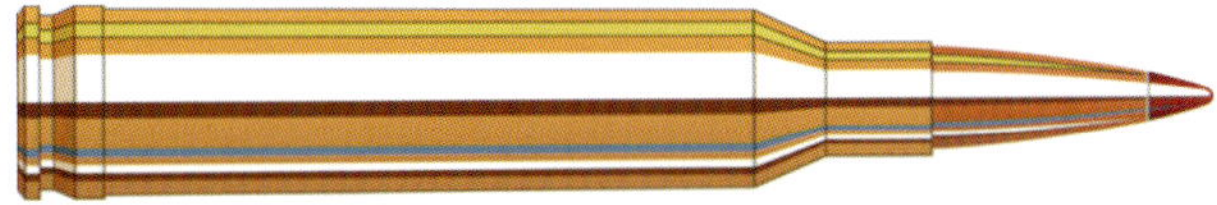

▲ A boattail cartridge is known for its accuracy at long distances, which makes it a good choice for hunters who shoot game at extended ranges. Credit: Hornady

Bonded Bullet (BB): A bonded bullet is more correctly referred to as a bonded jacketed bullet that has been chemically or molecularly bonded to a lead alloy core via heat, adhesive, or by electronic means. By bonding the lead core to the jacket, a bullet is produced that will stay intact even during the harshest conditions. Bonded bullet ammunition is designed for deep penetration. This is done in jacketed "solids" when hunting dangerous game. Bonded bullets remain intact as they penetrate game animals.

Copper-Alloy: There are pros and cons to hunting with copper bullets. When it comes to accuracy, copper bullets shoot well. Many hunters enjoy shooting copper alloy bullets, but others do not find them endearing. Like many bullets, though, some rifles shoot copper bullets well, while others do not. According to the ammunition industry, a lot of effort has been put into making copper bullets as accurate and as consistent as lead-core bullets. Copper-alloy bullets are lighter and harder than lead, and therefore they are less likely to fragment. In the past it was claimed that they caused barrel wear and fouling. Nowadays, most copper-alloy bullets have driving bands, which reduce copper fouling and pressure spikes and can increase accuracy. Copper-alloy bullets are flat flyers and have performed superbly at the distances most hunters actually shoot game. However, they are more expensive.

▲ Copper Impact® ammunition is specifically designed for use by big game hunters. The tough solid copper expanding bullet provides more impact trauma, better energy transfer, and larger wound cavities for excellent knockdown. Credit: Winchester Ammunition.

Flat Nose (FN): A flat-nose bullet is often referred to as a "full metal case flat nose," which is essentially the identical type of ammo. They are distinguished by a flat front area of the bullet. Flat-nose bullets are extremely well-received because of their accuracy. They are mostly used in rifles with tubular magazines. While these bullets are highly popular, they do not demonstrate their qualities until they have passed 200 yards downrange, making them more desirable to a select group of long-range hunters than they are to the masses.

Hollow Points (HP): While hollow points are excellent bullets for hunting, it does depend on the type of quarry to be hunted. They are not a good choice for larger deer species such as moose, elk, or caribou. But they are a good choice for whitetails and mule deer. Hollow points are fine for hunting game at reasonably close ranges; they are not good for hunting game at long-ranges.

With their hollowed-out tip, hollow-point bullets expand quickly upon impact. When contacting soft tissue, the pressure in its tip makes the soft lead core immediately expand outward. The bullet is specifically designed so that it slows as it moves through an animal's body cavity, generally stopping without exiting.

Due to hollow points having rapid expansion, they are not suitable for smaller deer species like Coues and Sitka black-tailed deer, because they destroy too much edible meat and tissue. However, if the object is to eradicate nuisance animals such as feral hogs, coyotes, fox, or even annoying groundhogs, hollow-point bullets can serve this purpose well.

For hunting white-tailed deer, hollow-point bullets work out to be a fine choice. They expand rapidly, creating quick trauma, and the heavy bullets retain enough weight to penetrate deeply, while creating a large wound channel immediately upon impact. Because they rarely pass right through the body cavity, it leads to more energy being released within the animal. The concussion results in a great deal of internal damage to large sections of a deer's vital organs. Consequently, most times, if the deer does not drop in its tracks, it will quickly bleed out before traveling more than 20 yards. With good shot placement, hollow points will drop deer quickly with one shot.

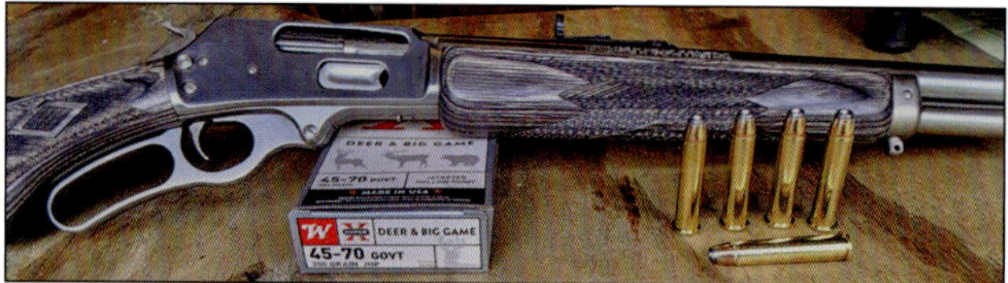

▲ Hollow points match up well with deer guns chambered for straight-walled cartridges including but not limited to Remington's .360 Buckhammer, Winchester's .350 Legend, .45-70, etc. Credit: Fiduccia Enterprises

Hollow points also work well out of slower, large-caliber rifles. They match up well with deer guns chambered for straight-walled rifle cartridges like Remington's .360 Buckhammer or Winchester's .350 Legend a.k.a. .350 LGND, or the .45–70 Government.

Jacketed Soft Points (JSP): A soft-point bullet, a.k.a. a soft-nosed bullet, is a jacketed expanding bullet with a soft metal core enclosed by a stronger metal jacket left open at the forward tip. A soft-point bullet is meant to expand the instant it contacts the animal's body. It causes a wound width greater than the bullet diameter. Soft points ranging from 130 to 150 grains and shot out of classic standard, straight-walled, and magnum deer calibers work exceedingly well on whitetails and other deer species. Refrain from standard soft points, though; they expand too rapidly, causing the bullet to shed too much material and weight to penetrate adequately. Soft points expand more than full metal jackets and penetrate better than hollow points. They have a wide array of uses when hunting large and small game.

Lead Round Nose (LRN): The lead round-nose bullet is a bullet type designation indicating the projectile is made entirely of lead with no jacket. It is a common traditional bullet style in current use. The nose of the bullet has a rounded, smooth shape with no pocket or hollow recess. It offers more penetration than a flat nose, but less expansion than a hollow point. Its large, uncovered lead fore-section is a perfect choice for medium-velocity cartridges at midranges. Round-nose bullets enlarge and penetrate game animals well when combined with medium to lower velocities. The good old-fashioned round-nose bullet, which seems to have been passed over in the history of bullet evolution, is still a viable choice for hunting many deer species.

▲ This partition bullet's dual-core design assures rapid expansion of the foremost core. It promotes the expanded mushroom, allowing the enclosed rear core to remain intact, retaining more than two-thirds the original bullet weight for deep penetration. This ammunition provides undeniable reliability on all game. Credit: Federal Ammunition.

Partition Bullet (PB): This premium hunting bullet is one of a kind due to its unique design that is almost like two bullets fused together to create an "H" shape.

Like bonded bullets, partition bullets can achieve reliable expansion without overexpanding, preventing the bullet from falling apart and reducing its effectiveness. There are two cores in the partition bullet separated by the copper alloy that jackets the bullet, except for the tip and the base.

Polymer Tip (PT): This ammunition is loaded exclusively with Nosler's line of Ballistic Tip® Hunting bullets. The bullet is a polymer-tipped projectile made popular by the company when they introduced it in 1984. It was touted as a premium choice for hunting medium-sized game such as antelope and wild hogs, as well as whitetails, mule deer, and Coues deer. Upon impact, the plastic drives into the hollow point, and the bullet performs like a standard hollow-point, mushrooming to a larger diameter. These bullets possess the aerodynamics for longer, more accurate flights, and the performance to ensure high lethality.

Semi-Jacketed Hollow Point (SJHP): A semi-jacketed hollow-point bullet is a type of expanding bullet that expands on impact, causing a more lethal hit without penetrating further than necessary. For deer hunting, they work well out of large-caliber rifles. They still expand rapidly, creating quick trauma, but the heavy bullets retain enough weight to penetrate deeply and do the job. Think of using these bullets for deer guns chambered for any of the straight-walled rifle cartridges.

Spire Point: A manufacturer's name for their own spitzer-style bullet. The word "spitzer" comes from the German word spitzgeschuss—literally "pointed shot (bullet)." In simple English, a spitzer bullet is a pointed bullet.

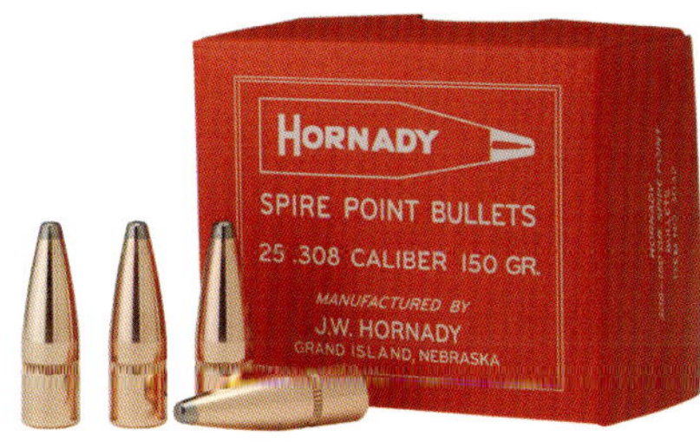

▲ Spire points are an excellent choice when hunting large game, including all the species of deer and even dangerous game animals. When hunting dangerous game, penetration is more important than expansion; hence spire-point bullets are a good choice. Credit: Hornady

Spire-point bullets are an excellent choice when hunting large game like Alaskan/Yukon moose and/or dangerous game like the great bears (polar, Kodiak brown, and grizzly bears). For example, a decent load is the .300 Weatherby Magnum with 180-grain spire-point bullets. When hunting large or dangerous game, penetration is more important than expansion. That's what makes spire-point bullets a good choice. Spire-point bullets are designed to be fired at high speeds over long distances, and their design minimizes air friction and maximizes spin stability. Spire points are also designed to be tapered, meaning they are longer without becoming heavier. The longer length also means it's easier for the bullet to stay stable for longer distances.

A word of caution about spire-point bullets: not all are created equal. Each type must be carefully evaluated to ensure it meets the hunter's specific needs and expectations. For instance, spire-point hollow-point boattail (HPBT) bullets are usually non-expanding. However, there are some exceptions such as the Berger Hunter Hybrid. Manufacturers design many polymer-tipped bullets like the Hornady ELD Match strictly for accuracy. They design others for accuracy and terminal expansion, like the Hornady ELD-X.

Soft-point bullets are always a safe and affordable bet for hunting. When a hunter makes a choice between a round-nose or a pointed soft-point bullet, his or her accuracy will benefit from the spire-point profile's low-drag ballistics.

I want to end this chapter with a reminder. When it comes down to killing big game, especially dangerous game, there are three main elements hunters need to totally focus on: shot placement, shot placement, and shot placement. If a hunter cannot hit what she or he is aiming at, no cartridge, rifle caliber, grain load, bullet design, et al. is going to help the hunter to kill game quickly and humanely.

SOME OF THE AUTHOR'S FAVORITE BULLET TYPES

1. Winchester Silvertip
2. Barnes TSX
3. Nosler Partition
4. Hornaday ELD-X
5. Federal Trophy Bonded Bear Claw
6. Remington Core-Lokt

▲ The most common rifle actions are bolt, lever, semi-auto, break-action, and pump. The bolt action is the most popular choice due to its ease of operation and dependability. The second most popular action is the reliable lever action. Credit: Fiduccia Ent.

Chapter Seven

LIGHTS, CAMERA, ACTIONS! Choosing a Rifle Action

I hold a shotgun in high regard; but rifles—well, I love the darn things.
—JACK O'CONNOR

Selecting a rifle action is as important as choosing an appropriate caliber. Yet, some hunters are not sure what type of action will work best for their type of hunting. There are varied types of actions to choose from, with each having its own advantages and disadvantages. Some of the considerations a hunter has to ponder include the types of terrain that will be most hunted; his or her ability to use a certain type of action accurately, quickly, comfortably, and competently; and how the action works in diverse types of weather conditions. When it comes to rifle actions, some of the more common selections include bolt, lever, pump, break, and autoloading actions.

▲ Bolt-action rifles have a reputation for being simple working devices that provide ongoing reliability. They are known for their dependability and lack of failures. Credit: Fiduccia Ent.

Today, the available rifle action mechanisms far exceed the options in years past. In all likelihood your grandfather and great grandfather's choices were much more limited to lever actions, and even single-shot rifles. Not so anymore. Now there are diverse types of actions that offer specific benefits. To lessen the confusion, it is best to follow the adage KISS: "keep it simple, stupid."

In other words, start with the basic necessities that will work best for you. The first step in selecting the perfect action for a rifle is to determine your primary shooting purpose. In this case, that would be an action for hunting and not target shooting. Matching the action with your intended purpose will ensure the most favorable performance in the field.

Once you have a clear understanding of your shooting needs, begin your research process. Become familiar with the distinct types and brands of actions that are available. Go online and read what experienced gun writers say.

.30–30 LEVER ACTION

The types of manual-repeating rifle actions to consider include the quintessential lever action, the exemplary bolt action, pump action, semi-automatic, and the single- or double-barreled break actions.

The classic rifle action is undoubtedly the time-honored lever-action .30–30. The Winchester Model 1894 rifle was the first firearm to use this cartridge. Referring to the rifle as a .30–30, though, would be incorrect. That's because in cartridge designation, the first 30 denotes the caliber and the second 30 refers to the gunpowder load, 30 grains.

In the mid-1960s, my first hunting rifle was a Gold Trigger, .30–30 Marlin lever-action 336. The rifle was more than likely the first deer rifle for generations of American hunters. Back then, the other two primary lever-action rifle models were the Winchester 94 and the Savage 99. However, the Marlin 336 etched its way into the hearts and minds as a favorite firearm among all rifles then and now. It is a timeless firearm. According to statistics from outdoorlife.com and other sources, more white-tailed deer have been killed by hunters using the .30–30 lever action than any other rifle action.[1] It also accounted for killing more than its share of black bear, elk, and mule deer.

Throughout my sixty years of hunting big game animals across numerous deer camps in North America, I frequently encountered hunters who were shooting a Marlin 336 lever-action .30–30. Many hunters at these camps relied on this rifle, and it was universally agreed that the Marlin 336 provided a sense of comfort and familiarity when held. When I lived in Colorado during the early 1970s, it was common to see big game guides, out-of-state hunters, and residents using Marlin lever-action rifles, although some preferred the Winchester 94 or the Savage 99. After all, they were cowboys—and a lever-action rifle was the ideal match-up for a cowboy. Many chose it not only for the rifle's renowned firearm components but also for its convenience factor. The rifle's action was handily flat, which made it perfect to slip snugly into a scabbard hung from a horse's saddle. Countless western movies show a .30–30 lever-action rifle strapped to one side of the saddle on the horse.

During that period, and certainly today, hunters have chosen a .30–30 lever action because of its ideal weight and length. As such, they can carry this classic rifle comfortably as they still-hunt through mature timber, thick cover, and even open parks. A "park" in western states is referred to as open fields in the east. Lever-action rifles are an excellent choice for different landscapes and game types where speed matters. Firearm guru Ron Spomer, who is a know-it-all firearm authority (yes, I mean it, he is credibly a know-it-all firearm authority), once said about shooting a .30–30:

▲ The .30-30 has been present and accounted for as a reliable and lethal firearm for hunting a wide variety of big game. Pictured here is my first rifle: a Gold Trigger, Marlin .30-30 lever-action 336. Credit: Fiduccia Ent.

"You must train to shoot as quickly as you start your truck and pull out of your driveway. Full confidence. No hesitation. Smooth and fast."[2] Excellent advice.

▲ Some believe lever-action rifles do not cycle as quickly as bolt actions. That's factually incorrect. Lever actions can be cycled extremely quickly. Credit: Henry Repeating Arms USA

Lever-actions are also a perfect rifle to make a first shot with rapid fast chambering for a follow-up shot. They have weathered the test of time and don't appear to be going out of style anytime soon. Some of the more prominent manufacturers of lever-action rifles include Winchester Arms, Henry Repeating Arms, and Marlin Firearms.

Some still-hunters (stalkers) prefer to not equip their lever-action .30–30 with a scope and opt to hunt with open sights. Ideally, though, when still hunting in thick cover, the .30–30 lever-action can be paired with a straight 4x scope. The best type of scope for a lever-action rifle is typically a low- to medium-magnification scope with a wide field of view. This allows for quick target acquisition and is well-suited for the shorter-range shooting often associated with lever-action rifles.

The lever-action is not only well-balanced, accurate, and flat shooting, but it can be zeroed in at 200 yards. Moreover, the recoil factor is about a fifth less than the recoil from other calibers (about 12 lbs. of recoil compared to 15 lbs.).

The .30–30 lever-action rifle is remarkably effective on most species of big game including whitetails, mule deer, elk, caribou, eastern moose, and black bear. This is particularly the case because most of these animals are usually shot at distances of less than 200 yards. That fits nicely into the .30–30's wheelhouse. I personally would not use a .30–30 for longer-distance shots greater than 200 yards. Nor would I choose it for larger and thicker-skinned game animals like an Alaskan moose, or dangerous game like the great bears and the like. Clearly, it would not be a viable choice to hunt Africa's dangerous Big Five either. With all that said about the quintessential .30–30 lever-action, though, today there are other actions to consider that can be paired with countless other types of cartridges.

Alas, lever actions do have some pitfalls. For instance, tubular magazines restrict it to flat-nose bullets that effect long-range trajectory. There are also not as many bullet weight choices in factory ammo. Though the .30–30's 150-grain bullet at around 2,300 fps is big game capable at modest ranges, the desire for more reach has pushed most hunters to more modern cartridges and hence, bolt-action rifles. Lever actions can be occasionally susceptible to bullet jam.

BOLT ACTIONS

The timeless bolt-action rifle has been around for nearly two centuries. It is the most common rifle action choice for hunters today. As I have mentioned, my first rifle was a .30–30 lever action, but when I started to hunt western big game at much longer distances, I chose to use a bolt-action rifle. At the time, it simply offered me better options. Although I have several types of rifle actions, I am a die-hard and totally dedicated fan of bolt-action rifles. There, I said it. Bolt-action rifles are my steadfast choice of all the action types.

▲ Bolt-action rifles are among the most commonly used hunting rifles today. Bolt-action rifles are manually operated and provide reliable cycling action. They are known for their soundness. Credit: Winchester Ammunition

Today's modern bolt-action rifles exemplify some of the toughest, most accurate, and most reliable actions in existence. Moreover, there can be no argument that the dependability of the bolt-action rifle is renowned. As with any other mechanical tool, reliability is job one! Therefore, the straightforward design of the bolt action shines in its steadfast consistency to work properly time and time again. I call it unflinching workability. The reason for its unwavering performance is simple—the design is so uncomplicated that there is not much that can go wrong with it. In my humble opinion, the single factor of a bolt action's relentless dependability is the chief advantage bolt actions hold over all other actions, especially semi-automatic rifles. These factors contribute to a bolt-action rifle having a long-established positive field record. The action has proven repeatedly that it gets the job done time and time again, even in bone-chillingly frigid temperatures, or other harsh weather conditions with which other actions could potentially have problems.

Like many tools today, the more complicated they are the more vulnerable they are to breaking down. That is my chief complaint about semi-automatic actions. They are complex with lots of moving parts. That is why an overwhelming number of hunters of African dangerous game choose the trouble-free bolt-action—for its dependability. No one wants an internal moving part, like operating rods and bolt carriers, to fail. That could end rather badly by having a 1,600 pound African buffalo charge, and not being able to load a second cartridge in the chamber! That can spoil a day afield in a hurry. Truth be known, semi-automatic actions are vulnerable to feeding ammunition problems and other various potential negative issues.

A bolt action's ease of operation comes from its nearly perfect design. As it has often been written, the bolt action's design is basic. Lift the bolt handle, pull back, push forward, press down, and you are good to go! Some benefits of a bolt-action rifle include a reduction of the overall weight of the rifle, greater ammo and caliber choices, and the options of adding a wider variety of scopes. Additionally, here are valuable reasons why a bolt-action rifle will outperform other actions:

- Capable of handling extremely high-pressure cartridges;

▲ The popularity of bolt-action rifles is due to their reliability and ease of operation. It doesn't take a rocket scientist to cycle a cartridge with a bolt-action rifle. Credit: Nosler

- The rifle doesn't use some of the round's energy to eject spent cartridges;
- Firmly locks the cartridge in a steadfast position for firing;
- The bolt is LOCKED during the entire time of firing, resulting in no loss of gas;
- Most times the chambers are cut tighter than other action rifles;
- It is a sturdier design that produces less flex when fired as compared to other actions;
- Bolt actions are also somewhat quieter when chambering a round;
- A bolt action works better for suppression; and
- A bolt action has better range and accuracy than a semi-auto.

Equally important, bolt-action rifles are available in almost every caliber manufactured. Not only that, but bolt-action rifles do not limit the kind of ammunition used for any particular caliber, and they are very compatible with custom brass ammunition as well. The bottom line is that a bolt-action rifle offers significantly more versatility than a semi-automatic rifle. Period. End of story.

▲ Bolt-action rifles do not limit the kind of ammunition used for any particular caliber, and they are very compatible with custom brass-ammunition, as well. Credit: Winchester Ammunition

One last thought about bolt-action rifles. Arguably, a bolt-action is claimed to deliver more pinpoint deadly accuracy than the semi-automatic. It is a subject that is hotly debated. However, my take on settling that argument is this: if they aren't pinpoint deadly accurate, why then do military snipers *always* choose a bolt-action rifle? Explain that point—huh?

BREAK ACTION

We've all seen movies with hunters using a two-barreled break-action rifle in Africa as they are being charged by a pissed-off Cape buffalo. Break-action rifles are also known as single-shot rifles or double-barreled rifles. They have distinct advantages and disadvantages compared to other types of rifles. Break-action rifles are renowned for their straightforward simplicity of operation and reliability. They have fewer moving parts compared to semi-automatic or even bolt-action rifles, which means there are fewer components that can malfunction. This reliability makes break-action rifles well-suited for hunting in harsh environments or in situations where reliability is paramount.

Another advantage is their accuracy. Break-action rifles can be highly reliable due to their rigid barrel and simple action. Furthermore, with the proper ammunition and shooting technique, break-action rifles can deliver exceptional accuracy, making them popular choices, especially for the precision shooting needed to hunt dangerous game.

There is a great deal of safety with break actions. Break-action rifles typically have exposed hammers or a visible cocking mechanism, allowing the shooter to easily verify whether the rifle is cocked and ready to fire. The design of a break action makes it simple to load and unload: snap open, load, slam shut, fire, break open, and eject shells. This simplicity can be advantageous in some situations.

▲ Like a bolt-action rifle, break-action rifles are easy to operate. They can deliver exceptional accuracy, which makes them popular choices for hunting dangerous game. Credit: Henry Repeating Arms

However, break-action rifles do have some drawbacks, with the most commonly mentioned being their limited ammunition capacity. Typically, single shot or double-barreled, these rifles can only hold one or two rounds at a time. This limitation can be significant in scenarios where additional shots may be necessary, particularly when hunting dangerous game.

Break actions also have slower follow-up shots. Reloading a break-action rifle after firing requires manually opening the action, ejecting the spent cartridge, and loading a new cartridge. This process can be slower compared to the cycling of a semi-automatic or bolt-action rifle, making follow-up shots more difficult.

High-quality break-action rifles, especially double rifles, can be expensive due to their craftsmanship, materials, and specialized design. This higher cost may deter some shooters from choosing a break-action rifle.

Recoil is a key factor to consider when thinking about buying or using a break-action rifle. Break-action rifles can have more felt recoil compared to rifles with other action types, especially in larger calibers. Without a semi-automatic or bolt-action mechanism to absorb and distribute recoil energy, shooters may experience significant kickback. So, if the shooter is oversensitive to recoil, a break action may not be the best choice.

Overall, break-action rifles excel in reliability, accuracy, and simplicity, but they may not be ideal for every shooting situation due to their limited capacity and slower reloading process. As a rifle option for hunting whitetails, they are not a popular choice. With that said, I have a hunting companion who, over many decades, has killed countless whitetails with a 16-gauge, single-barrel, break-action rifle with iron sights.

PUMP-ACTION

The pump-action, a.k.a. "slide action" or "trombone action," is a manual action. It is operated by sliding the handguard on the firearm's forestock. The action-release button initiates loading the first shell from the magazine into the chamber, and it also unloads the shell from the chamber if the gun is unfired. This button is often found directly behind the trigger guard. Sliding the forestock forward toward the muzzle closes the action and readies another rifle cartridge or shotgun shell for loading. After a cartridge or slug is fired, a shooter must pull the action back to eject the spent casing or shell and push it forward to load a new cartridge or slug.

Pump-actions are known mostly for their mechanical simplicity and ease of use. A pump-action rifle or shotgun can be accurate, but their accuracy almost entirely depends on the hunter's skill at operating a pump-action and, of course, the quality of the rifle. With proper technique and a well-maintained rifle, though, pump-actions can be used quite effectively for hunting big game.

Pump-actions are available in several rifle calibers including but not limited to a .308, .30–30, and .30–06 (and in different shotgun gauges, generally 12-gauge). For many years, pump-action shotguns were very popular actions to hunt deer with, particularly in the Northeast and New England areas.

Pump-actions allow hunters to choose a cartridge or slug suited to their hunting style, environment, and preferences. This versatility makes them suitable for hunting deer and other big game in various terrains and at different distances. They also have relatively few moving parts, which reduces the likelihood of jamming issues or other malfunctions compared to semi-automatic rifles, making them rather dependable firearms in various hunting conditions, including foul weather.

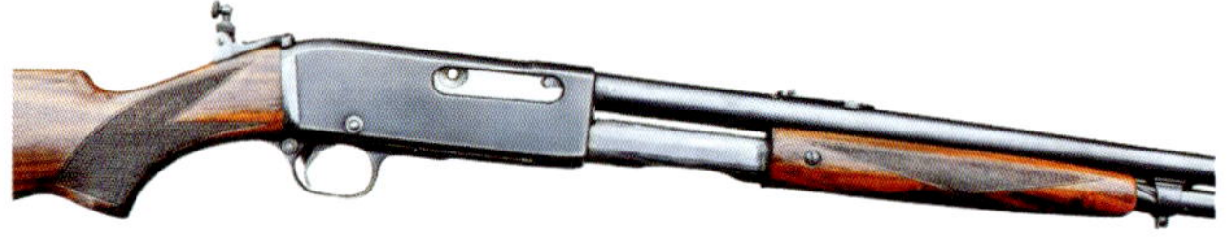

▲ Pump-action rifles are dependable firearms. They have a hardcore following among big game hunters. Credit: Davide Pedersoli

When compared to a single- or double-barrel break-action, pump-actions allow for relatively quick follow-up shots, enabling hunters to take advantage of opportunities for successive shots. The simple operating mechanism can be advantageous for hunters, especially those who prefer a rifle that is easy to maintain and operate in the field.

But pump-actions are not without a few negative issues, one of which is the tubular magazine only holds a limited number of cartridges. Nevertheless, some manufacturers offer models with removable magazines that house more ammunition. While the recycling process can be done quickly, there is a potential for short stroking the action, which can lead to feeding or ejection issues. Also, pump-actions are noisier to operate than most other actions.

Lastly, Baba Yaga boogeyman type of heavy recoil can be an issue in pump-action rifles, specifically when using heavier cartridge loads. For instance, a .30–06 Springfield, with an 8-pound rifle firing 165 grains at

▲ One of the knocks on pump-action rifles is that they deliver noticeable felt recoil when chambered with high-powered cartridges. Credit: ID 219534611 © Iakov Filimonov | Dreamstime.com

2,900 fps produces a recoil energy of 20.1 ft-lbs. That's meaningful felt recoil, which inevitably causes most hunters to flinch. Consequently, heavy kickback can affect a hunter's ability to execute an accurate shot. Therefore, when shooting a pump-action with heavy loads, it may require additional practice to manage the recoil effectively, particularly for inexperienced or light bodied hunters.

SEMI-AUTOMATICS

The term semi-automatic is interchangeable with autoloading rifle. These terms describe rifles that automatically load the next round into the chamber after firing but require the shooter to release and pull the trigger for each individual shot.

In a semi-automatic or autoloading rifle, the energy from firing the cartridge is used to cycle the action, eject the spent cartridge case, and load a new round from the magazine into the chamber, allowing for relatively rapid follow-up shots compared to manual actions like bolt-action or lever-action rifles.

In my mind's eye, the primary reason for choosing a semi-automatic is to reduce the impact of recoil associated with heavy-caliber bolt-action rifles. A longtime knock about bolt-action rifles, mostly made by semi-automatic advocates, is the claim that semi-automatics reduce recoil (both perceived and felt). This is a valid claim. Semi-automatics have greatly reduced recoil, and for some hunters, that single factor makes a semi-auto rifle worth buying.

However, the amount of recoil experienced when firing a rifle depends on several factors, including the caliber of the cartridge, the weight of the rifle, the design of the firearm, and even the shooter's stance and technique. In general, semi-automatic rifles tend to have slightly less perceived recoil compared to manually operated actions like bolt-action or lever-action rifles.

▲ For anyone who enjoys hunting with an AR rifle or thinks about owning one, Montana's Big Horn Armory's AR500 Automax put an unparalleled amount of power into a pleasant shooting, rapid firing, versatile rifle. Credit: Big Horn Armory

This reduction in perceived recoil is often due to the design of semi-automatic rifles, which typically feature mechanisms to absorb and mitigate some of the energy generated during firing. For example, semi-automatic rifles may have recoil-operated or gas-operated systems that help to reduce the felt recoil by spreading out the impulse (kickback) over a longer period of time compared to bolt-action rifles, where the shooter directly absorbs the full force of the recoil.

However, some firearm gurus claim the difference in recoil between semi-automatic and other action rifles may not be significant enough to be noticeable in all cases, especially when considering factors such as the specific cartridge being fired, the weight and design of the rifle, and individual shooter preferences and perceptions.

There is absolutely no doubt that a semi-automatic rifle is superior to a bolt-action rifle when it comes to the rate of fire. No matter how skilled a hunter is to quickly operate a bolt-action rifle, he or she will never reach the same rate of fire that a semi-automatic rifle delivers. While I understand this could come into play in some hunting situations, my feeling is that most hunters don't need to fire another round within a second of shooting the first round. This is definitely true if the hunter makes an accurate first shot.

Therefore, unless the problem of recoil is at the very top of a hunter's reason for buying a semi-automatic rifle, there seems to be fewer reasons why they should choose anything but a bolt-action rifle for hunting. However, you should still take a look at several options if possible. It is always better to get a feel for what you really like to shoot before spending money on a certain gun just because someone told you it was the best choice.

Selecting the proper action is a very personal decision. It may be wise for any hunter, particularly a newbie, to actually shoot several types of actions before making a final choice to actually zero in (pun intended) on which type of action to buy. The most critical point to remember, however, is that, undoubtedly, a rifle's action is a crucial element to a hunter's ability to make accurate shots. Therefore, selecting your most efficient action to hunt with is a particularly paramount decision. Consequently, it is wise to do your due diligence before selecting your action.

▲ The BAR features accuracy and performance that will make auto loading enthusiasts out of even the most skeptical shooters, including those who are hard to tear away from bolt- or lever-action firearms. Credit: Browning.

▼ Recoil is the nemesis of big game hunters. It can often result in wounding or missing game. By using mitigating recoil methods, a hunter will shoot game more accurately. Credit: Winchester Ammunition.

Chapter Eight

TAMING THE BOOGEYMAN OF FELT RECOIL: Mitigating Recoil for Improved Accuracy

The recoil of heavy-caliber rifles has been described as a 'push.' With a .700 Nitro, such a silly description doesn't apply unless having a 130-pound sandbag dropped on you can be called a push. There was also a momentary impression that my nose and jaw were no longer in alignment.
—JIM CARMICHEL, "The Day I Shot the .700 Express"[3]

As I thought about writing this chapter, I wondered how I could best describe, and drive home, the point to readers about the effects of a firearm's recoil. Then it came to me. In the 1960s, I boxed as a light-heavyweight in the Police Athletic League (PAL) in Brooklyn, New York. I was told by my coach that I had "very fast hands." Nonetheless, before every fight, "Coach" as he was known, *always* reminded me, "It's always the punch you don't see coming that puts you down." This axiom has been voiced time and time again over the years.

For instance, in the third installment of the Riddick franchise, *The Chronicles of Riddick: Riddick*, Vin Diesel's character Riddick was *badly* wounded and verbalized how dissatisfied he was with himself for letting his guard down. He remarked, "It's always the punch you don't see coming that puts you down." In real life, the late professional boxer George Foreman, perhaps one of the top most powerful punchers of all time, was once quoted as saying, "It's not the hardest punch that knocks you out, it is always the punch you don't see coming." The punch that you don't see coming has been described as a "sucker" punch. Why? Because it delivers a powerful, *unexpected* force that is rarely braced for, rolled with, nor able to be blocked . . . hence, it delivers a punch with unexpected kickback power.

▲ Light heavyweight boxer Michael Moorer, a master of delivering felt recoil, had a 52-4-1 professional record with forty knockouts. He was known for his ferocity and ability to quickly adapt to each of his opponent's style. Moorer is one of my favorite boxers of all time—save the heavyweight boxers Foreman, Frasier, Holyfield, and Tyson. Credit: PCFImages.

I learned this truism the hard way. It was during a boxing match that would have placed the winner in a bout for first place. As I stood up off the stool for the first round, Coach placed his two hands on my shoulders and robustly warned me that my opponent had, "Superfast hands and a wicked power punch. Be prepared for both." My overzealous young ego led me to disregard his cautioning words. I never saw the punch coming—but I sure as hell felt it.

I was later told by Coach, "It was a lightning-fast right cross that knocked you out." My overconfidence landed me, literally, in third place in the competition. Are you wondering what my point is with this anecdote? It's this: don't permit a rifle's recoil to be the punch that you don't see coming!

Recoil (a.k.a. kickback, push, or knockback) is a general term that refers to the backward movement a shooter feels when a rifle is fired. In scientific terms, recoil is a result of conservation momentum, which is a result of Newton's third law of motion, a.k.a. the law of action and reaction. If object A exerts a force on object B, then object B must exert a force of equal magnitude and opposite direction back on object A. The force of the bullet gunpowder pushing the bullet forward is balanced out by an equal and opposite force exerted back on the firearm via the escaped gases from the exploded powder that propels the bullet. The larger the caliber of the rifle, the greater the recoil will be. This law represents a certain symmetry in nature: forces always occur in pairs, and one body cannot exert a force on another without experiencing a force itself.

The terms free recoil (a.k.a. recoil energy) and perceived recoil (or felt recoil) are somewhat interchangeable. Free recoil is the rearward energy that is thrust into the shooter when a bullet is fired. A more fundamental description for free recoil is that it refers to recoil of a free-standing firearm, such as a hunter shooting a firearm freehanded. This is in contrast to a rifle or other firearm that is securely fixed, bolted, or braced by a vise or other stout backing. Perceived recoil is also referred to as felt recoil. It is the backward force, a.k.a. push, thrust, kick, and kickback, a hunter experiences after firing a firearm. The two are related because the force that propels the bullet forward also powers the gun backward.

So when discussing the *technicalities* of recoil, there are differences between the terms recoil, free recoil, and perceived recoil. As mentioned, free recoil and felt recoil are different but directly related to one another. With that said, though, when I use the words recoil, free recoil, or felt recoil don't be confused. I am always referring to the general terms associated with recoil.

Recoil sucks. Pardon my frankness. Factually, many times shooters fail to properly prepare for free recoil's coming energy. Without a doubt felt recoil is a hellish inconvenience for big game hunters. Hence, I liken it to a Baba Yaga boogeyman—a mythical creature. Worse yet, it is unavoidable, and it can make shooting a rifle intimidating to some and downright hurtful to others. It is recognized as the number one shooting nemesis of every big game hunter (and even target shooters). Hunters nearly always encounter felt recoil.

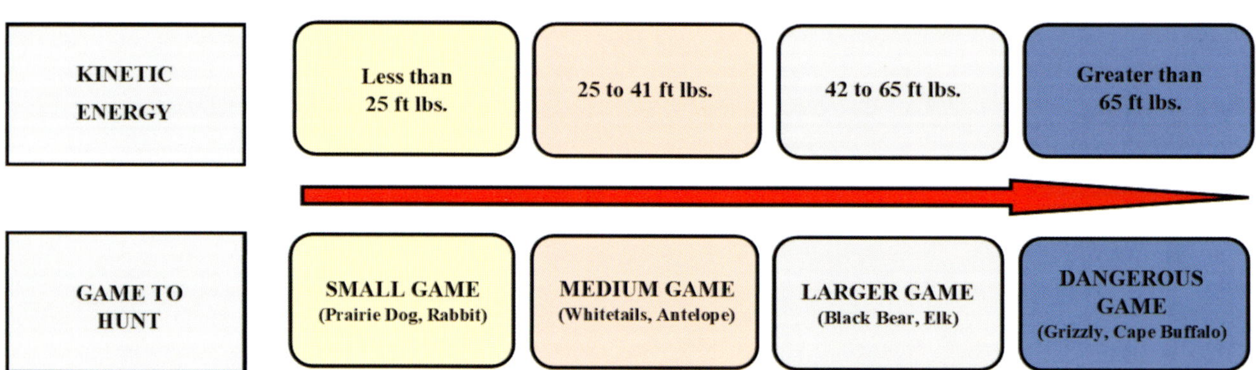

▲ This chart demonstrates the amount of kinetic energy—or recoil—suggested for various game animals. Credit: Fiduccia Ent.

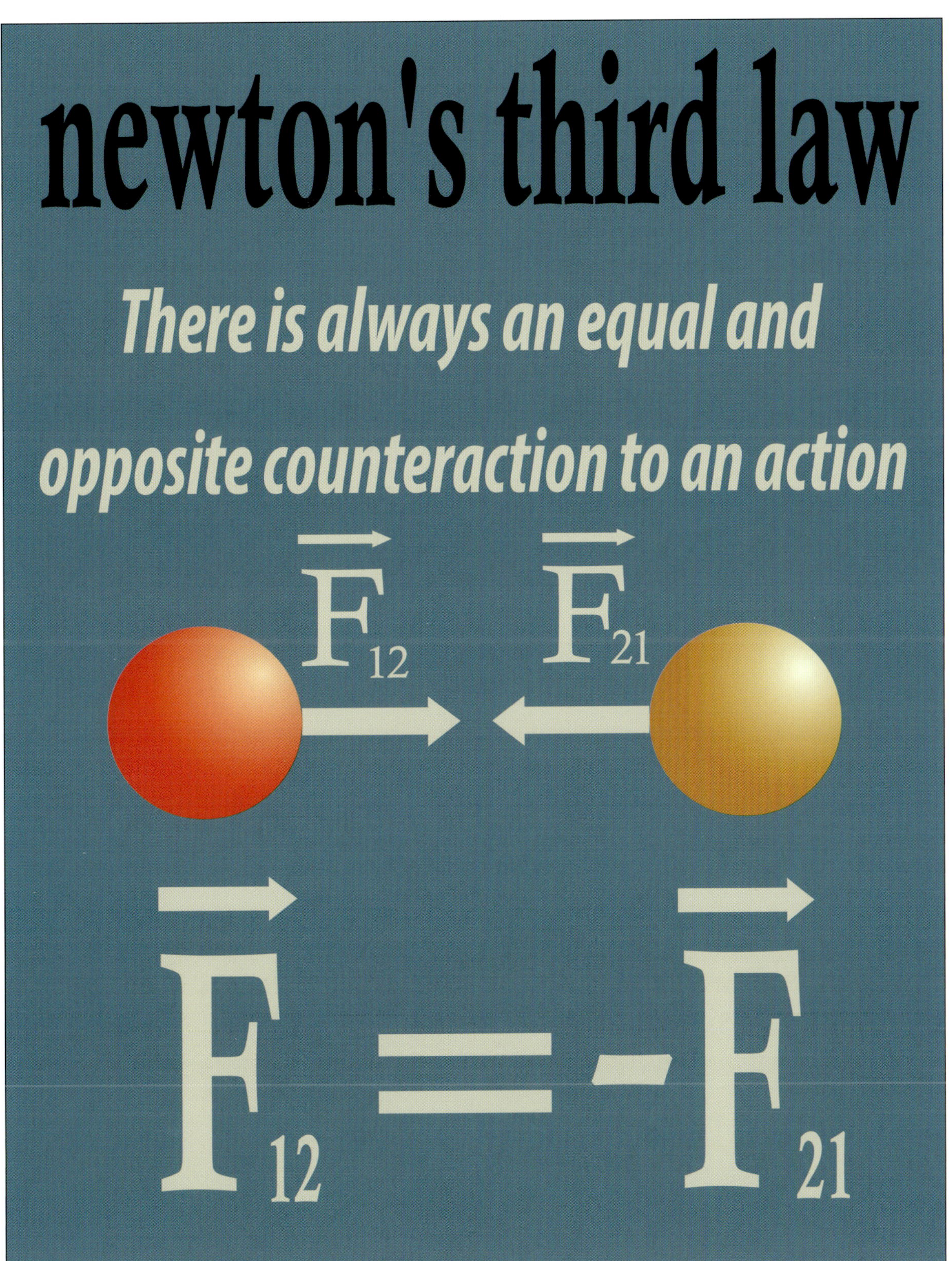

▲ With Newton's Third Law, the action is the cartridge firing and the bullet's movement. The reaction, and a few other factors, refers to the firearm's recoil or rearward thrust. Credit: ID 291216955 © Serhii Verbovskyi | Dreamstime.

Large calibers deliver more felt recoil than a majority of shooters want or can tolerate. But here's the good news. While felt recoil is never pleasant to deal with, there are ways to considerably mitigate it. For instance, one can use a *high-end* recoil pad or install a muzzle brake or a suppressor to help tame felt recoil. Note that I didn't say eliminate it. Mitigating options are discussed in more detail later in the chapter.

Factually, perceived recoil is *the* number one shooting nemesis to every big game hunter. And as such, it is a pain in the ass as *the* primary cause of flinching or even closing one's eyes. Famed gun writer Jack O'Connor had an eccentric way of describing recoil. O'Connor wrote, "Flinching is like halitosis. It is almost impossible for an individual to know whether he has it, and his best friends seldom tell him. But it is something he should know." To me that's a distasteful description but an undeniably accurate one.

Flinching, or shutting one's eyes, also causes many complications when a hunter prepares to shoot a deer or other big game animal. Therefore, felt recoil can lead someone to develop an intense inner fear of pulling the trigger, blinking early, excessively shaking the rifle, firing with eyes closed, and other similar issues. Because felt recoil results in pain, the *brain* quickly trains itself to preempt the impact by blinking or shutting the eyes at the sound of the blast.

The realization of having the rifle butt slam into your shoulder is this: no hunter wants to feel like he or she has just been punched by a world-class superheavyweight boxer every time they squeeze the trigger of the rifle. The human brain and body are simply not designed to experience an explosion within inches of the face. Nor does the brain like its body getting smacked in the shoulder and cheek. Unfortunately, no hunter escapes the ravages of a rifle's free or felt recoil. All such reactions to recoil adversely affect a hunter's ability to shoot game with consistent accuracy.

All big game calibers deliver recoil. However, recoil ranges from low to high in its delivery of energy (ft-lbs.). For instance, a .25–06 Remington has a recoil energy rating of 18.5 ft-lbs., which is noteworthy on recoil charts that range from an ultralight kick rating or score of 0.2 to an immense shoulder-crunching 28.8 ft-lbs. One of the better charts available is the late Chuck Hawks's Recoil Table (available at chuckhawks.com/recoil_table.htm).

Recoil is an absolute. Just how much recoil hunters have to endure, and how the recoil is reacted to, is what can make or break a hunt. When a rifle is fired, like the visible universe, its rearward motion is looking to hurt something. There is a tremendous amount of energy being delivered after the shot is fired. The instant expansion of powder gas pushes a tight-fitting bullet through the barrel from zero to 3,000 feet per second, which is equivalent to 2,045 mph. That kind of force can move a rifle with extreme prejudice. Unfortunately, a hunter's shoulder is the *only* object that stops this force. Trust this—no matter your size or toughness, you will react to the punishment delivered by a rifle's felt recoil.

▲ No big game hunter escapes the abuse of free recoil, unless of course, recoil-mitigating tools are used. Credit: ID 190196264 © Denis120386 | Dreamstime.com

Here are some interesting stats about recoil:

- **Over 28 ft-lbs.**—Can be considered massive recoil that can be difficult for even well-seasoned shooters to shoot accurately.
- **Over 25 ft-lbs.**—In a lightweight rifle, even experienced shooters can struggle to shoot more than 15 rounds without pain or developing a flinch, UNLESS a muzzle brake, suppressor, or a heavier rifle is used.
- **Over 15 ft-lbs.**—Begins to be very difficult to spot the bullet impact on the target through the scope because of the recoil.
- **Under 10 ft-lbs.**—Even newer shooters can easily spot impacts through the scope during recoil. Ideal for youth shooters.

- **Under 4 ft-lbs.**—Feels more like a vibration than a "smacking push."

At this point, I am going to steer away from the technical mumbo-jumbo. This chapter is not about the science of recoil. Instead, it focuses on the problems felt recoil can cause during a hunt, and equally important, how to reduce the effects of recoil. Although no one gets away with avoiding dealing with recoil, again, there are ways to lessen it.

Believe it or not, it is well known that the number one cause for missed shots in big game hunting is flinching. The obvious reason for flinching is our mental awareness of how recoil is about to hurt. The mental anxiety of that alone can be a key factor when flinching. Once a hunter removes the flinching factor, though, he or she will, without question, become a more deadly accurate shooter. Once a flinch becomes a habit, though, it will undoubtedly take full control over the hunter's ability to keep the flinch from becoming a dominant issue.

OWN UP TO THE BOOGEYMAN

I suppose this is the best place to explain why I included the Baba Yaga boogeyman in this chapter. It is because I describe felt recoil as the Baba Yaga boogeyman. In folklore, Baba Yaga is known as a boogeyman, witch, or demon. In the John Wick movie series, the character John Wick is referred to as the Baba Yaga and is one scary dude! This creature casts evil spells, curses, and causes *unmitigated fear*. I have always thought that felt recoil is a scary curse, delivered by an evil demon to cause pain, hence fear, thus flinching. So a Baba Yaga boogeyman causes a lot of problems. Therefore, when I refer to recoil as the Baba Yaga boogeyman now you know why. Baba Yaga boogeyman is scary, and so is felt recoil. 'Nuff' said.

▲ Flinching can cause a clean miss or, worse yet, wounding of an animal. It takes practice and determination to eliminate flinching. But it is doable. Credit: Winchester Ammunition.

▲ The Baba Yaga boogeyman is scary and so is felt recoil. Credit: ID 288418520 © Igor Georgiev | Dreamstime.com

▲ While each of my son's friends flinched when they first began shooting rifles, it only took some practice before they learned to control it. Eliminating the flinching reflex ends up with success like this. Credit: Fiduccia Ent.

Over the years, I have introduced many of my son's friends to deer hunting. Before they go on their first deer hunt on our farm, one of the initial requirements is to demonstrate to me that they can properly handle and fire a rifle accurately at 100 yards. Inevitably, I have seen each of them flinch the first time they fire a rifle. The target is hit, but usually not near the bull's-eye. When I remark that it is due to flinching, almost all of them don't believe they flinched. That is not unusual; most people do not realize they flinched after firing a rifle or don't like to admit they flinched. Before I learned how to stop flinching due to recoil, I, too, denied that I flinched. I think denial of flinching is simply human behavior—or perhaps a small dose of bravado. Importantly, though, to stop flinching when you shoot, you first have to admit to yourself that you are flinching.

Adding to the mental aspect is the fact that there are other cumulative contributing factors that cause perceived recoil. They include, but are not limited to, recoil energy, recoil velocity, and muzzle blast. Additionally, a heavy load, improper placement of the rifle butt into the shoulder, an inexpensive recoil pad, an ill-fitting rifle, a poor shooting rest, an improper shooting stance, and more are all factors that can increase flinching.

SELF-CHECK

Some important self-help tips include making sure the rifle stock is not too long to prevent proper cheek contact. Rifle stocks that are too short can be even worse as the odds of having the riflescope knock you in the head are greatly increased.

Protecting your ears from the loud muzzle blast will go a long way to reduce flinching. For four decades plus, I suffered from severe tinnitus and subsequent hearing loss. I have trouble hearing in both ears but mostly from my right ear, because I am a right-handed shooter. As I have told many hunters, numerous older shooters I know are hard of hearing. When I began hunting in the 1960s no one told me about hearing protection. It was ignored. It wasn't until the 1980s that hearing protection became popular. Do not make the same mistake I made. Wear well-made hearing protection or, at the very least, a pair of moldable earplugs. Wearing ear protection will definitely cut down the collateral effects of free recoil and, in turn, will help a hunter shoot more accurately. More than that, it has been years since I have experienced hearing a deer's hooves crunching leaves as it approaches my stand. I sorely miss that. I can no longer hear a buck grunting unless it is extremely close. Nor can I enjoy hearing a tom turkey's gobble from a distant ridge. To do so,

▲ Not only will quality hearing protection protect you from a potential loss of hearing, but it will also dampen the "bang" of the fired bullet. The sound of a fired rifle often leads to flinching. Thus, quality hearing protection serves two purposes. Credit: Winchester Ammunition.

I have to wear hearing aids. For those reasons alone, protect your hearing.

SHOOTING TECHNIQUES

There are a few standard shooting techniques that, when followed diligently, help to reduce flinching. One simple step is to press the rifle's stock tightly into the shoulder pocket and place the cheek firmly on the stock. There should be no space between the butt-pad of the rifle and the shoulder, nor between the cheek and the stock. To prevent the muzzle from rising, use the hand holding the forearm of the rifle to pull it snugly into the shoulder.

In addition, an improper trigger pull can move shots left or right and is one of the most critical aspects of causing recoil. Jerking the trigger down can result in misplaced shots at the target. Therefore, learning proper trigger disciplines is important to reduce felt recoil. Remember to *gently squeeze* the trigger until the rifle fires instead of *jerking* it. To accomplish this, practice safely dry-firing the rifle several times before actually shooting it. Don't be concerned about dry-firing a firearm. Today's firearms are designed to tolerate dry-firing. In the event you are using an older firearm and want to protect the firing pin and striker, use a Snap Cap (it looks like a cartridge). It prevents damage to the firearm. Carlson's makes a Snap Cap for various calibers.

Another way to manage recoil is to lean forward with the bulk of your weight over your knees while standing on the balls of your feet. With this stance, the body will take in more of the recoil and your shoulder will roll with the kick. Felt recoil is also more noticeable when shooting from a seated (like from a shooting house) or prone position.

Another very popular practice idea is to use a light .22 handgun. Have someone else load it leaving a few chambers empty (unloaded). Fire the pistol slowly and take note of what happens when the hammer strikes an empty chamber. The odds are very high that the shooter will probably blink and jerk the gun as if it had actually fired. To get past this type of perceived or anticipated recoil reaction, practice with the .22 pistol until you no longer blink. Remember to squeeze the trigger slowly so that it surprises you when the muzzle blast takes place.

What helped me take control of my flinching in the early 1970s was first learning to think through the pre-shot moments. Like many hunters, I get excited before I shoot an animal. But that's okay. Hunters are supposed to be excited or nervous as long as they can quickly control it. To be frank, there are times when I feel as if I am in a controlled state of high angst. This is especially true when I am hunting moose. But over my six-plus decades of hunting big game, I have learned how to quickly shelf my excitement or nervousness.

▲ It was when I lived in Colorado that I learned how to control flinching by talking to myself through the pre-shot moments. It worked well and helped me take my first bull elk. Credit: Fiduccia Ent.

I quickly double-check that the rifle and I are in a solid, ready-to-shoot position and mentally remind myself to calm down. Then, with a single squeeze of the trigger I fire the rifle. My inner thoughts not only steady my nerves and build my confidence, but, more importantly, they also help me prepare for the inevitable forthcoming Baba Yaga boogeyman felt recoil.

Proper breathing techniques also go a long way to help reduce flinching. The key to breathing techniques is once again to use the KISS method. This method of breath control requires a shooter to stop breathing while aiming and firing the shot. So, what is the best way to control breathing? According to the NRA's "Basics of Shooting: Breath Control" article, the best time to control the breathing cycle is during the "respiratory pause." This is when you're finished exhaling. Don't force air out, because forcing air out makes you contract chest muscles, which is a no-no. During the respiratory pause, chest muscles are relaxed, making it easier to stop breathing longer without feeling uncomfortable. To breathe correctly, breathe in for a continuous count—one, two, three, four. Stop momentarily at the count of four. Then exhale for a count of four. If needed, the sequence can be repeated. This method will calm down a case of the heebie-jeebies before sending the bullet on its way.

Another tip about flinching is not to shoot too much at the range. Instead, limit the number of rounds you fire. Also take time between each shot. By doing so you avoid taking too much recoil punishment and limit any conditioned or felt recoil reactions like flinching. Moreover, always shoot a rifle you feel comfortable with. You'll react less to its recoil. Don't go overgunned if you don't have to. For instance, when hunting whitetails, a .338 Lapua Magnum with 285-grain cartridges is more gun than is necessary. It delivers a muzzle energy of nearly 4,800 ft-lbs. The recoil is a whopping or, better stated, shoulder-*crushing,* body-vibrating, 32.08 ft-lbs. of felt recoil energy. I bet there are darn few hunters who can shoot it without flinching. If you do, don't be surprised if you end up having to get your nose realigned.

MUZZLE BRAKES

There are three basic muzzle brake designs with almost unlimited variations. Carefully research which muzzle brake is best for you before selecting one. So how much does a muzzle brake reduce recoil? The answer is any amount is enough, but a quality muzzle brake can reduce felt recoil by up to 50 percent, even when shooting a heavy large-caliber rifle with a heavy cartridge load.

A muzzle brake's intended purpose is to vent the gases that propel a bullet out of the barrel in a direction that will significantly mitigate recoil and, sometimes, even muzzle rise. Brakes can be significantly valuable for making large hunting calibers more manageable to shoot. In short-action cartridges a muzzle brake can negate almost all of the felt recoil.

◀ A muzzle brake will help make any hunter a more accurate shooter. The muzzle brake's holes are designed to vent the troublesome gases that cause recoil. Do your due diligence and research muzzle brake manufacturers before purchasing one. Credit: Griffin Armament.

A good-quality muzzle brake can also subdue the muzzle rise enough to see the impact on the intended target through the scope. This helps a hunter to know if there was a successful hit or not. Muzzle brakes are great for taming rifles, primarily if a child or a small-statured shooter is going to use the rifle. Muzzle brakes usually thread onto the end of the barrel, though clamp-on brakes do exist. If your rifle does not have a threaded muzzle, an experienced gunsmith can easily thread your barrel. I want to repeat that. An *experienced* gunsmith. Another benefit of a brake or any muzzle device is that it can protect the crown of your barrel. Brakes change harmonics and the point-of-impact, so once installed, the rifle needs to be re-zeroed.

Like anything else, muzzle brakes have their downside. And in this case, it is a considerable disadvantage. They can be deafening and cause **permanent** hearing loss if hearing protection is not used. This can be a huge issue as most hunters do not wear hearing protection while hunting. A majority of hunters feel that a single shot cannot be that detrimental to their hearing. That is a foolhardy belief if you are shooting a rifle with a muzzle brake. Hearing damage can happen almost immediately from shooting a braked rifle. Consequently, hearing protection is a must when shooting with a muzzle brake. Moreover, when other hunters are around when someone is sighting in with a muzzle brake, they need to wear quality hearing protection, too.

Additionally, eye protection should be worn when shooting at the range. Muzzle brakes are known for kicking up a lot of dirt and other debris, thereby threatening an eye injury and/or a potential body injury. You really didn't think something as helpful as a muzzle brake that could tame the infamous Baba Yaga boogeyman recoil wouldn't come without some issues, did you?

The absolute best option is to add a suppressor to the rifle's barrel. Undoubtedly, it is the most effective way to reduce perceived recoil. Suppressors are attached to the muzzle of the rifle and are generally tube-shaped and detachable. Some firearms, however, are available with nondetachable suppressors that are constructed onto the barrel. There are many types of suppressors from which to choose. Most, if not all, do not hinder a rifle's weight nor handling. Suppressors also muffle the noise made when firing the rifle, since it is the noise that often causes the shooter to flinch, negatively affecting the accuracy of the shot. Not only will suppressors enhance a hunter's accuracy when firing a rifle, but they will also go a long way to save on hearing loss.

THE WORKINGS OF A SUPPRESSOR

When a hunter fires a rifle, it obviously ignites the gunpowder within the cartridge. In turn, this instantly releases hot gases that expand and generate pressure.

The pressure is what propels the bullet through the barrel and out of the muzzle at an exceptionally high speed. At the instant the bullet departs the muzzle, the built-up pressure follows. The explosive release of the pressurized gases is what causes the accompanying loud gunshot noise. When a suppressor is attached to the muzzle, it decreases the gunshot noise by catching and diverting the suddenly released gases through its baffles. When the gases are diverted through the baffles, it slows down the escaping pressured gases, and thus, leading to considerably less felt recoil and a noticeably quieter gunshot.

SELECTING RECOIL-REDUCING ACCESSORIES

The use of a suppressor is *not* legal in every state. Therefore, prior to purchasing a suppressor accessory it is necessary to first research if it is legal to use in the state in which one hunts or lives. If it is legal, they can be purchased via many online sites. However, make sure the site you choose is reliable. Another option is to buy a suppressor from a reliable local sports store or gun shop. That will allow a hunter to see and feel a suppressor. If you prefer to shop online, here are some sites that offer suppressors and other recoil-reducing devices: www.nosler.com, www.griffinarmament.com, www.athlonoutdoors.com, www.brownells.com, www.wittmachine.net, www.pewpewtactical.com, and www.silencerco.com.

BLAST SHIELDS

Blast shields, however, are another potential choice if what I just stated about muzzle brakes is overconcerning for you. Cutting to the chase, blast shields are simply another name for muzzle blast control devices. They are a practical choice for hunters to consider. A blast shield, a.k.a. blast diffuser, blast diverter, or blast cone, produces the same effect: they direct all of the gases, debris, and some of the noise straight forward and directly away from the shooter. Do your homework to select the best blast shield.

All the described and other felt recoil-reducing tips can save you from being scared of the Baba Yaga boogeyman and the curse of recoil.

▲ Nosler suppressors turn down the "bang" volume without turning down accuracy or performance, so you can protect your hearing. The noise made from the rifle firing is also a major contributing factor to flinching. Credit: Nosler.

▲ For a bullet to precisely hit its target, accuracy begins with properly zeroing a big game rifle. Credit: Fiduccia Enterprises

Chapter Nine

ON TARGET: Your First Shot Matters—Here's How to Make It Count

Windage and elevation, Mrs. Langdon. Always remember, windage and elevation.
—COL. JOHN HENRY THOMAS, *The Undefeated*

As each new deer season approaches, inevitably an annual question arises, "What is the best way to zero a rifle?" Well, realistically, there is no one "best" way that is superlative because there are a lot of elements to consider when answering that question. First and foremost, a scope and rifle must initially be calibrated to one another in order for the bullet to accurately hit its target. This tune up, so to speak, will ensure the bullet will impact where the scope is aimed. This is often referred to as zeroing. Here's how to zero a scope so it will allow the bullet to hit where the hunter is aiming.

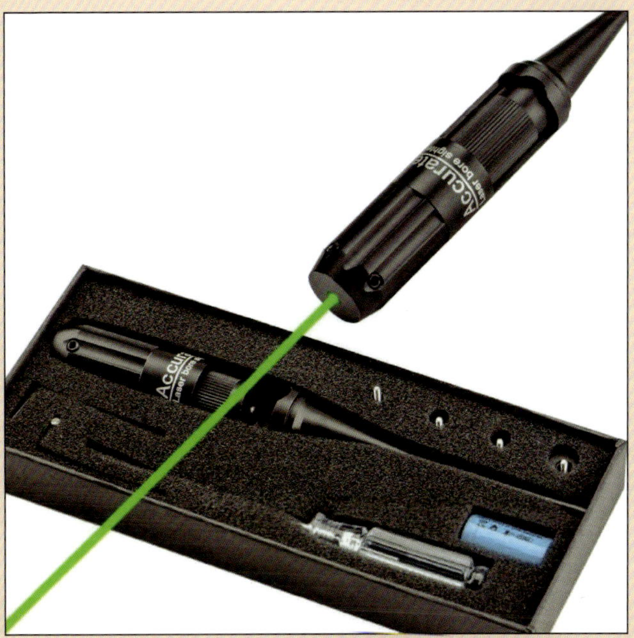

▲ Today's boresighters, available in nearly every caliber, are high-tech laser tools that have replaced the older types of boresighting products. They are most helpful for putting a bullet on paper after mounting a new scope. They are also used to check that a rifle is still on from a previous season. Using a laser boresighter to zero in a rifle does so without wasting ammunition. It also decreases the frustration of the process to zero in—by leaps and bounds. Credit: Accurate.

BORESIGHTING

The least expensive way to zero a rifle is to boresight it before going to the range. By boresighting a rifle a hunter will save time and money when actually sighting in. The zeroing process should begin by boresighting the scope first. Once the scope is boresighted it will allow the shooter to put a bullet hole on a paper target, giving the shooter instant information of exactly what direction the crosshair needs to be adjusted, if any.

CHECK ALL SCREWS

Next, check all screws to make the process of zeroing go quicker. Before sighting the rifle, take the time to be absolutely sure the scope is mounted properly to the rifle and that all screws on the rifle and the scope parts are *tight*. Do not overtighten the screws but make sure they are snug. Loose screws cause zeroing problems.

EYE RELIEF

The scope should be mounted with 3 to 4 inches of eye relief. Eye relief simply means the distance from the eyepiece or the rear lens to the shooter's eye. Next, adjust the ocular focus ring of the scope so that the target and the reticle (the crosshair) are clear at the same time. Also check that the reticle is aligned at a 90-degree axis to the bore.

BENCH RESTS

This step is really important as it is responsible for problems when zeroing a rifle. Always use a solid bench rest, sandbag, or a rest like a Caldwell Lead Sled (or any sled of your choice) to cradle the rifle snugly so that it points toward the target naturally. Use additional sandbags to secure it so that it rests on its own, making it hard to easily move.

TARGET PLACEMENT

A bullet follows the bore axis out of the muzzle. Therefore, it will travel almost parallel to the line of sight until the universe's greatest force—gravity—intervenes and forces the projectile downward and, thereby, off its course. Gravity begins its force on the bullet the precise instant it exits the rifle barrel. From that point on, a bullet's course is *never* entirely straight. When zeroing a rifle (or any firearm) you adjust the sight, so your straight line of vision intersects a bullet's parabolic path (a bullet's trajectory is referred to as being parabolic). Past that point, the bullet continues to succumb to gravity, and it drops even further away from the line of sight.

▲ Eye relief is the distance between the rear of the scope and your eye. If the eye relief is too short, a shooter will need to squint to see through the scope and recoil could result in a black eye. If eye relief is too long, there could be an issue with seeing the entire field of view. Credit: Fiduccia Ent.

Sighting in, therefore, is simply a method that aligns the iron sights, or a riflescope's crosshairs, so the bullet accurately strikes the intended aimpoint from a prescribed distance. A shooter cannot adjust the rifle in order for the rifle to change the bullet's path. Logically, it is the rifle's sights that have to be adjusted to accomplish that.

Furthermore, it's a common mistaken belief that a bullet rises above the line of bore during its trajectory. It does not. It cannot. It is virtually impossible to do because of the force of gravity. Sightline is not parallel to bore line, but, rather, at a slightly converging angle. The line of sight dips below the bore line and the bullet's arc. The sightline is doomed never to meet the bore line. Both are straight and, after crossing, they diverge. A bullet hits above the sightline at midrange because the sightline has been purposefully angled down through its trajectory. The bullet falls to intersect it at a greater range. If the sightline were parallel with the bore, it would never touch the bullet's arc.

Consequently, you may be content with zeroing in a rifle at 100 yards. In fact, again, it is quite common for hunters to sight in a rifle at an inch or two high at 100 yards. This allows a hunter to strike a target at the same aimpoint at 200 yards. The end goal is to zero a rifle in order for it to have a bullet consistently strike a particular aimpoint at more than one prescribed distance, in this case between 100 and 200 yards.

Most hunters are satisfied with sighting their rifle an inch or two high over the center of the target at 100 yards. That will be a bullet extremely near or in the bull's-eye at 200 yards. Another way is to zero the rifle in at 25 yards and then move out to 100 yards. As mentioned in other chapters, the fact is, a majority of the time, deer are generally killed at less than 100 yards away. Thus, a 100-yard zero is perfect in this scenario and is appropriate throughout most of the

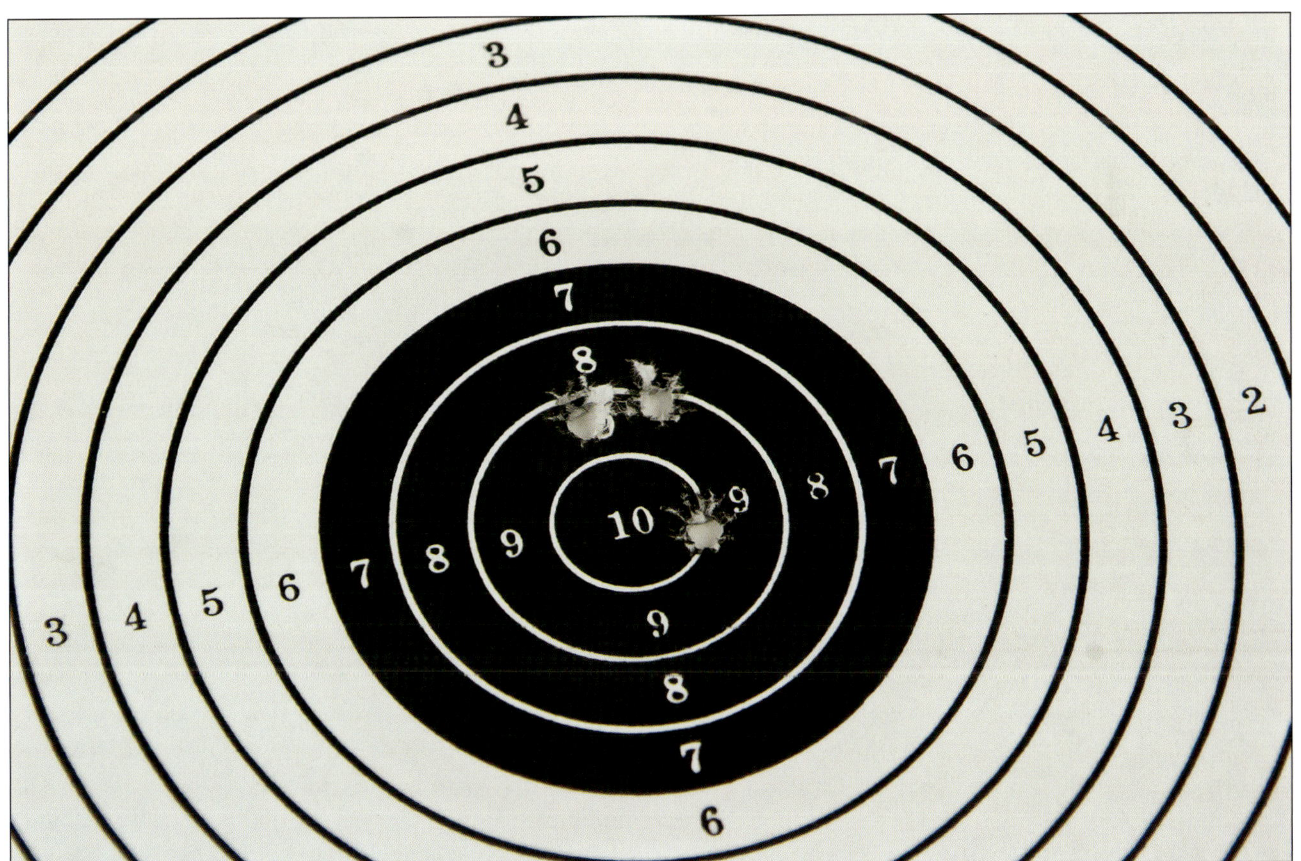

▲ Sighting at an inch or two high at 100 yards will allow the bullet to strike a target at the same aimpoint at 200 yards. Credit: ID 15932686 © Karen Sarraga | Dreamstime.com.

Northeast, New England, and a majority of the midwestern states.

SAFETY EQUIPMENT

This may sound obvious to seasoned veterans, but for the sake of novices to the sport, it needs to be said. When using a loud, potentially dangerous tool, such as a rifle, always include personal protective equipment. When sighting in, it is wise to use quality eye and ear protection. If affordability is an issue with using the more expensive ear protection devices, then at least use earplugs, earmuffs, or a combination to protect your hearing. Similarly, wearing eye protection will keep your vision safe from any wandering materials, such as an ejected shell.

AMMO CHECK

Another important tip is to always zero a rifle with the same type of ammunition you will be hunting with. Sometimes hunters don't give that advice serious enough consideration. I have witnessed hunters mixing ammo from different manufacturers and even using cartridges of different bullet types and grain weights. For instance, generally, the bullet from a 150-grain cartridge will strike at a different point on the target than a bullet from a 180- or 200-grain cartridge. So, mixing different ammo brands and cartridges is a recipe for problems.

▲ It is always a wise idea to zero in a rifle using the same ammunition with which you plan to hunt. Credit: Weatherby.

To ensure your bullet will perform exactly the same way it did when you sighted it in, the same ammo and brands should be used. This includes a specific bullet type and weight, shape, and grains. Changing any of these variables will affect your zero. A good plan, therefore, is when buying ammunition, consider buying a few boxes of the same ammunition. By doing so, there will be enough ammunition to zero the rifle and to hunt. In most cases, if the rifle is sighted in properly and good shot placement is executed, there will be plenty of ammo for the next hunting season.

SIGHTING OR ZEROING AT 100 YARDS

Zeroing a rifle starts with the hunter knowing the average expected range for the game that will be hunted. As mentioned, many hunters prefer sighting in their rifles at 100 yards, but some like to shoot at a 25-yard target in order to confirm that the rifle is going to shoot a bullet that ends up on paper at 100 yards. Shooting at a 25-yard target may not result in a pinpoint accurate bull's-eye at 100 yards, but it will generally place a bullet close to the bull's-eye. So close in fact, that when the rifle is sighted in (zeroed) at 100 yards, it can be accomplished with a minimum of time and shots fired.

▲ It is often recommended to zero a rifle in first at 25 yards and then move out to a 100-yard target. Remember that a bullet striking 1 inch high at 100 yards will be in the bull's-eye at 200 yards. Credit: ID 123455628 © Hackisan Dreamstime.com.

This process begins with shooting at a target set up 25 yards away from the shooting bench. First adjust the ocular on the rear of the scope to provide you with sharp focus on the crosshairs. With the rifle secured in a rifle rest, fire one round at the 25-yard target's bull's-eye. Then with the rifle safely set aside, check the target to see where the bullet impacted. Measure the horizontal and vertical distance from the point of impact (POI) to the center of the target (the bull's-eye). At this point, it is not necessary to worry about shooting tight groups.

For instance, if the bullet impacted the 25-yard target at 1¾ inches to the right and 1¼ inches below the bull's-eye, you would need to calculate the number of clicks needed to adjust a quarter minute of angle (MOA) riflescope. In this case, one click equals one-quarter inch or four clicks equal one inch. You will need to adjust the turrets accordingly. Once the 25-yard shot is where a shooter wants the bullet to strike, fire three more shots at the bull's-eye to confirm consistency.

For maximum accuracy it is particularly important to let the rifle barrel cool after firing each shot. This is time-consuming, but you will be amazed by how much more accurately the rifle shoots by letting it cool off between shots. Then fire one shot aimed directly at the bull's-eye to confirm that the adjustments you made are correct. Don't fret if the bullet did not impact the bull's-eye smack-damn in the center. My rule of thumb is as long as you are within 1 inch of the center of the bull's-eye you are good to go.

Now it is time to shoot at the 100-yard target. Take the next shot and remember to let the rifle barrel cool down between shots. If the rifle is zeroed to hit an inch or two high at 100 yards—it will be centered at 200 yards.

This information involved a trip to the range and shooting from a bench and a stable rest: a rock-solid shooting position. As noted earlier, bench rest shooting at a range is to ensure a rifle's scope and the rifle itself are fine-tuned to hit the same point of impact by reducing or eliminating human error. One last thought

▲ To achieve maximum accuracy when zeroing in, it is necessary to let the rifle cool between shots. While this step takes more time, it enhances accuracy tenfold. Credit: Winchester Ammunition.

on bench shooting at the range. Even if the rifle did not print a grouping of shots that could fit in a half dollar, albeit that is every hunter's end goal, and instead it demonstrated a grouping within an inch or two, I would not hesitate to say the rifle is zeroed in and is ready for the hunt.

It might be advisable after zeroing at the range to schedule another sight-in day to practice shooting under real-world hunting conditions. Basically, that means shooting freehand under different scenarios: prone, sitting, kneeling, and standing. Also include shooting freehand using the rifle sling to steady the shot. An additional exercise is to shoot from one-, two-, or three-legged shooting sticks. This method of practice will build confidence under real-world hunting shooting conditions. Truth be told, 95 percent of big game hunters do not shoot from a bench rest or other secured shooting vise when sighting in. Although most hunters do not get quarter-size groupings when shooting freehand, they should be able to consistently have groupings within a 4- to 6-inch bull's-eye. Once you've accomplished this practice along with your range practice, you will be ready to compete against Annie Oakley. Since she's dead, you're guaranteed to win.

ZEROING-IN EQUIPMENT

1. Quality ear and eye protection for each person at the range.
2. Two boxes of the same ammo that will be used on the hunt.
3. Rifle sled, sandbags, or bench rest.
4. Paper targets with a centered bull's-eye and a 1-inch grid. Targets with grids allow for more precise calculation adjustments.
5. Spotting scope/10 x 50 binoculars to check where bullets have hit the target.
6. Staple gun and staples to set up targets (a staple gun that works!)
7. Screwdriver to adjust windage and elevation turrets.
8. A gun case.

▲ A high-quality spotting scope is essential when zeroing in. It helps to determine exactly where bullets hit the target. This is especially true when zeroing in at 200 yards or more. Credit: TRACT Optics.

▲ After zeroing in at a range, it is critical to practice freehand shooting as it is the most real-world position used on a hunt. Credit: Montana Rifle Company

▶ There is a significant difference between bench rest precision and hand-held accuracy. Making the transition is an all-important factor to hitting game accurately in the field. Credit: Browning.

Chapter Ten

BRIDGING THE GAP: Translating Bench-Rest Accuracy to Freehand In-Field Accuracy

If your rifle groups well off the bench, all the better. In the field that one-inch grouping means nothing. The only meaningful factor is your ability to put your bullet in the vitals of your game at any time, from any angle, and from any reasonable distance with which you feel comfortable.
—CRAIG BODDINGTON, *Shots at Big Game*, 1989

The process of sighting in at a range stands in stark contrast to the challenges encountered in offhand shooting, also known as freehand shooting. Alternatively termed as "shooting from your back legs," this technique entails firing a rifle while standing without any support apart from the shooter's arms and legs. This discussion focuses solely on scenarios where hunters find themselves sitting on a stump, leaning against a tree, or stealthily walking through woods or fields while on a hunt. It excludes considerations of other forms of support such as shooting sticks, slings, or common shooting positions.

▲ An overwhelming number of times hunters, like the one seen here, find themselves having to place the crosshairs on a game animal while shooting offhand. Credit: Weatherby.

Zeroing a rifle at a range typically involves securely resting the firearm in a gun vise, shooting sled, or sandbag, to ensure tight bullet groupings. This process effectively minimizes the human element's influence on zeroing the rifle. However, offhand shooting introduces a myriad of accuracy-compromising factors into the equation. Indeed, shooting offhand at a paper target will not yield the consistent tight groupings achievable with bench-rest shooting. As the esteemed Craig Boddington aptly remarks, "If your rifle groups well off the bench, all the better. In the field, that one-inch grouping [from the bench] means nothing."[4]

In reality, the standing offhand position is perhaps the most commonly assumed stance by hunters when aiming at deer or other big game. Yet, it is undeniably one of the most challenging positions in which to maintain accuracy, particularly when neither arm is supported. This difficulty often leads to missed or, worse, wounded game. Holding the rifle barrel steady in the standing offhand position is virtually impossible—unless, that is, one commits to rigorous practice.

While mastering the offhand stance may seem daunting, dedicated practice can significantly mitigate its challenges. I know this is true because I have practiced it and achieved the end goal. With relentless repetition, the offhand position becomes second nature. Consistent practice *markedly* improves accuracy, with benefits accruing year after year. Initially, the primary focus lies in minimizing the erratic movement of the rifle barrel, gradually enhancing steadiness with each session.

Furthermore, time management is a paramount factor during freehand shooting. Prolonged aiming diminishes accuracy as the reticle is destined to bounce around the target. In my six-plus decades of hunting experience, I've learned when I am about to shoot at an animal, I must swiftly shoulder the rifle, align the crosshairs with a kill zone, and squeeze the trigger. However, this is not the military technology procedure rapid target acquisition (RTA) that is often incorrectly referred to when describing time management in a hunting scenario. In hunting time management, it's really better said that time is of the essence. It is merely the practice of immediately shouldering a rifle, quickly placing the crosshairs on a kill zone, and firing as soon as the reticle acquires the target. By employing the time management method, a hunter will increase his or her kill ratio dramatically when shooting offhand.

Although mastering offhand shooting can be a challenge, it's entirely achievable with focused, diligent training. The brain steps up significantly to help achieve this goal. The concept of neuroplasticity underscores this potential for improvement, as the brain adapts and strengthens neural connections in response to *repeated* experiences. With consistent repetition therapy, offhand shooting can become second nature to any dedicated hunter, drastically reducing missed opportunities and promoting ethical hunting practices.

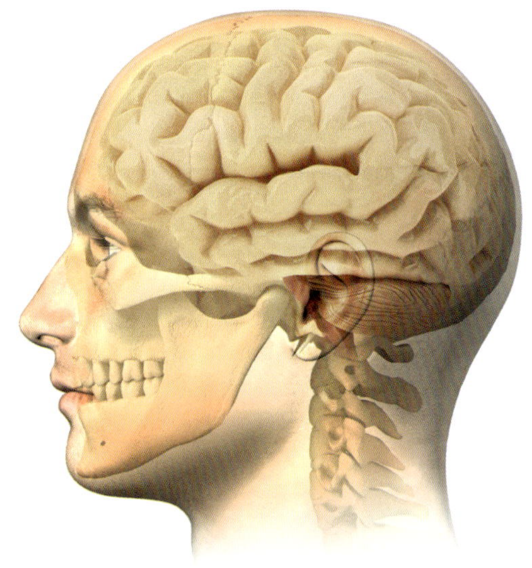

▲ Accurate offhand shooting can be achieved with diligent repetitive training. The more a hunter shoots offhand, the quicker the brain adapts to this type of training. Moreover, the training reduces the potential of a misplaced shot. Credit: ID 30313835 © Leonello Calvetti | Dreamstime.com.

Therefore, when the time arises to take an offhand shot, there is little hesitation by the hunter as he or she is trained to be confident when shooting a freehanded shot. Confidence builds success—of that fact there is no doubt.

▲ For successful offhand shooting, hunters must practice this technique often in order to be consistently skillful at making accurate shots that result in quick and humane kills. Credit: Browning.

▼ Whenever there is doubt about shooting an animal at a very long distance, the savvy hunter will choose a better option, like closing the distance rather than taking the extended shot. Credit: Leupold.

Chapter Eleven

HOW FAR IS TOO FAR? Understanding the Limits of Responsible Shooting Distances

If in doubt, stretch the stalk and not the shot.
—Boone & Crocket Position Statement—Long Range Shooting[5]

In this chapter, I want to have a frank discussion about shooting big game at long, and particularly exaggerated, distances. Is shooting game at extra-long distances appropriate, objectionable, or even unethical? What I say here may not sit well with some hunters, but it needs to be addressed.

The shooting distances for big game hunting can be categorized as follows:

- **Short range**: 100 yards or less
- **Medium range**: 100 to 300 yards
- **Long range**: 300 to 500 yards
- **Extreme long range**: 500 yards or more

▲ I may take some criticism for the following: I think shooting extreme long distances, even at large game such as the elk seen here, is nothing but bravado. Credit: Canstock.

In my view, shooting big game animals at distances beyond 300 yards should be reserved for target shooting or hunting varmints with smaller-caliber rifles, which are generally not recommended for big game hunting. Once a shot exceeds 300 yards, a hunter must either hold over or adjust the elevation on their scope to compensate for bullet drop.

THE LIMITATIONS OF LONG-RANGE SHOOTING

Long-range shots at game should not exceed the limitations of the firearm, cartridge, and the hunter. Some hunters argue that modern hunting rifles are specifically designed for extreme distances. They are correct—there are rifles capable of shooting big game at remarkable distances. For example, the .300 Remington Ultra Magnum and the .300 RUM can deliver flat-shooting performance with hard-hitting capabilities at ranges of 1,000 yards or more. Other notable long-distance rifles include the Nosler Model 21, the Savage Model 10 GRS, the Weatherby Model 307, and the Browning X-Bolt. These rifles can launch heavy bullets at high velocities, reaching distances of 1,000 yards or more.

However, such performance comes with a price: significant recoil (approximately 30 ft-lbs. of free recoil energy) and substantial noise. But the real question is not whether these rifles *can* shoot at such exaggerated distances, but rather *should* hunters be doing so? In my mind, just because a rifle is capable of hitting a target at 1,000 yards does not mean it is an appropriate or ethical choice for hunting big game.

A PERSONAL PERSPECTIVE

I firmly believe that most hunters, including myself, have no business shooting big game at distances beyond 300 yards. This was made clear to me during a visit to the NRA's Whittington Center in New Mexico. While there, I had the opportunity to shoot a target set at 1,000 yards. It didn't take long for me to realize that 1,000 yards is an immense distance, well beyond my ability to consistently hit a target with precision. If I couldn't hit a stationary target, why would I risk a long-range shot on a living animal?

THE ETHICS OF LONG-RANGE HUNTING

At distances of 500 yards or more, many factors can negatively affect the bullet's flight path, increasing the likelihood of wounding the animal rather than making a clean kill. Many responsible hunters strongly believe that shooting at an animal from half a mile or more is unethical. Furthermore, shooting from such distances puts big game at a significant disadvantage. An animal's natural defenses—olfactory senses, hearing, and eyesight—are virtually useless against a hunter positioned 1,000 yards away. This raises fair chase concerns and brings the ethics of such a hunt into question.

Conversely, proponents of extreme long-range hunting argue that it cannot be categorized as ethical or unethical. They claim that technological advancements in firearms, the species being hunted, and their own exceptional shooting experience justify long-range shots. However, this argument falls short for many hunters who prioritize reducing suffering. Ethical hunters strive for swift and humane kills rather than seeking the thrill or challenge of hitting a target from extreme distances. One long-range hunter even told me, "I feel a buzz when I shoot a big game animal at 1,000 yards or more." To me, hunting should be about ethical decisions and respect for the animal, not about seeking a "buzz."

A COMMONSENSE APPROACH

Many seasoned hunters, professional guides, outdoor gun writers, and industry experts discourage extreme long-distance shooting for moral and practical reasons. Even shooting at 300 yards should be left to experienced hunters with extensive shooting skills.

▲ Just because a rifle caliber and cartridge are designed to achieve accurate distances of 1,000 yards or more, doesn't mean they should be used for big game hunting. If you want to shoot nongame targets at that distance, I say, "Have at it!" Credit: Leupold.

Esteemed gun writer and big game hunter Craig Boddington is a trusted authority on these matters. In his book *Shots at Big Game*, Boddington writes, "I edit *Petersen's HUNTING*, [and] I shudder when a contributor writes about a shot in excess of 300 yards. I usually edit the copy to read, 'the animal was a long way out.'" He further states that another publication has a firm rule against publishing shots exceeding 250 yards. This demonstrates a commonsense approach that many ethical hunters embrace.

THE REALITY OF HUNTING DISTANCES

Field & Stream ran an experiment and found that the average shot distance for whitetail deer hunting is about 100 yards or less. While there may be instances where a 300-yard shot is warranted, their findings indicate that threats to deer (and other big game) increase beyond this range. This is a subtle way of acknowledging that long-range shots often result in wounded or unrecovered animals. In reality, most deer and other big game animals are harvested at distances under 200 yards.

EXPERT OPINIONS

My longtime friend, Wayne van Zwoll, PhD, is another well-respected author and firearms expert. He states that hunters should limit their shots to 200 yards if they are average shooters and 300 yards if they are highly skilled. His perspective aligns with my own: hunters must be honest about their shooting capabilities and recognize their limits.

▲ My son took this mule deer in Wyoming. It was 213 yards away. Cody used a .300 Win Mag, with a Nosler 180-grain load and partition bullet, which is quite capable of shooting game at that distance. The buck was well within Cody's proficient shooting range. Credit: Fiduccia Ent.

All hunters should know when they have exceeded their comfortable shooting range. Hunters attempting shots of 300 yards or more must diligently assess their personal shooting skills and the limitations of their equipment. Reading an article, watching a YouTube video, or seeing a TV show about long-range hunting does not make someone a competent long-range shooter. Mastering such a skill requires extensive practice and knowledge. Sending a bullet 300 yards or more to kill a mule deer two ridgelines away should never be taken lightly.

A HARD-EARNED CONCLUSION

For me, shooting a big game animal at over 300 yards contradicts my hunting ethics. No emails or texts, please—I said it's against *my* ethics. But, more than that, the hardcore reality is that shooting a game animal at more than 300 yards is beyond most hunters' shooting abilities.

After over sixty years of hunting across North America and Africa, and thirty-five years producing *Woods N' Water Big Game Adventures*, I have reached an inescapable conclusion: accurately shooting game beyond 300 yards is far more challenging than many hunters realize. The risks increase dramatically at extreme distances, particularly when the animal is moving. I have witnessed countless long-range shots that resulted in misjudged distances, complete misses, poor shot placement, or worst of all, wounded and unrecovered game.

FINAL THOUGHTS

So, is shooting game at extreme long-range distances objectionable or unethical? Yes, I believe it can be both. Many prominent hunters and firearms experts agree. Hopefully, I have given you something to think about. I will end with this: When you spot an animal at a distance that gives you hesitation, don't take the shot. Better yet, follow the guidance of the Boone & Crockett Club, which advises, "If in doubt, stretch the stalk and not the shot." I couldn't have said it better myself.

▲ I shot this moose in Newfoundland, Canada. My rangefinder put him at a distance of 547 yards. It took us nearly two hours to sneak up to a distance of 155 yards. I always choose to shorten the distance rather than taking a risky long shot. Credit: Fiduccia Ent.

▼ After most traditional rifle seasons end, hunters can extend their big game hunting using muzzleloaders. Today's muzzleloaders can achieve accuracy comparable to rifles. Credit Ted Rose

Chapter Twelve

MODERN MUZZLELOADERS: They Ain't Your Father's Muzzleloaders Anymore

Muzzleloaders can be extremely effective in the right hands.
—RON SPOMER, www.ronspomeroutdoors.com

In the realm of firearms, muzzleloaders stand as the venerable elders, steeped in history and tradition. Yet, despite their earliest roots, modern muzzleloaders have undergone a remarkable transformation. No longer relics of a bygone era, today's muzzleloaders represent the epitome of cutting-edge firearm technology. As the saying goes, they truly aren't your grandfather's or father's muzzleloaders anymore. Consequently, it would be imprudent of me not to include a chapter about hunting deer and other big game with the highly effective modern inline muzzleloaders available today.

▲ Using muzzleloaders for hunting big game is legal in most states. Nearly every state in the country has designated muzzleloader hunting seasons. Muzzleloader hunting is a highly popular way to extend hunting after regular big game firearm seasons end. Credit: Traditions®

Today's modern .45 and the much more popular .50 caliber muzzleloaders are remarkably ballistically similar to the big-gunned straight-wall cartridges. The .50 caliber muzzleloaders deliver a strike akin to a professional heavyweight knockout punch. The three types of aerodynamic projectiles that muzzleloaders use are the bullet, round ball, and shot. The bullets are preferred for hunting because they are more aerodynamic and accurate, especially at longer ranges. When hunting whitetails or other larger deer species, either 245- or 250-grain bullets will certainly provide excellent knockdown power along with equally good accuracy out to about 175 to 200 yards. So the question is, then, why shouldn't today's modern inline muzzleloaders have their kudos mentioned in this book? In fact, they most certainly should, the new inline modern muzzleloaders, like traditional and straight-walled rifles, are also appropriate firearm choices to hunt a wide variety of big game.

THE EVOLUTION OF MUZZLELOADERS

The year 1985 marked a significant turning point in the history of muzzleloaders with the advent of the first "inline muzzleloaders." This innovation paved the way for a wave of advancements in safety and performance, propelling muzzleloaders into the modern era. Manufacturers seized the opportunity to refine and

▲ Ever since the development of inline muzzleloaders, companies have continued to improve their technology and innovations, which accounts for their popularity. Credit: ID 306087239 © Guy Sagi | Dreamstime.com.

enhance these firearms, resulting in the most sophisticated muzzleloaders to date.

POPULARITY AND PRACTICALITY

The surge in popularity of modern muzzleloaders can be attributed to their versatility and practicality. Not only do they boast a dedicated following among enthusiasts, but they also serve as invaluable tools for extending hunting seasons. Additionally, the inherent thrill and satisfaction in shooting today's muzzleloaders makes them a favorite among hunters. There is definitely something satisfying about taking big game animals using a muzzleloader. Perhaps it is a feeling of slipping back to a time when our forbearers hunted game with smoke-poles.

UNPRECEDENTED OPTIONS

Today, the market abounds with a considerable array of muzzleloader options, catering to diverse preferences like a hunter's budget and the type of game to be hunted. From tighter barrel tolerances to innovative projectile designs, these advancements have propelled muzzleloaders to new heights of performance and accuracy.

While adhering to traditional elements, modern muzzleloaders have embraced innovation with the adoption of compressed pellets for enhanced precision. This shift reflects a commitment to maximizing accuracy and efficiency, setting a new standard for modern inline muzzleloader performance.

CHOOSING THE RIGHT LOAD

Selecting the optimal load is paramount to achieving success in the field. Today's loads are all exceptionally capable of taking big game like whitetails and all of the other deer species. They are also quite competent to hunt black bear, wild hogs, and even bison and musk ox. But when hunting the superstrong bovines, keeping shots to 100 or so yards is an exceptionally good idea. Notably, renowned experts like Ron Spomer and others offer invaluable insights into crafting effective muzzleloader loads, ensuring hunters are equipped for success.

▲ Sabot bullets are a good option because they allow a smaller-diameter bullet to be fired at a faster speed than a bullet of the same caliber fired alone. Some popular sabot bullet brands for muzzleloaders are Hornady, Precision Rifle, MMP, Barnes, and Powerbelt. Credit: ID 129662640 © Bill H | Dreamstime.com.

CHALLENGES AND CONSIDERATIONS

Despite their myriad benefits, muzzleloaders present unique challenges, notably the issue of smoke obscuring visibility after firing. The smoke can block out the view of whether or not the shot actually hit the intended game animal. It can also complicate seeing if the animal is dead where it stood or determining in what direction it ran off. This factor underscores the importance of making every shot count, as the reloading process of a muzzleloader takes more time than traditional rifles, no matter how fast a hunter becomes in the reloading process. While the smoke issues are generally not a deal-breaker for a majority of muzzleloader hunters, it is worthwhile mentioning for those who have never shot a muzzleloader. With that said, though, the unparalleled experience of hunting with a muzzleloader transcends these minor obstacles by embodying the essence of the hunt.

NAVIGATING THE MARKET

With a plethora of manufacturers vying for attention, selecting the right muzzleloader can be daunting. However, by exploring reputable brands and consulting resources, hunters can navigate this landscape with much more confidence.

In the ever-evolving world of firearms, modern inline muzzleloaders stand as a testament to innovation and ingenuity. With their blend of tradition and technology, they offer hunters an unparalleled experience, redefining the boundaries of what is possible in the pursuit of game. As hunters continue to push the limits of their craft, the legacy of the modern muzzleloader remains as enduring as the spirit of the hunt itself.

I have included brief overviews of the more popular muzzleloader choices here. If they do not include your favorite manufacturer, you can find a list of other gunmakers in the Muzzleloader appendix section and search the web for more information about their product offerings. For the sake of impartiality, the selections below are in alphabetical order.

.50 CALIBER CVA ACCURA® LONG-RANGE X

The .50 Caliber CVA Accura LR-X offers hunters exceptional long-range performance and accuracy. Its stout 30-inch barrel manages magnum powder charges, enhancing velocity and flattening trajectory. With a threaded barrel for easy muzzle brake attachment and a breech plug for tool-free cleaning, the Accura LR-X is a top choice for hunters seeking precision.

- **Overall Length:** 45"
- **Barrel Length:** 30"
- **Weight:** 8.1 lbs.
- **Sighting System:** Iron Sights & Drilled/Tapped for Scope Mount or with Mounted Scope
- **Caliber:** .45 or .50 Caliber Magnum
- **Ignition System:** 209 Primers

CVA ACCURA MR-X

The Accura MR-X is a break-action muzzleloader with easy breech access for quick priming and cleaning. Available in .50 and .45 calibers, it boasts compatibility with 209 primers and a maximum magnum charge of 150 grains for optimal performance in the field.

- **Overall Length:** 41"
- **Barrel Length:** 26"
- **Weight:** 6.7 lbs.
- **Sighting System:** Durasight scope rail
- **Caliber:** .50 Caliber Magnum
- **Ignition System:** 209 Primers

CVA® OPTIMA™

The Optima V2 features a redesigned trigger-guard with an actuated breeching lever for improved usability. Its ambidextrous stock and CrushZone recoil pad offer comfort, while the 26-inch stainless steel fluted barrel ensures maneuverability. Equipped with quality features like the Quick Release Breech Plug and DuraSight DEAD-ON one-piece scope mount, the Optima V2 provides exceptional value for its price.

- **Overall Length:** 41"
- **Barrel Length:** 26"
- **Weight:** 6.65 lbs.
- **Sighting System:** Includes One-Piece Scope Mount
- **Caliber:** .50 Caliber Magnum
- **Ignition System:** 209 Primers

CVA PARAMOUNT™

With its nitride-treated stainless steel Bergara barrel and fully adjustable stock, the Paramount delivers remarkable accuracy and muzzle velocity. Available in .40, .45, and the more popular .50 caliber, it's designed for long-range shooting and accepts Remington 700 Pattern Scope Mounts for enhanced versatility.

- **Barrel Length:** 26"
- **Weight:** 9.8 lbs. (Paramount) or 8.2 Pounds (Paramount Pro & HTR)
- **Sighting System:** Accepts Remington 700 Pattern Scope Mount
- **Caliber:** .45 Caliber Magnum (Paramount and Paramount Pro), .40 Caliber Magnum (Paramount HTR and Paramount Pro), or .50 Caliber Magnum (Paramount Pro)
- **Ignition System:** Vari-Flame Ignition

CVA WOLF™ V2

The lightweight and adjustable Wolf V2 offers ease of handling and customization. Its ambidextrous stock and Quick-Release Breech Plug ensure user comfort and convenience, while its affordability makes it an attractive option for hunters seeking performance without breaking the bank.

- **Overall Length:** 39"
- **Barrel Length:** 24"
- **Weight:** 6.25 lbs.
- **Sighting System:** Includes One-Piece Scope Mount
- **Caliber:** .50 Caliber Magnum
- **Ignition System:** 209 Primers

REMINGTON 700 ULTIMATE MUZZLELOADER

The Remington 700 Ultimate Muzzleloader features a 26-inch barrel and iron sights, making it suitable for both close and long-range shooting. With a weight of 8.5 lbs. and compatibility with Remington UML Ignition, it offers reliability and accuracy for muzzleloader enthusiasts.

- **Overall Length:** 47"
- **Barrel Length:** 26"
- **Weight:** 8.5 lbs.
- **Sighting System:** Iron Sights & Drilled/Tapped for Scope Mount
- **Caliber:** .50 Caliber Magnum
- **Ignition System:** Remington UML Ignition

TRADITIONS® BUCKSTALKER XT YOUTH

The Buckstalker XT is a compact and affordable muzzleloader designed for youth hunters. Equipped with an Elite XT Trigger system and Accelerator Breech

Plug™, it offers safety and ease of use without compromising on performance.

- **Overall Length:** 40"
- **Barrel Length:** 24"
- **Weight:** 6.35 lbs.
- **Sighting System:** Truglo Fiber Optic Sights & Drilled/Tapped for Scope Mount
- **Caliber:** .50 Caliber Magnum
- **Ignition System:** 209 Primers

▲ An advantageous feature of the Traditions® Youth Buckstalker™ XT Muzzleloader 13" is its length of pull, making it one of the shortest stocks in the industry. It is a compact, maneuverable firearm that combines many of Traditions® best features into one rifle. Credit: Traditions®.

TRADITIONS® KENTUCKY FLINTLOCK KIT

For enthusiasts who yearn for the traditional appeal of a flintlock Kentucky rifle, look no further than the Traditions® flintlock kit. This build-it-yourself package promises immense satisfaction for those adept at following step-by-step instructions. With all the necessary components included, such as a full-length walnut stock, an octagonal rifled barrel, and solid brass furnishings, assembling this handsome rifle is a fulfilling endeavor.

Upon completion, this meticulously crafted recreation of yesteryear stands ready for the hunt, exuding authenticity and craftsmanship. Designed to evoke a sense of time travel, this rifle beckons muzzleloader hunters to embark on a nostalgic journey with authentic black powder and a 1:66" rifling twist rate ideal for patched round balls.

The sheer joy of crafting and wielding a primitive muzzleloader for hunting purposes is unparalleled, offering a unique and immersive experience reminiscent of bygone eras. With each shot, hunters can connect with a rich heritage and a simpler time, making the Traditions® flintlock kit a cherished relic brought to life.

- **Overall Length:** 49"
- **Barrel Length:** 33.5"
- **Sighting System:** Open Sights
- **Caliber:** .50 Caliber
- **Ignition System:** Flintlock or Percussion Cap

TRADITIONS® NITRO FIRE® VAPR

Simplifying loading with Federal's FireStick system, the NitroFire® VAPR requires just two fingers, ensuring ease and safety. Its 1:24" rifling twist rate and Traditions® VAPR barrel deliver remarkable accuracy, particularly with heavier bullets. Cleanup after the hunt is straightforward, but buyers should be aware of potential state restrictions on its use.

- **Barrel Length:** 26"
- **Weight:** 6.5 lbs.
- **Sighting System:** Drilled/Tapped for Scope Mounts
- **Caliber:** .50 Caliber Magnum
- **Ignition System:** Federal FireStick

▲ Traditions® NitroFire features the Federal FireStick system. The FireStick system includes a new ignition system that charges from the breech, while the projectile is loaded from the muzzle. The design was destined to change the face of muzzleloading. Credit: Traditions®.

TRADITIONS® PURSUIT VAPR XT

Weighing a mere 5.75 pounds, the Pursuit VAPR XT offers exceptional lightweight performance for extended hunts. Featuring a VAPR barrel with a 1:24" rifling twist, it excels with both heavy and light bullets, providing versatility in the field. With an Accelerator Breech Plug for easy maintenance and comprehensive safety features, it's a reliable choice for hunters seeking accuracy and convenience.

- **Overall Length:** 42"

- **Barrel Length:** 26"
- **Weight:** 5.75 lbs.
- **Sighting System:** Drilled/Tapped for Scope Mounts
- **Caliber:** .45 Caliber or .50 Caliber Magnum
- **Ignition System:** 209 Primers

TRADITIONS® VORTEK STRIKERFIRE® LDR

The Vortek Strikerfire® LDR boasts a 1:24" twist VAPR barrel for enhanced accuracy and faster lock times, ensuring precise shots in any conditions. Its patented StrikerFire system enables quick and quiet cocking with a simple button press, improving usability in the field. Packed with features like the TAC-2 Trigger System and Dual Safety System, it represents the pinnacle of Traditions® muzzleloader technology.

- **Overall Length:** 46"
- **Barrel Length:** 30"
- **Weight:** 6.8 lbs.
- **Sighting System:** Drilled/Tapped for Scope Mounts
- **Caliber:** .50 Caliber Magnum
- **Ignition System:** 209 Primers

▲ The Vortek StrikerFire represents one of the most advanced muzzleloaders on the market thanks to the StrikerFire system and the TAC-2 Trigger. Credit: Traditions®.

CLEANING AND MAINTENANCE OF MUZZLELOADERS

One of the most common pitfalls encountered with muzzleloaders is neglecting their maintenance. Unlike conventional rifles, muzzleloaders require immediate attention after each use. The adage holds true: "If you shoot it, you'd better clean it." Failure to do so allows residual chemicals to accumulate within the barrel, leading to detrimental effects on its internal components. While traditional firearm cleaners suffice for basic maintenance, specialized muzzleloader cleaners are often preferred for their efficacy. These cleaners are specifically formulated to address the unique residues left behind by black powder and substitutes, ensuring thorough cleansing of the barrel. Additionally, proper lubrication is essential for maintaining optimal functionality. When storing a muzzleloader for an extended duration, a moderate application of oil to all moving parts is recommended, albeit without excessive saturation. Before venturing into the field for hunting season, a brief cleaning session is advisable to ensure peak performance.

▲ An important maintenance routine when storing a muzzleloader at the end of the season is to make sure all moving parts are lightly oiled. Credit: OTIS.

OTHER PROTOCOLS FOR MUZZLELOADERS

Many state regulations stipulate that a muzzleloader is considered "unloaded" only when the cap is removed from the ignitor (nipple) and the primer is extracted. This provision offers the convenience of transporting the firearm without the need to discharge it after every outing. However, it's imperative to avoid leaving the bullet in the muzzleloader for an extended period, ideally no more than two to three days.

Upon returning from a day afield, refrain from bringing the firearm indoors immediately, as the abrupt change in temperature can precipitate moisture accumulation within the barrel and powder. Instead, store the muzzleloader in a designated area in an unheated space to acclimate gradually. If the firearm remains unloaded for three days or longer, it's prudent to discharge and clean it before embarking on subsequent hunting endeavors.

The journey of the modern inline muzzleloader is one of evolution and adaptation, guided by the steadfast commitment of enthusiasts and manufacturers alike. In the ever-evolving landscape of hunting firearms, modern muzzleloaders stand as superb examples of time-honored tradition embraced with innovation.

▲ Modern muzzleloaders have taken the sport to a new and exciting level of popularity. Muzzleloaders provide hunters a unique rifle option to hunt big game which should not be overlooked. Credit: Traditions

▼ Making quick and humane kills is the result of thorough knowledge of big game anatomy. The three best kill-zone areas are the double lung, shoulder, and heart. Credit: Fiduccia Enterprises

Chapter Thirteen

THREE BEST KILL SHOTS: Target These Vital Areas for Quick, Ethical Kills

Be not afraid of any beast, no matter what it's size. When danger threatens, wield me, and I shall see to it's demise.
—Engraving on The Ultimatum from *Fallout 4*

During my first several years of hunting, I regularly hunted whitetails on a 130-acre farm in Ulster County, New York. The property was near the hamlet of Sundown and adjacent to the Big Indian Wilderness Area: a 33,500-acre expanse of forest known for its superb whitetail hunting. Weisman's land was a mixture of abandoned apple and pear orchards, hay fields, and mature woods.

My third deer hunt took place on opening day of the firearm season in 1967. Although it ended disappointingly, it taught me a valuable lesson. My post overlooked a vast section of woods that rarely failed to provide deer sightings.

▲ Weisman's Farm provided splendid color in the fall along with memorable deer hunts. Credit: Fiduccia Enterprises.

Shortly after legal light, I heard the telltale crunching of deer hooves on dry leaves. Then, suddenly—silence. Minutes later, a striking eight-point buck emerged about forty yards in front of me and stopped broadside (there were no rangefinders back then). My heart pounded as I raised my .30–30 Marlin loaded with Winchester's Deer Season XP ammunition. Winchester ammunition specifically designed it for deer hunters at that time (I still have a full box). I was about to place the crosshairs of my 4x Leupold M8 scope on the middle of the buck's chest, when the buck stepped behind a large oak tree. With its chest safely hidden, I hesitated to shoot. Only its neck and rear end were visible. Without forewarning, the deer turned and walked away without offering me a clean shot. I never saw the buck again.

Back then, I simply did not understand the nuances of shot placement. During the offseason, I educated myself on all aspects of the subject. I learned that I could have shot the buck in the neck. At 40 yards, the bullet would have severed the spinal cord in the cervical vertebrae, rapidly dispatching the deer where it stood. In the articles I read, a recurring point was that

▲ This is the standard broadside shot. It provides the perfect opportunity to shoot the boiler room or lung area. Credit: Canstock.

deer and other big game are *hardcore survivors*. If their central nervous, circulatory, or respiratory systems are not disabled on the first shot, they can still manage a clean getaway. Another constant point mentioned was that fatal kill shots are a result of using the proper types of cartridge loads and bullet designs, as they go hand-in-hand with accurately placing the shot to vital areas. These factors, combined with precise shot placement, are critical elements to putting big game down swiftly and ethically.

THE BEST BIG GAME POSITIONS

To achieve dependable one shot kills, animals must present a favorable angle, ideally a standing broadside position. It allows hunters multiple shot placement options. I fully understand not every animal presents

▲ The buck pictured here offers the perfect position for a shot to the shoulder blade or a double-lung shot. Credit: Canstock.

a broadside standing or walking opportunity. So, I get it. But, putting the crosshairs on broadside standing animals is *the* golden ticket to taking big game down consistently and successfully.

Here is why I swear by it. I spent many of my early years testing different shot placement strategies. I listened to old-timers at hunting camps, read everything I could find on ballistics, and practiced shooting targets that included the full body anatomy of deer relentlessly, and I shot different kill zones. It became clear to me that when a hunter places a broadside shot on a standing big game animal, it is just as important—if not more so—than the caliber of their rifle. Hunters can debate the merits of a .30–06 versus a .270 all day long, but if you do not hit any of the best kill zones accurately, no amount of firepower will make up for it.

I also discovered that shooting running game is like playing Russian roulette with your hunt. It is a recipe for disaster, end of story. Period. My favorite gun writer was the legendary Jack O'Connor. He once claimed in an October 1970 issue of *Outdoor Life* magazine that "A running buck makes for as big a target as a stationary one." *Yikes!* I respectfully disagree. There can be no logical argument that shooting at running game *nullifies* excellent shot placement opportunities. Even if the animal is as large as a bull moose, a running shot opens the door to big trouble. Consequently, five-plus decades ago I made it a steadfast personal rule never to shoot at running game. It has paid off to the nth degree. *Trust this;* if you stick to taking shots at standing or walking game, especially when they are clueless about your presence, your kill rate success will increase exponentially. And that is a hardcore fact you can take to the deer hunting bank.

TOP NOTCH SHOT PLACEMENT CHOICES

During my 61 years of hunting a variety of different types of big game animals throughout North America and Africa, I have confirmed that selecting the broadside standing position coupled with an appropriate kill

▲ Shooting at running game is risky. An ill-placed shot can end up wounding game. Credit: 6533875 © Photomyeye | Dreamstime.com.

zone choice played a crucial role in providing me with *consistent* successful shots at big game (note: *I am not being braggadocious;* I am relating a fact that will help you achieve the same kind of success).

When it comes to accurate shot placement on standing broadside big game animals, it boils down to the KISS principle, "keep it simple, stupid." That means aiming at areas on an animal that result in a quick demise. These zones include the boiler room, the heart, the lungs, and the large scapula (shoulder blade). Sometimes you just have to let an animal walk away rather than shoot at it.

BOILER ROOM SHOT

For decades, hunters have referred to the lung area as the boiler room or breadbasket. The term was commonly used in the 1960s and 70s in *Outdoor Life*, *Field & Stream*, and *Sports Afield*. This area provides the largest and most forgiving kill zone. A well-placed shot here causes massive hemorrhaging, because the chest cavity encompasses its main organs, including the heart and lungs, and the most concentration of major arteries and veins. The result is a quick kill. The boiler room is located directly above, and slightly behind, the front leg of a big game animal when it is standing broadside to the hunter. A common mistake is assuming the boiler room shot works from any angle. Not so. When a hunter shoots it from a severe angle, the vital organs could be missed.

Therefore, it is *most* lethal when big game animals are standing broadside in relationship to the hunter. Lastly, a misplaced shot to the boiler room, like one caused by shooting a running animal, can lead to hitting the rear portion of the animal's body, which could result in a lengthy tracking job.

▲ The lungs are a very dependable shot to shoot a deer. The lungs present the largest kill zone. Image courtesy of www.onxmaps.com.

HEART SHOT

Most big game hunters believe the best kill zone to aim for is the heart, because many hunters mistakenly believe a heart shot kills a deer flat out. Unfortunately, it usually doesn't—but sometimes, it does. An animal shot in the heart is more apt to run off than fall down dead where it stands. For instance, a healthy adult whitetail buck can run up to 250 yards before it expires and collapses from a heart shot.

When a big game animal does collapse and die on the spot after being shot in the heart, it is most likely due to the bullet severing the large veins and arteries that connect to the *top* of the heart (specifically, the aorta, the largest artery). When that occurs, the animal's blood pressure drops to zero and it dies quickly due to shock and extreme blood loss. But that does not usually happen because hitting the top of the heart often happens by mistake. In other words, a hunter probably did not deliberately aim for the arteries and veins on the top of the heart.

Another drawback for targeting the heart is it is a small target, in an adult buck, the heart is only about 4 to 6 inches from top to bottom. It is about 6 to 8 inches in length in larger big game species. Therefore, when *intentionally* aiming at the heart of a white-tailed buck or any other big game animal, it is a *must* for the animal to always be at a close range in a *standing* broadside position for the absolute *best* results.

There is no doubt a heart shot is a lethal kill shot on any big game animal, but experienced big game hunters know a single shot into the heart/lung area is by far a much better combination. Targeting just the heart should be left to longtime big game Dead-eye Dans or Dianes with years of experience shooting the heart. This needed to be addressed because so many hunters, especially novices, think the heart shot is a top-notch kill target.

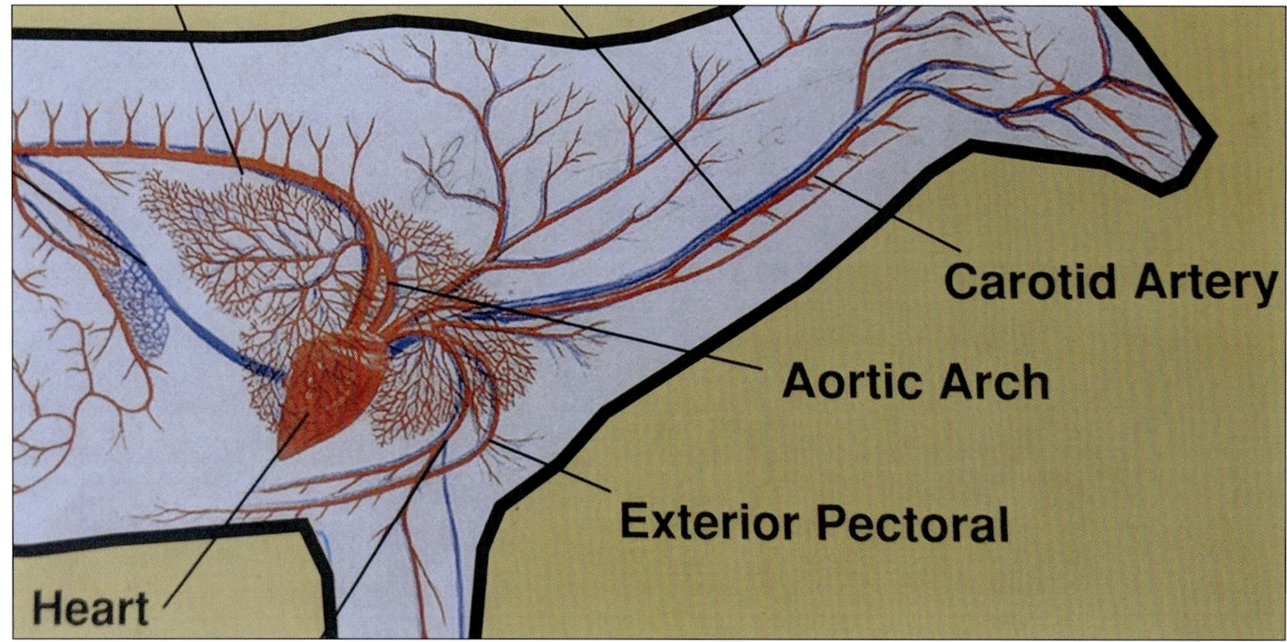

▲ I am not a fan of making the heart a primary target, even though it is a deadly kill shot. It is *always* better to target the heart in a combination heart/lung shot. Photo Credit: *Deer & Deer Hunting* magazine.

THE SCAPULA SHOT

The scapula (shoulder blade) is the most effective and humane shot placement zone. A well-placed shot to the shoulder can drop any big game animal instantly. It's a top-notch kill zone to target, particularly when an animal is standing broadside.

A shoulder shot can destroy three vital body parts: the heart, lungs, and spine. With the correct ammunition, like a bonded or partition bullet, it can also penetrate or pass through the opposite shoulder. Additionally, a bullet penetrating the shoulder blade destroys the brachial plexus, which consists of nerves, veins, muscle, and tendons. Destruction of the brachial plexus results in *instantaneous* paralysis of the animal. As if that is not enough, the fragmentation of the bullet often incorporates shock to the spinal column.

One example of a scapula shot happened during a Newfoundland hunt in 2008. I had a twenty-point bull broadside at 210 yards. I placed my crosshairs just above the center of his shoulder and squeezed the trigger. He collapsed instantly where he stood. Once again, that shot reaffirmed my belief in the effectiveness of the scapula shot. That hunt and many other one-shot big game kills can be seen on my YouTube channel Woods N' Water.

The shoulder shot is my go-to shot placement position. When I see a big game animal in a standing broadside position, I relax, knowing my chances of an instantaneous kill just skyrocketed exponentially. Hunters who master this shot, along with shooting broadside standing game, will significantly increase their big game kill success rates while imparting an absolute minimum amount of distress to the animal. While the other two shot placement zones are excellent choices, targeting the scapula is a top-notch choice bar none!

▲ This buck presents a shoulder shot. It will kill the deer before it hits the ground. Photo Credit: Canstock photo.

▼ By correcting poor finger placement on the trigger, hunters will improve their shooting skills tenfold. Proper trigger finger placement is key to accurate shooting 101. Placing a shot one-inch high of the bull's eye at 100 yards will result in a bull's eye at 200 yards. Credit: Fiduccia Enterprises

Chapter Fourteen

CRITICAL STEPS TO SHOOTING TIGHTER GROUPS: Elevate Your Hunting Success

You know, if you need a hundred rounds to kill a deer, maybe hunting isn't your sport.
—ELAYNE BOOSLER, comedian

If you're struggling to shoot tighter groups, it might not be the rifle, an error in the setup, or your execution. It may be due to other less recognized issues. Learning to spot subtle shooting mistakes inevitably helps hunters to execute better groupings at the range and in the field. There is skill involved in all types of shooting, but generally, rifle accuracy from a bench rest is about consistency and eliminating outside influences that can limit a firearm's capabilities. Once you learn to recognize these eight frequently overlooked errors, you will see better results when hunting big game.

IMPROPERLY MOUNTED SCOPE

While mounting a scope can be done at home, there is a learning curve. If you feel even the slightest hesitation, it is wiser to have a sporting goods store or gunsmith professionally mount your scope. However,

◀ This scope has all the elements of a properly mounted scope. For those who are unsure about mounting their own scope, it is always wise to have this done by a professional gunsmith. Credit: TRACT Optics.

these days anyone can learn to do anything by watching a YouTube video. You can also find videos and tutorials on many riflescope and gunsmith tool manufacturer's websites. Top-notch scope mounting always begins with *high-quality* bases and rings.

STABLE REST

When zeroing in a rifle, a stable rest is a no-brainer. It allows a shooter to test the rifle accuracy and not your ability to hold it steady. Once the rifle is on target you can practice shooting offhand, which is a more real-world situation when actually hunting.

SHOOTING IN BAD CONDITIONS

It is best to zero a rifle early in the morning on calm days. This is when the temperature is lower and mirage issues are nearly nonexistent. Shooting in poor visibility conditions will result in having to shoot more ammunition and waste more time.

TRIGGER PULL

Trigger pull is not a "pull" at all. It is more of a trigger press. Once a shooter gets in the habit of pulling the trigger, it will inevitably cause you to yank it. Learning to press a trigger is moving it straight to the rear of the trigger housing without disturbing the sight picture. It takes time and practice to achieve. Dry firing practice helps. Use snap caps to prevent damaging a firearm from excessive dry firing practice. After enough practice, a shooter should be able to take up all the trigger slack first, so at the instant you want to fire the firearm it will break the trigger. What should be achieved is to pull the trigger and have as little external influence on the rifle as is possible.

TOO MUCH BARREL HEAT

Erratic shot placement when zeroing a rifle is often from not cooling off the barrel between shots. It requires patience to wait for the barrel to cool, but the result will be greater accuracy.

LACK OF FOLLOW-THROUGH AND FOCUS

The Achilles' heel, for many shooters, is failing to follow through. The shot should not end until after impact. Try to visualize the bullet impacting the target by keeping your head pressed to the stock of the rifle throughout the shot. If that doesn't work, shoot a smaller target.

▲ A key to Accurate Shooting 101 is the placement of the finger on the trigger. It may not seem important, but I assure you it is. The reason is because, depending on where your index finger is placed on the trigger, it triggers (pun intended) different muscle interactions with the gun. Credit: Fiduccia Ent.

It will help your concentration because an impact point must be picked rather than an impact area.

USE THE CORRECT AMMO

It is critical to always sight in with the same type of ammunition you plan to hunt with. Shoot several types of loads and bullet designs through your rifle. It will help to discover which bullets shoot most accurately. It will cost more money to do this test, but it is definitely worth it.

A QUALITY SCOPE

As I have mentioned in other chapters, a quality scope pays big dividends in achieving top-notch accuracy. It

▲ Trust this: A higher-end scope will always provide better accuracy and more successful kill ratios—bar none. Credit: Leupold.

is a wise investment to buy a quality scope, rings, and mounts. A quality scope will also have more precise windage and elevation adjustments. It will also tolerate the pounding from firing the rifle and provide clearer images in low light and foul weather, etc. Quality optics include TRACT Optics, Swarovski, Leica, Zeiss, Vortex, Steiner, and Leupold. I can't emphasize this enough: quality rings reduce the bending forces on a scope tube. Inexpensive rings and mounts will eventually cause accuracy problems.

Here are some additional pointers for more accurate shooting:

DON'T SCREW UP

I mentioned this earlier, but it pays to repeat it. *Always* check the rifle and the scope for loose screws. The bedding screws that secure your rifle to the stock are particularly important for accuracy. They should be tightened periodically to the manufacturer's specifications, which can be found in the rifle's manual. It is important to tighten bedding screws only to their proper torque. Overtightening them will generally end with the screw snapping or getting stripped.

A CLEAN BARREL

With an unloaded rifle, remove the bolt and look through the muzzle in good light. If there is accumulated gunk, it is time to clean the barrel. Accuracy decreases as a barrel accumulates heavy powder residue and copper fouling. Hunters rarely give cleaning kits much thought and usually end up buying inexpensive gun-cleaning kits. A quality cleaning kit will cost about $50 to $75. Using it will enhance a rifle's accuracy. Also consider buying high-end cleaning rods, which can cost $20 or more, but they are a must-have item. Use a rod guide specifically designed for your rifle's chamber. A rod guide prevents solvents from running back into the chamber and the trigger group. The rod guide centers the cleaning rod of the bore and prevents rod damage to your chamber, throat, and bore. Solid, one-piece cleaning rods with freely rotating handles allow the rod to spin with the twist of the rifling in the barrel.

BREAK IN A RIFLE BARREL

A rifle that is broken in correctly will help to minimize fouling that reduces accuracy. Rifles that are not properly broken in are prone to become over-fouled in as little as 12 to 20 rounds, which results in reduced accuracy. Many shooting gurus believe breaking-in a rifle is critically important to optimize the accuracy of a hunting rifle. It helps to eliminate the worry about a rifle becoming over-fouled during the hunting season.

The break-in process is simple but time-consuming. When breaking in a rifle, use any affordable ammo. Start with a clean barrel, fire a single shot, and then clean the barrel. Be sure to remove all the copper. Repeat this process after taking another five shots. Next, fire *two* shots and reclean the barrel three times. Then take *three* shots and clean and repeat this three times. Going forward, cleaning the barrel will become much quicker and easier and copper fouling should be minimized.

TRIGGER CREEP

Again, trigger pull is *essential* in making an accurate shot. The worst hunting triggers have "excessive creep," which means the shooter is never sure when the trigger will break. Should this occur, the most practical suggestion is to take the rifle to a gunsmith. Trigger repair generally costs about $100 to $150—sometimes more, but it is well worth the investment. A fully adjustable replacement trigger will cost more.

CUSTOM BEDDING

Custom bedding will definitely improve a rifle's accuracy. Bedding work costs about $200 or more. As soon as a rifle no longer shoots tight groups, and

▲ Breaking in a rifle barrel is only performed on rifled bores. There are many ways to break in a new barrel, albeit they use the same fundamental process. One popular method is to thoroughly clean the barrel between each of the first 15 to 25 shots, then between every two or three shots for the next 10 shots. Credit: Winchester Ammunition.

other probable causes are ruled out, it is more than likely time to get a bedding job done by a professional gunsmith.

USING THE RIGHT CARTRIDGE

This quest is where the pedal meets the metal. Unfortunately, there are no quick answers to discovering what the right cartridge is. It is all a matter of trial and error. By testing a rifle, you will soon discover which cartridges and bullet types it does or does not prefer.

The way to resolve this issue is to fire several different cartridges and bullet designs at the range. Clean the barrel between each type of load. Shoot about five shots of each type of ammo to settle in the bore. If you clean the bore, allow two fouling-shots with the new ammo. If you are going from coated to non-coated bullets, give the bore a thorough cleaning. Then, add two fouling shots with the non-coated bullet before testing for accuracy. The point of this test is that you will marry the right loads to the rifle for the rifle to perform its best.

By following the advice and suggestions contained herein, you will help yourself to achieve better shooting habits and greater accurate shooting techniques. Shooting accurately is not out of range (pun intended) for anyone who is willing to devote the time and energy to developing good shooting habits.

▲ Rifles can be likened to a relationship. They will quickly tell you what type of ammunition they like or dislike. Once you discover the type of cartridge your rifle prefers, it will provide you with more reliable accuracy afield. Credit: Hornady.

▲ Some experts say buck fever is not curable. But many hunters have learned to stop bouts by using quick target acquisition, breathing techniques, and disregarding the antlers. Credit: 36563438 © Mikael Males | Dreamstime.com

Chapter Fifteen

BUCK FEVER: Did You Know It Can Kill You?

Its telltale adrenaline surge is so instant and convulsive that a blood-pressure check at that moment would bust the machine that takes it.
—Robert Ruark, *The Old Man and the Boy* (1953)

You may wonder why I included a chapter on buck fever in this book. The reason is simple: buck fever can be dangerous to big game hunters. This condition can strike any hunter regardless of age, skill, strength, or experience.

A report from the *Journal of Mountain Hunting* states that, "Buck fever has afflicted just about every big game hunter at some point."[6] It triggers physiological reactions: shaky hands, sweating, racing heart, difficulty breathing, tremors, fainting, and, sometimes, loss of speech. It's no surprise that the medical community recognizes buck fever as a *real* physical condition. It is classified as *Acute Coronary Syndrome* and *Acute Extreme Excitation*. In severe cases, buck fever can even lead to a heart attack.

A study by Verba, Jensen, and Lynn in 2016 monitored nineteen hunters using electrocardiogram (ECG) patches. Fifteen experienced buck fever, with heart rates spiking dramatically. Some hunters' heart rates doubled at the mere sight of a buck, jumping from 78 to 168 beats per minute. One subject recorded ventricular arrhythmias, highlighting the cardiovascular risks of extreme hunting excitement.[7] Furthermore, the American Heart Association (AHA) confirms that buck fever, especially for those with clogged arteries, *definitely* increases the risk of a heart attack.[8]

Over the last sixty years I have read countless studies about this affliction. One was conducted by Texas A&M.[9] It classified buck fever as an

▲ Buck fever shows no partiality to age, gender, or physical fitness. Any hunter can be affected. Credit: TRACT Optics.

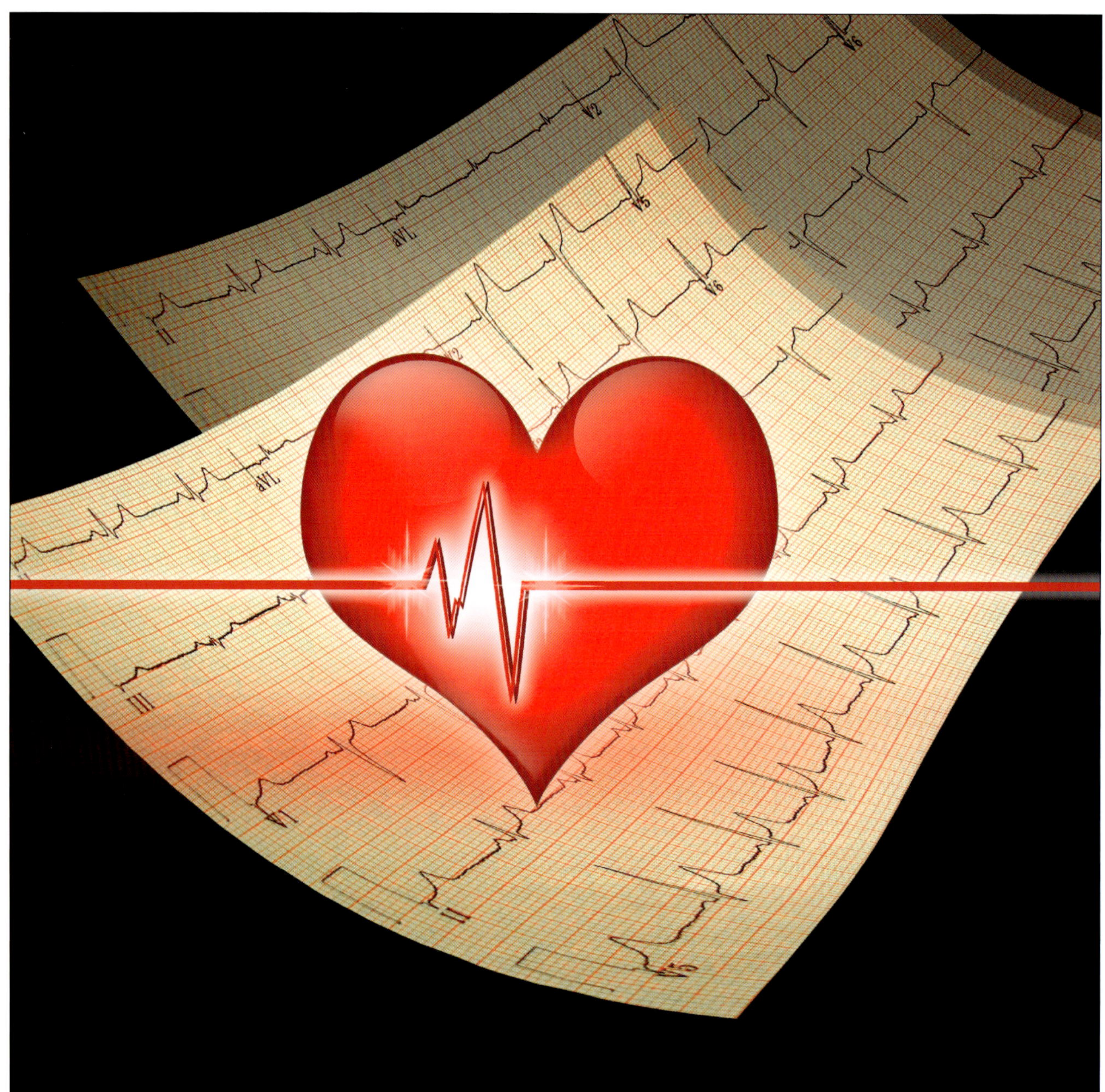

▲ Buck fever can be more serious than most hunters suspect. Credit: Eti Swinford | Dreamstime.com.

anxiety disorder. Researchers Tom Heberlein and Rich Steadman explained that the body's response to an antlered game sighting triggers nervous system activation, altering heart rate, blood flow, and breathing. The result: impaired motor function, irrational actions, and missed or wounded game as their projectiles have no real dedicated target. Hence, bullets and broadheads can fly helter-skelter. That can cause hunters in the midst of a buck fever attack not to be safe around other hunters.

But here is the most serious potential result about buck fever. In its most *extreme* form, it can kill you by causing a massive heart attack. Additionally, buck fever can render a hunter incapable of rational thought

▲ Even a small antlered buck can trigger an episode of buck fever. Credit: Canstock photo.

▲ Buck fever can interfere with routine rifle functions. Credit: Weatherby.

or safe firearm operation. That is what I experienced firsthand in 1964 while hunting Breakneck Ridge. After seeing a large-antlered buck, my next reaction was to eject every shell from my shotgun. Even in a light-headed and nauseous condition, I continued cycling the action minutes after the buck had disappeared from my view. When I started to regain some coherence, I decided it was time to immediately go home.

▲ A representation of the buck I saw that day on Breakneck Ridge. Credit: Canstock Photos.

The Texas A&M Health Science Center found that "there is no cure for buck fever," but there are ways to manage it. I respectfully disagree. I do agree that buck fever is serious, and that it can be controlled, but I also believe it can be cured, at least for some big game hunters. However, understanding the nuances of buck fever and the ways to prevent it are the *keys* to considerably reducing future bouts or potentially curing it.

Excitement is a natural part of hunting, but control of a hunter's emotions is essential. Therefore, the best way to prevent buck fever is to focus on placing your crosshairs on a specific aimpoint on the animal and *not* get immersed into staring at its antlers.

Thankfully, numerous techniques exist to help manage buck fever. However, be wary that the internet includes a lot of unreliable advice. So, just how does a hunter achieve the goal of considerably reducing or potentially eliminating cases of buck fever? Well, the first step is to admit that buck fever is a real medical condition. That single admission is the first step to recovery.

Here are the three steps that I used to cure my buck fever attacks after my first encounter with it decades ago. I do not promise a lot of hunting tactics I recommend will *always* work. However, I promise my three tactics will work if the advice is followed *exactly,* each and every time you see antlered game.

Quick Target Acquisition. Whenever you are at the range or just out shooting, use a full-bodied antlered game target. With control of the firearm, place your crosshairs on one of the two most deadly kill zones on any big game animal—the scapula (shoulder blade) or the lungs. The instant the crosshairs find a kill zone, fire the rifle. Firstly, this practice develops training your brain to concentrate only on these two kill zones that you are completely comfortable shooting—and not pay a bit of attention to the animal's antlers.

▲ The scientific community agrees that buck fever is an "acute anxiety disorder." Credit: Designer491 | Dreamstime.com.

▲ Practicing shooting at a target that includes an image of a buck or another type of antlered big game serves two purposes: (a) It helps a hunter become instinctively used to shooing a particular kill zone, and (b) it helps to learn how to disregard the antlers and immediately focus instead on a fixed kill zone. Credit: PCFImages.

Breathing Techniques. Learn to use breathing techniques when firing a rifle. You can search the web for breathing exercises, or you can read dozens of articles on the subject. Controlled breathing is a big step to eliminating the fast breathing that buck fever is known to cause.

Disregard the antlers. Those damn antlers. This tip is golden! It is *the* number one element to drastically reduce, or potentially eliminate, bouts of buck fever. The microsecond you see a big game antlered animal and you decide to take it, *never* look at the antlers again. Instead, completely focus on one or the other kill-zone aimpoints (shoulder or lungs). The time to admire the antlers is when you approach your expired big game animal.

▲ Hunters who focus on antlers are more susceptible to buck fever. Credit: Canstock.

A FINAL THOUGHT

The time to get excited is when you walk up to your dead buck. However, if you have a heart condition or high blood pressure, stay relaxed and channel your inner *Cool Hand Luke*. Buck fever is real, but with the right strategies, it can be controlled or even eliminated.

▼ Too few big game hunters realize the importance of using a quality scope. Some gun writers say a riflescope should cost as much as the rifle. I agree. Credit: TRACT Optics.

Chapter Sixteen

THROUGH THE LENS: Factors to Consider When Selecting Riflescopes

If you hunt big game with a bolt-action rifle, odds are you own a 3–9x scope, a scope that's as common in deer camps as cold coffee and old boots. If you do not own a 3–9x, it's about time you bought one.
—WAYNE VAN ZWOLL, PhD, 2005[10]

Choosing a riflescope for hunting big game can become somewhat of a time-consuming ordeal. For instance, eastern hunters' needs for a scope vary widely from the requirements of a western hunter. Therefore, what I write here is a more general overview of scopes that can be viewed as versatile for either eastern whitetails or western game animals. What should stand out about a hunter trying to purchase the perfect scope is this: there is not such a thing as *the* perfect rifle scope. I can say this, whether you hunt mostly whitetails but also other big game, such as elk, moose, etc., choosing a scope that first offers versatility above all else is always more practical.

▲ An important element when selecting a riflescope is to select the scope to the type of game and terrain to be hunted (stump sitting, still hunting, tracking, etc.). Credit: Canstock

Not only are there a lot of decisions to make about a scope's components, but there is also narrowing down an ideal choice from one of the myriad of scope manufacturers. The multitude of selections that have to be carefully thought about are considerable, and sometimes mind-bending, especially to novice hunters. Such considerations, in no order of importance, include the scope's magnification, field of view (FOV), type of reticles, fixed or variable, objective lenses, lens coatings, defogging options, waterproof or water resistant, focal plane, windage, elevation turrets, parallax, scope weight, flip covers, and warranty. The key factor that always comes into play, of course, is the price of the scope.

Some hunters think riflescopes are superfluous. Those who believe this are often hunters who regularly still-hunt or track whitetails in thick cover. Therefore, their opinions can be understandable because trackers and still-hunters generally have to make quick snapshots at close ranges. Most often, they hunt in dense cover and in the low light of hemlock stands and other overgrown topography.

Realistically, though, a riflescope can be used effectively in these scenarios. The caveat is that a scope used in heavy cover should be one of fixed power, and it should have low magnification. Low-power scopes have a wide field of view, which allows hunters to make fast and accurate target acquisitions. Therefore, riflescopes even have a place when hunting in thickets and low-light environments. This is the opposite of a scope that offers versatility; it is very specific to a hunting style and even hunting location. From here on, the type of scope information provided is more general. My point here is this—a quality riflescope is an important and useful hunting tool, no matter the terrain or method of hunting being used. A hunter can benefit greatly when the rifle is equipped with a quality scope.

I firmly believe riflescopes up the ante of achieving more successful kill ratios by tenfold. That in itself should be enough for any big game hunter to equip his or her rifle with a scope, rather than shooting with iron sights. Unless, of course, if one enjoys the challenge of hunting during primitive seasons and with fundamental methods and equipment. According to dozens of well-versed hunting pros, gun writers, and guides, a quality riflescope is a critical tool where its "cost should not be compromised." In fact, there are countless articles written that suggest a hunter should spend the same amount of money to buy a riflescope as he or she paid for their rifle.

Frankly, many hunters just do not believe that a quality scope can absolutely make or break a hunt. Therefore, the wisest strategy when planning to buy a riflescope is to budget enough money in order to purchase a high-quality scope rather than an economical one. Selecting an inexpensive or, worse yet, a cheap riflescope will almost always prove to be problematic.

Riflescopes are available in a wide range of price points. A quality scope offers two of the most critical benefits: versatility and durability. Think of it this way: a less-expensive scope will not last as long as a higher-end scope. Therefore, it is wiser to buy once, rather than twice. Most times the lowest-end scopes, which cost $100 or less, are usually not going to be trouble free. I liken them to a multi-time divorcée. Thus, they come with "issues." One of these issues is crucial—longevity.

▲ Too often hunters fail to realize the importance of a high-quality riflescope for their hunt. Without a doubt, a riflescope and its components are a crucial element to the success of a big game hunt. The cost of a quality scope should not be compromised. Credit: Monte Loomis.

For instance, in 1970 I bought a Redfield Wide Angle scope. At the time, the Redfield Company was a top riflescope brand. I don't recall what I paid for it, but it was probably within the quality range I refer to today. That scope has been on my Winchester .270 for more than fifty years, and it is still functioning like a well-oiled machine. Durability is a crucial element to take into consideration when purchasing a riflescope.

My thoughts about the different cost points of riflescopes are basic and, of course, are my own views.

ENTRY LEVEL—There are scopes that retail for less than $100. But, in my mind, it makes little sense to put

Chapter Seventeen

RIFLE CLEANING FREQUENCY: Schedule It Based on Usage and Conditions

A clean rifle shoots straight, and a straight shot brings meat to the table.
— Unknown

One of the most asked questions by novices and seasoned veterans is, "How often does a rifle need to be cleaned?" If that question were asked of 100 gun writers and firearm experts, you would most likely get a multitude of different responses. Years ago, the answer would have been, "After the rifle has been fired several times." Moreover, most firearm authorities would have recommended a rifle be cleaned every time one returns from a hunt (when the rifle was fired).

There's an old axiom that claims, "Things inevitably change; nothing remains the same forever." Today, that adage can be applied to the query of how often a rifle should be cleaned. With today's high-tech rifles, cartridges, bullet types, synthetic stocks, stainless steel barrels, etc., the thought about thoroughly deep cleaning a rifle each and every time it is used is no longer compulsory—things change. Note, though, that doesn't mean even the most high-tech types of rifles should not be cleaned attentively—just not as often nor as thoroughly as was recommended in years past.

I will start with this: The first step is to change your vocabulary about cleaning a firearm. Thorough cleaning is not the same as a maintenance cleaning of a firearm. Instead of thinking of the routine as cleaning a rifle, think of it as maintaining the firearm. So exactly what does that mean? Well, before pushing a wire brush through the barrel and using too much solvent to clean the bolt, first inspect the firearm to determine just how dirty it really is.

▲ Decades ago, firearm pros recommended a rifle be cleaned thoroughly every time a hunter returned from a hunt. This was particularly the case if the gun was fired. Today, it is recommended to *thoroughly* clean a rifle less often. Credit: OTIS.

Moreover, when it needs a cleaning, don't spend a lot of time trying to eliminate every speck of carbon from the barrel. While it may seem important to clean a rifle to a state of spotlessness it can actually do more harm than good. Too much thorough cleaning can cause detrimental effects on the rifle's barrel. Therefore, many gun pros do not recommend thoroughly deep-cleaning a rifle too frequently anymore because it can lead to "excessive wear on the bore," and even wear and tear on other parts of the gun including screws, springs, and scope rings. Therefore, regular light cleaning, a.k.a. maintenance, of the internal bore and other rifle parts is still essential to prevent the negative impact from bullet residue on your rifle's performance.

FOULING IMPACTS BULLET TRAJECTORY

Each time a cartridge is fired a layer of powder and copper coats the barrel's bore. Additionally, the faster the velocity of the powder and bullet, the quicker the carbon and copper fouling accumulates and the thicker it becomes. Consequently, the impact of a shot will change from slight to substantial depending upon the stage of fouling. Some rifles are very sensitive to fouling and therefore they need to be cleaned after less than a dozen shots. Other rifles seem to shoot better with fouling, even considerable fouling, and can go without cleaning for 100 or so shots. So checking the stage of the fouling is always a good idea to determine if it needs maintenance or a cleaning.

▲ Once the carbon and copper fouling accumulates, it will change the impact of the bullet from slight to substantial. Credit: Fiduccia Ent.

On the other hand, there is a camp that states there is a "window" where the fouling of a barrel stabilizes and does not affect the grouping of the placement of the bullets. Of course, that claim depends on other factors. For instance, the types of cartridges, the quality and size of the rifle's bore, type of rifling, and the powder and bullets being used may allow a hunter up to 100 shots of quality accuracy before the bore becomes over-fouled enough to affect accuracy and needs to be cleaned. Think of that for a moment: 100 shots for a hunting rifle including confirming a zero from one season to another, could take a couple of years.

On the other hand, some rifles are oversensitive to fouling and need to be cleaned after a maximum of a dozen shots. Most often a hunter will be warned that fouling has built up noticeably as accuracy begins to decrease. One such alert will be when bullets begin to "walk" around the target. So paying attention to your rifle's needs regarding fouling is an ongoing concern.

Lead deposits that accumulate in the bore can cause similar troubles to the bullet's trajectory. At some point, when accuracy begin to decrease—yup. You got it. It's time to lightly clean fouling from the bore. Keep in mind that once the barrel is cleaned and all the fouling has been removed, the spotless barrel may send a bullet to a different place than intended. For that reason, I don't clean the inside of my rifle's barrel once the window of stabilization is reached—which is usually after the first several shots. Regular light-bore cleaning

▲ A snake is an ideal way to execute regular cleaning. It removes the fouling buildup preserving the accuracy of the rifle. Credit: OTIS.

removes fouling, reduces friction, and preserves the integrity of the rifling, ensuring your rifle performs optimally over time.

Each rifle has its own needs. For instance, my 1964 Winchester Model 70 .270 positively doesn't like a squeaky-clean barrel. It shoots more accurately if the bore is slightly fouled. Mind you, I did not say over-fouled. So, I rarely deep-clean it, especially before hunting season. On the other hand my Kimber Model .270 WSM Classic and my Kimber .308 Win. Classic simply do not like a fouled barrel. Therefore, I pay closer attention to the buildup of the fouling on these two rifles.

SO, HOW OFTEN SHOULD A RIFLE BE CLEANED?

The short answer is not as often as it was once believed. If the barrel is damaged by continuous deep cleaning with harsh metal brushes, it will affect the spin of the bullet, which in turn diminishes accuracy. It's little things like this that are important to pay attention to when thoroughly cleaning a rifle, particularly with harsh cleaning methods. In the end, the best course of treatment can simply be running a cleaning bore snake through the barrel (from breech to barrel) to accomplish a less coarse, quick cleaning method. This will lessen the risk of a cleaning rod causing any damage to the rifling or other parts of the barrel.

▼ Three of the most common ways to clean big game rifles are abbreviated, thorough, and deep cleaning. Credit: OTIS

Chapter Eighteen

INNOVATIONS IN RIFLE CLEANING: Beyond Traditions

A clean rifle is an accurate rifle.
—PJ DELHOMME, Crazy Canyon Media, LLC[17]

How a hunting rifle is cleaned is mostly based on the experience of the hunter. For instance, novice hunters are not generally aware that cleaning and oiling a firearm should always be done from the receiver end of the barrel. There are four cleaning methods to consider for the outside and inside of the barrel. They are a wipe down; an abbreviated cleaning; a thorough cleaning; and a deep cleaning.

WIPE DOWN

An external cleaning is often referred to as a wipe down. A wipe down should occur each time a hunter returns from a day afield in foul weather, particularly rain or snow. It's incredible how fast both exterior and interior parts of a rifle can be damaged by the elements. Basically this entails attentively wiping down the entire exterior of the rifle to make sure each and every cranny is dry and free of debris. It is also wise to run a clean rag through the barrel to remove any moisture. During a wipe down, it is wise to remove the bolt. Wipe it thoroughly dry, and lightly oil it. Wipe downs prevent rust and wear and tear on the exterior and internal parts of a rifle. Even "all-weather" hunting rifles that offer high-tech finishes and stainless-steel parts require this type of cleaning and maintenance under these types of foul weather circumstances. This type of cleaning method should never be overlooked anytime a rifle has been exposed to foul weather.

▲ Wiping down a firearm after a day afield is a good habit to practice. It can keep the firearm looking good and operating well. Credit: OTIS

ABBREVIATED CLEANING

An abbreviated cleaning is simply cleaning and lubricating the rifle's bore. It can be accomplished by using cleaning patches or bore snakes, but not harsh brushes. It pays most attention to the fouling that has accumulated in the bore. Run a dry patch down the barrel until the patch only has a light color. The patch doesn't have to be entirely spotless. An abbreviated cleaning can usually be done in less than thirty minutes.

THOROUGH CLEANING

This option is a more comprehensive way to clean a rifle. It is the cleaning method that is most often recommended by firearm authorities and hunting pros. It requires some basic firearm cleaning tools (kits). However, unlike a deep cleaning, it is not necessary to do what soldiers do with their rifles in basic training. In other words, you do not have to *entirely* strip down the rifle, trigger mechanism, and such and then put everything back together again.

A thorough cleaning involves several parts of the rifle. It includes cleaning and properly lubricating the bore, chamber, barrel, bolt, magazine, all exterior metal surfaces, and both the exterior and interior stock. It also consists of cleaning and tightening all screws under the stock, on the scope and the scope mounts.

▲ When performing a thorough cleaning, take the time to clean as many rifle parts as possible without performing a total breakdown of the firearm. This includes cleaning the bolt, magazine, bore, safety catch, etc. Credit: OTIS

Additionally, the safety catch (a.k.a. safety) is the device that is used to commence firing a firearm. It, too, should be visually inspected and cleaned. A trigger is the mechanism that activates the function of the firearm. Both the trigger and its external housing should be wiped clean with a wet patch and dried, as well.

What is also especially important is to remove the stock for a complete cleaning. Rifle stocks collect dirt in places that are hidden from view by the stock. Disturbingly, on occasion, I have sometimes discovered a dab of rust after removing a stock. If you catch rust early, it can be prevented from getting worse and doing any real damage. Once the stock is removed, coat the exterior of the action and barrel sparingly with a rust inhibitor.

Years ago, a thorough cleaning included running harsh steel wire brushes through the barrel several times to ensure the barrel was cleaned thoroughly. No longer is it advised to use harsh steel wire brushes. There are now bore brushes made of brass and softer bronze and nylon. Many times hunters will reach for a bronze brush to get a thorough clean. The type of brush you use is really a personal preference. For instance, I am a big fan of Otis Technology's cleaning products. I find their nylon and brass brushes work exceedingly well. There are numerous other companies with fine cleaning products. Use what works best for you.

Some hunters are fans of nylon brushes because they work well in removing loose carbon and fouling. Nylon brushes also work well with solvents like copper removers, as the chemicals won't break down the nylon the same way they might affect brass. Brass brushes work well with solvents that remove powder, lead, metal fouling, carbon deposits, and rust. A caveat with bronze brushes is that they can give you a false indication that the bore is clean, because some ammonia-based copper removers will turn blue or green when they react with the bronze brush, rather than any copper left in the barrel. Other softer cleaning tools for quick abbreviated cleanings include a bore snake. A bore snake is especially helpful to take on a destination hunt when taking along a full cleaning kit is not practical. Soft cotton bore mops are another option.

When it comes to oiling or lubricating a rifle, it is always advisable to do so in moderation using only quality gun oil products. Do not leave too much oil or

Chapter Nineteen

FLIGHT READY: Preparing Firearms for Air Travel

A vote is like a rifle: its usefulness depends upon the character of the user.
—THEODORE ROOSEVELT

The above quote may seem a bit obscure. However, in the context of this chapter, it emphasizes the importance of responsibility and adherence to airline regulations when traveling with firearms. As most hunters know, before 2001, packing a hunting firearm as baggage on a plane was more or less not a big deal. After 2001, though, it became much more complicated. In fact, if you do not follow the rules precisely it can be nothing less than a huge PITA. Many hunters have heard about the problems encountered with the Transportation Security Administration (TSA) regarding flying with firearms and ammunition. With that said, however, once you have the correct information on how to transport firearms and particularly ammo when flying from state to state and especially out of the country, the TSA's procedures can be rather straightforward, albeit more time consuming. By following the rules *precisely,* hunters will save themselves a lot of aggravation and potential complications.

▲ To eliminate problems with hunting firearms, it is wise to check all current rules and regulations of the TSA and the airlines you are flying. Credit: besttravelluggage.com.

TIME

When flying with firearms, it is wise to pay attention to the airline's recommendations about arrival times. Most, if not all, airlines recommend passengers arrive two hours early for domestic flights and three hours early for international flights, and that does not include the time it takes to find parking and to get back to the terminal. More importantly, it does not take into consideration the extra time needed for checking in firearms, particularly if things do not go smoothly.

Therefore, the first point about transporting firearms on a plane is to recognize it takes *more* time than usual. You must consider the potential of having issues checking in a firearm. If things go smoothly, it can take anywhere from about 20 minutes to well over an hour. On a few occasions, I have had it take more than 90 minutes at some of the busier metropolitan airports. This was entirely due to the airline personnel having to call for a TSA agent to handle and personally inspect not only the rifle but also the interior of the rifle case. Ammunition must be checked separately from the firearm. Thus, it is very wise to plan to arrive with more time than the usual airline recommendations. Earlier arrival will alleviate a lot of potential headaches and frustration.

The reasons why the airlines require arriving early are based on security, as well as dollars and cents. The truth is, the airport, TSA, and the airlines each have their own motives for early arrival. First and foremost, the TSA prefers airline travelers get to airports at least 90 minutes early because the TSA does not want its agents to rush their screenings no matter how long the security line is. Factually, that's a good strategy; after all, these days it is better to be safe than sorry! Another reason the airlines want passengers to arrive early is so they can keep their departures on time. Even the airport itself benefits from early arriving patrons. It gives flyers more time to stop at a restaurant or a shop before boarding. If a flyer is in a rush to get through security and get to a gate, he/she obviously can't stop to eat or browse through some stores. When I have firearms and ammunition to check in, I arrive three hours before a domestic flight. When traveling to Africa or other countries, I arrive 3.5 hours before the flight.

FIREARM DECLARATION PROCESS

Basically, the airline Firearm and Ammunition Declaration process is rather straightforward. It allows passengers to travel with firearms in checked baggage if they are properly packaged and declared at the airline ticket counter. Firearms must be unloaded, packed in a hard-sided locked case, and packed separately from ammunition. A gun case must be a hard-sided container. The TSA rules regulate that "the container must completely secure the firearm from being accessed."[20] If a locked gun case can be easily opened, the airline will not accept it. The locked case should be taken to the airline check-in counter to be declared.

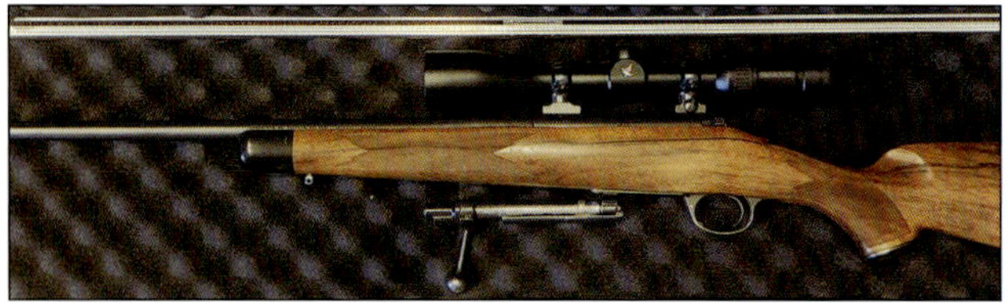

▲ Airlines require firearms to be packed in hard-sided cases. The firearm must be unloaded and available for the TSA agent's inspection. Credit: PCFImages.

At that point, a majority of the time the airline counter personnel will call for a TSA agent for further inspection. A TSA agent will have the passenger open the locked firearm case, and then the agent will personally inspect the firearm to ensure it is unloaded. If it is a bolt-action rifle, the bolt should be removed and set aside from the rifle in the case. It makes the barrel inspection go easier for the TSA agent, and it saves some time. Be absolutely sure when packing a firearm in the gun case that there is no loose ammunition in a clip, or a stray cartridge lying in the case, including under the foam cushions. Loose ammo in a rifle case will cause a huge problem and delay as the TSA will then consider the firearm "loaded." Loose ammo, even a single cartridge (*not* in an ammo box) found in luggage or on one's clothing, will also cause a problem with the TSA. One may be delayed to the extent where a flight is missed.

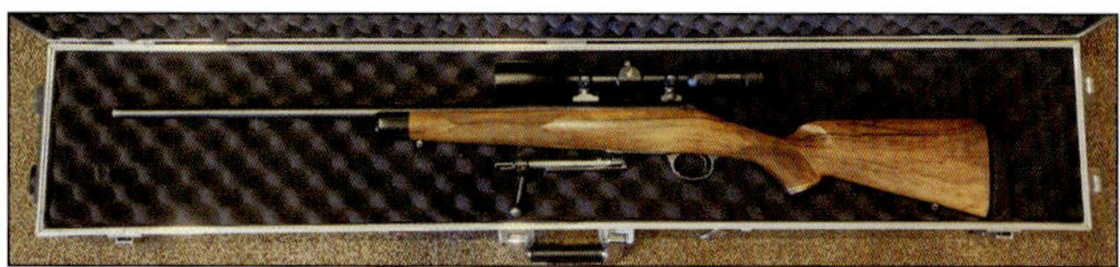

▲ To keep the TSA's inspection running quickly, the bolt should be placed by itself in the case in order for the TSA agent to check that the rifle's bore is empty. Credit: PCFImages.

When you are at the airline ticket check-in counter, be quick to advise the agent that your luggage includes an unloaded firearm in its own case and ammunition packed separately in your personal luggage. Firearms are considered baggage. The sooner you let the agent know you are traveling with a firearm and ammunition, the sooner the agent can call a TSA agent to come and get your firearm for inspection. The ticketing agent will also be able to put a paper document with the firearm in the case noting that the luggage has been checked for ammunition. For more information, go to: https://www.tsa.gov/travel/transporting-firearms-and-ammunition.

A rifle case without a lock or one that can be easily opened will not be approved by the TSA agent checking the firearm. Hence, it is wise to always secure the gun case with approved TSA locks. They are designed to be used with a universal "master" key. See the sidebar for more information about approved TSA locks.

Firearm airline regulations are subject to change without notice. Therefore, it is highly advisable to contact the TSA Center prior to your flight with questions you have regarding TSA firearm and ammunition regulations so you are clear about what you may or may not transport in your carry-on or checked baggage.

▲ TSA agents prefer locks on gun cases (or any luggage) to be TSA accepted. Credit: PCFImages.

To prevent a delay in baggage inspection, it is a good idea to buy locks that are TSA "approved" for a gun case and all other baggage.

The TSA screens all checked and carry-on luggage before allowing the luggage onto any commercial airline flight. In the majority of cases, pun intended, baggage can be electronically screened, which doesn't require the bag to be opened. However, sometimes a flyer's luggage may need to be opened by a TSA agent.

Some TSA-approved locks also come with an indicator to let you know if the TSA opened your bag. The indicator will be red after an inspection or remain green if your bag wasn't opened. You can easily reset the indicator in seconds using a pointed object, such as a pen or paper clip, so you can reuse the indicator for each trip.

TRAVELING WITH FIREARMS

- When traveling, be aware and comply with the laws concerning possession of firearms as they will inevitably vary by local, state, and even international governments.
- If you are traveling internationally with a firearm in checked baggage, you should definitely check the US Customs and Border Protection website for their information and requirements. Do this long before you plan to travel.
- The TSA reminds flyers to declare *each* firearm *each* time they produce it for transport as checked baggage. It is prudent to check with your airline about the possibilities, limitations, or fees that may apply.
- Only the passenger checking in the firearm/ammunition is permitted to retain the key or combination to the lock of their gun case. The TSA agent may request the key to open the firearm container to ensure compliance with TSA regulations. You may use any brand or type of lock to secure your firearm case. I highly recommend using a TSA-approved lock as it demonstrates to the TSA agent that you are a seasoned traveler with firearms.
- Warning: Bringing an unloaded firearm with accessible ammunition to the security checkpoint carries the same civil penalty and fine as bringing a loaded firearm to the checkpoint. Be absolutely careful about this.
- Firearm parts, including magazines, clips, bolts, and firing pins, are prohibited in carry-on baggage, but may be transported in checked baggage. I often remove my rifle bolt and place it in a ziplock bag inside the firearm case alongside my rifle.
- Riflescopes are permitted in carry-on and checked baggage.
- After your firearm is checked in by the TSA agent, be sure to keep an ear out for any airport announcements. Sometimes the TSA needs to reopen a gun case for any reason they deem necessary. They will want you to be present to either open the case or to be there when they open it.
- Additionally, many of the Canadian provinces require registration forms and fees to bring in firearms. This process can throw a wrench in the spokes if not done properly. And that will affect your travel plans.

TRAVELING WITH AMMUNITION

Ammunition is a separate issue. Some airlines, including United, Air Canada, JetBlue, and Delta have their own guidelines for how ammunition is to be packed. I have also run into different regulations when traveling to and from various Canadian provinces and African countries. Next is some information and tips.

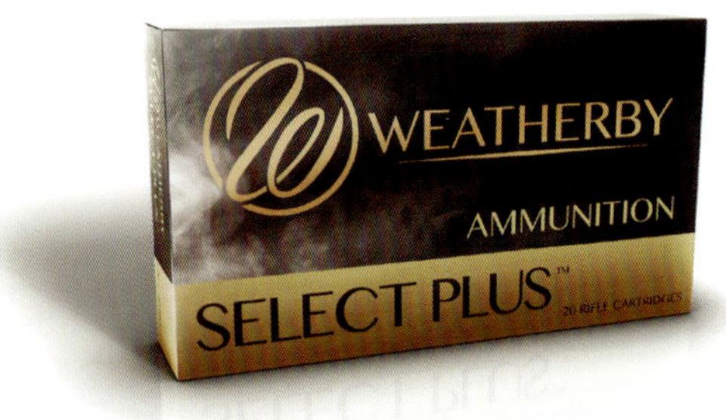

▲ It is absolutely critical you pack your boxed ammunition separately from your gun case. It is also critical that all ammunition be stored in the ammunition box and not loose in any other luggage. Miss this point and you are likely to miss your flight. At the time of this writing, four air passengers were jailed in a foreign country for having loose ammunition in their luggage. Don't make this mistake. Triple-check for loose ammo. Credit: Weatherby.

- Ammunition is prohibited in carry-on baggage, but it is allowed to be transported in checked baggage. Most airlines, if not all, however, will not allow the ammunition to be stored in the firearm case (which is regarded as baggage). It must be packed in luggage separate from your gun case.
- Empty ammunition clips must be securely boxed or included within a hard-sided case containing an unloaded firearm.
- Small arms ammunition (up to .75 caliber and shotgun shells of any gauge) are required to be packaged in cardboard, wood, plastic, or a metal box that is *specifically* designed to carry ammunition and declared to the airline ticket agent when you are checking in.
- Long before your flight, always check with your airline regarding quantity limits for ammunition.

IT'S A WRAP

In the end, to have a flight that is unencumbered with delays or other surprises when flying with firearms and ammunition, thoroughly do your homework at least two to three months *before* your scheduled departure date. Equally important is to remember to allow yourself plenty of extra time to deal with any unplanned contingencies. I like to include enough time to go to a restaurant before boarding and relax for a bite to eat and enjoy a cold Heineken or Corona. When the TSA and airline rules and regulations are followed, it will go miles to make sure everything goes more smoothly and quickly.

the area that can be seen in feet at 100 yards. Field of view is *directly* correlated to magnification. At a higher scope magnification, the field of view is smaller. A larger field of view is best in situations where the objects are moving.

Fire forming: The process of reshaping a metallic cartridge case to fit a new chamber by firing it within that chamber.

Firearm: A weapon that fires bullets, and of such a size that is designed for usage by one individual.

Firing pin: A spring-loaded bar that strikes the primer of a cartridge when the trigger is pulled to discharge a round from a firearm.

Firing pin dent: The dimple on the primer of a centerfire cartridge case (or in the rim of a rimfire cartridge) caused when it is struck by the firing pin.

First focal plane: The first focal plane is what is referred to when the reticle gets bigger as the shooter zooms in. It becomes smaller as the shooter zooms out.

Fixed reticle: A wire reticle typically appears in a crosshair and is stretched and fixed in the sleeve to form the aiming point. It is the most common variety of reticles in riflescopes as it has a low manufacturing cost.

Fixed riflescopes: As the name implies, a fixed riflescope scope is one that only comes with a certain amount of power of magnification. The magnification cannot be adjusted to be greater or lesser than what the scope is already set to. For example, a 4x scope will only have 4x of magnification.

Flash suppressor: A device that is attached to the muzzle of a firearm that lowers the temperature at which gases disperse upon firing.

Flat-nose bullet: A bullet with a flattened nose (front end). They are used primarily with tubular magazine rifles.

Flintlock: An obsolete mechanism for discharging a firearm.

Flip covers: A type of scope cover designed to stay locked when closed and flip back out of the way when opened. They protect the lenses on a scope from dust, dirt, grime, and grit.

Floating barrel: A barrel that avoids contact with the stock of the firearm.

Floor plate: The removable bottom of the magazine.

Focal plane: This riflescope term is also known as front and rear focal plane; this refers to the position of the lens etched with the reticle, in relation to the zoom mechanism. If the reticle-etched lens is in front of the zoom mechanism, it is referred to as a first, or front, focal plane scope.

Fog-proof: Fog and waterproof riflescopes are specifically designed instruments that provide effective protection against fog and water. These specially designed scopes offer enhanced durability and versatility when compared to traditional optics.

Follower: The portion of the magazine located between the spring and cartridges. It aids in properly feeding new cartridges into the chamber.

Foot pound (ft-lb.): A unit of energy commonly used for bullets; the force required to raise a one-pound weight one foot against the resistance of gravity.

Forearm: The forward part of a rifle stock associated with either one- or two-piece stocks. In pump-action rifles, the forearm is sometimes referred to as a slide.

Fouling: The accumulation of unwanted material on solid surfaces. Fouling material can consist of either powder, lubrication residue, or bullet material such as lead or copper.

Fouling shot: A shot fired through a clean bore that deposits a small amount of contaminants in the barrel. Subsequent firing prepares the bore for more consistent performance in ensuing shots. The first shot through a clean bore behaves aerodynamically differently from later shots through a bore with traces of powder residue. This results in the bullet's point of impact.

Free-floated: A procedure used to denote the relief of wood from the forearm area so that it does not touch the rifle barrel.

Full metal jacket bullet: A type of bullet designed to maintain its shape during impact and penetration. Full metal jacket bullets are unlike soft-point or hollow-point bullets that are designed to expand and create large wound channels.

Fully coated: A fully coated scope means that all the lenses in the scope received at least one chemical coating.

G

Gas-operated reloading: A system of operation used to provide energy to operate autoloading firearms.

Gauge: The gauge of a firearm is a unit of measurement used to express the diameter of the barrel.

Grain: Used to represent the amount of powder in a single cartridge or the weight of a bullet.

Grooves: The portion of rifling that is removed from the rifle's bore.

Gun control: The legal definition of gun control is a law regulating the purchase, sale, manufacture, and use of guns and, more recently, ammunition.

Gunpowder (black powder): The powder used in ammunition as the propellant charge. Generally, it is a mixture of sulfur, charcoal, and potassium nitrate. It burns rapidly, producing a volume of hot gas made up of carbon dioxide, water, and nitrogen, and a solid residue of potassium sulfide.

Gun serial number: A unique identifying series of numbers and sometimes letters given to a specific firearm.

Gunsmith: An individual expertly schooled and skilled in the repair, modification, design, and production of firearms.

H

Hair trigger: When a rifle's trigger is set to release at the slightest pressure. It is said a hair's width is all that is needed on a hair trigger to fire the rifle or other firearm.

Half-cock: The position of the hammer where the hammer is partially but not completely pulled back and cocked. Many firearms, particularly older firearms, had a notch cut into the hammer allowing half-cock. This position was designed to prevent the gun from firing and it also did not allow the hammer-mounted firing pin to rest on a live percussion cap or cartridge. The purpose of the half-cock position was as a safety-mechanism. However, like any firearm safety device, they should *never* be treated as a foolproof method of preventing a firearm to discharge a cartridge.

Hammer: A hammer strikes the firing pin to detonate the gunpowder. The hammer of a firearm was given its name for both resemblance and functional similarity to a hammer tool.

Hammer bite: The action of an external hammer pinching or catching the web of a shooting hand between the thumb and forefinger when the gun is fired.

Hammer block: A security device on some firearms that separates the firing pin from the hammer, except for when the trigger is pulled.

Handgun: A type of firearm that is compact enough that it can be held and used with a single hand.

Hang fire: An unexpected delay between the triggering of a firearm and the ignition of the propellant. Modern weapons can be vulnerable to this, particularly if the ammunition has been stored in an environment outside the manufacturer's specifications.

Headspace: The distance measured from the bolt face that acts as a cartridge stop when the round is fully chambered. Used as a verb, headspace refers to the interference created between this part of the chamber and the feature of the cartridge that achieves the correct positioning.

pin that protrudes radially from just above the base of the cartridge.

Pistol: A type of firearm that can be held and fired with one hand.

Pistol grip: A feature on some firearms that gives the user a slightly curved area to grip, just rear of the trigger.

Plated bullets: Plated bullets are constructed by applying a fine layer of copper to a lead core through an electroplating process. This procedure joins the benefits of jacketed and cast bullets, making them a popular choice among many shooters. Plated bullets are generally softer than jacketed bullets.

Plinking: Informal target shooting done at nontraditional targets such as tin cans, glass bottles, and balloons filled with water.

Point of aim (POA): Where the sight of the gun is pointed.

Point of impact (POI): The correlation between where the shooter is aiming and the exact area in which a bullet hits its target.

Point of view (POV): Refers to what a shooter is seeing.

Polymer-tip bullets: Polymer-tip ammunition is designed to enhance the ballistic coefficient of the bullet and enhance expansion on impact. The polymer tip aids the bullet to uphold a flatter trajectory and improves the likelihood of a successful strike on an animal.

Powerhead/bang stick: A specialized firearm used underwater that is fired when in direct contact with the target.

Primer: The part of the cartridge casing that ignites the powder.

Propellant: This is the powder or gas that ignites the powder.

Pump action: A rifle or shotgun in which the handgrip can be pumped back and forth to eject a spent round of ammunition and to chamber a fresh one. It is much faster than a bolt action and somewhat faster than a lever action, as it does not require that the shooter remove their trigger hand during reloading. In rifles, this action is also commonly called a slide action.

Pyrodex: The trade name of a black powder substitute with similar burning characteristics, but safer and designed to produce less fouling in the firearm.

R

Ramrod: A device used with early firearms to push the projectile down the barrel and up against the propellant (mainly gunpowder).

Rate of fire: The frequency at which a firearm can fire its projectiles. Usually measured in rounds per minute (RPM).

Rate of twist: A rifling measurement described as a ratio to indicate the number of rotations a bullet makes; 1:10 indicates that the bullet will make one complete rotation in 10 inches of the barrel.

Receiver: The part of a firearm that houses the operating parts.

Recoil: The backward momentum of a gun when it is discharged. In technical terms, the recoil caused by the gun exactly balances the forward momentum of the projectile, according to Newton's third law, often called kickback or kick.

Recoil operation: An operating mechanism used in locked-breech, autoloading firearms. As the name implies, these actions use the force of recoil to provide energy to cycle the action.

Red dot sight: A type of reflector (reflex) sight for firearms that gives the user a red light-emitting diode as a reticle to create an aimpoint.

Reflector (reflex) sight: A generally non-magnifying optical device that has an optically collimated reticle, allowing the user to look through a partially reflecting glass element and see a parallax-free crosshair or other projected aiming point superimposed on the field of view. It was invented in 1900, but was not generally used on firearms until reliably illuminated versions were invented in the late 1970s

Reticle: A reticle is anything in the scope that helps a shooter to aim. In its basic form a crosshair is a reticle. A reticle can be etched onto glass. This allows for the reticle to change in size as the scope magnifies or to change color based on user preference. To use a riflescope reticle properly, a shooter must first focus it to his or her eye.

Revolver: A repeating firearm that has a cylinder containing multiple chambers and at least one barrel for firing.

Rib: A raised surface along the top of a gun barrel that is used as a sight.

Ricochet: A rebound, bounce off, or skip off a surface, including rocks, water, metal, etc., particularly in the case of a firearm projectile.

Rifle (long gun): A gun fired from the shoulder level, which has a long, spirally grooved barrel.

Rifle bedding: A process of filling gaps between the action and the stock of a rifle with an epoxy-based material.

Rifling: Helical grooves in the barrel of a gun or firearm, which imparts a spin to a projectile around its long axis. This spin serves to gyroscopically stabilize the projectile, improving its aerodynamic stability and accuracy.

Rimfire (RF): A type of firearm cartridge that uses a firing pin to strike the base's rim to ignite it. This is in contrast to the firing pin striking a primer cap at the center of a cartridge's base in centerfire cartridges. The rim of the rimfire cartridge is essentially an extended and widened percussion cap that contains the priming compound, while the cartridge case itself contains the propellant powder and the projectile (bullet).

Riot gun: A gun that has been loaded for rubber bullets, smoke grenades, or any other projectile that is not designed to kill its target.

Rolling block: A form of firearm action where the sealing of the breech is done with a circular shaped breechblock able to rotate on a pin. The breechblock is locked into place by the hammer, thus preventing the cartridge from moving backward at the moment of firing. By cocking the hammer, the breechblock can rotate freely to reload the weapon.

Rotary cannon: A type of autocannon that contains multiple rotating barrels. If in a machine gun caliber, it is referred to as a rotary machine gun.

Round: A word that is often used as slang or colloquially for a single cartridge.

Round-nose bullets: A round-nose bullet has a tip that is one-half the diameter of the bullet. The tip is rounded, not hollow. It differs from other bullets with pointed tips.

RPM: Rounds per minute.

S

Sabot: A device used in a firearm to fire a projectile, such as a bullet, which is smaller than the bore diameter.

Safety: A mechanism used to help prevent the accidental discharge of a firearm in case of unsafe handling. Safeties can generally be divided into subtypes such as internal safeties (which typically do not receive input from the user) and external safeties (which typically allow the user to give input, for example, toggling a lever from "on" to "off" or something similar). Sometimes these are called "passive" and "active" safeties (or "automatic" and "manual"), respectively.

Sawed-off shotgun/sawn-off shotgun/short-barreled shotgun (SBS): A type of shotgun with a shorter gun barrel and often a shorter or deleted stock. Sawed-off or sawn-off shotguns are often used as home safety firearms.

Appendix B

Firearm Manufacturers

ANSCHUTZ NORTH AMERICA
205-655-7500 / 205-655-7502
www.anschutznorthamerica.com

BARRET®
615-896-2938
www.barrett.net

BCM® RIFLE COMPANY
877-272-8626
www.bravocompanymfg.com

BENELLI® USA CORPORATION
301-283-6981
www.benelliusa.com

BERGARA® NORTH AMERICA
877-892-7544
www.bergara.com

BERETTA/TIKKA/SAKO
800-Beretta
www.beretta.com

BIG HORN ARMORY
307-586-3700
www.bighornarmory.com

BLASER GROUP INC.
210-377-2527
www.Blaser.de/us

BROWNING®
800-333-3288
www.browning.com

BUSHMASTER® FIREARMS
800-883-6229
www.bushmaster.com

CHIAPPA FIREARMS®
937-835-5000
www.chiappafirearms.com

CHRISTENSEN ARMS®
888-517-8855
www.christensenarms.com

COLT
800-962-COLT (2658)
www.colt.com

CVA®
770-449-4687
www.cvabpishopping.com

DAVIDE PEDERSOLI®
39-030-891-5000
www.davide-pedersoli.com

FIERCE FIREARMS
435-462-0040
www.fiercearms.com

FREEDOM ARMS, INC.
307-883-2468
www.freedomarms.com

H&R 1871
203-239-5621
www.hr1871.com

HENRY®
866-200-2354
www.henryusa.com

HI-POINT® FIREARMS
419-747-9444
www.hi-pointfirearms.com

HORIZON FIREARMS
979-229-4664
www.horizonfirearms.com

INFINITY FIREARMS
800-928-1911
www.sviguns.com

ITHACA GUN COMPANY®
419-294-4113
www.ithacagun.com

KAHR ARMS®
508-795-3919
www.kahr.com

KELTEC® FIREARMS
321-631-0068 / 800-515-9983
www.keltecweapons.com

KIMBER® AMERICA
888-243-4522
www.kimberamerica.com

LAZZERONI®
520-624-7000
www.lazzeroni.com

MARLIN
203-239-5621
www.marlinfirearms.com

MAUSER
49 7562 61894 75
www.mauser.com/us

MCWHORTER RIFLES
229-782-5445
www.mcwhorter.com

MOSSBERG®
203-230-5300
www.mossberg.com

REMINGTON®
844-736-2767
www.remarms.com

RUGER®—STURM, RUGER & COMPANY
203-259-7843
www.ruger-firearms.com

SAKO
+358 10 830 5200
www.sako.global

SAVAGE®
413-568-7001
www.savagearms.com

SIG SAUER®/BLAZER/MAUSER
603-772-2302
www.sigarms.com

SMITH & WESSON®
800-331-0852
www.smith-wesson.com

SPRINGFIELD ARMORY®
800-680-6866
www.springfield-amory.com

TAURUS™
229-515-8464
www.taurususa.com

THOMPSON/CENTER
800-331-0852
www.tcarms.com

WEATHERBY
805-466-1767
www.weatherby.com

WINCHESTER FIREARMS
800-333-3288
WWW.WINCHESTERGUNS.COM

Appendix C

Muzzleloader Manufacturers

CVA
770-449-4687
www.bpioutdoors.com/CVA

GUNWERKS
307-296-7300
www.gunwerks.com

INVESTARM
39-030-896-0105
www.investarm.com/en

KNIGHT RIFLES
423-745-6213
www.muzzleloaders.com

LYMAN
928-524-6854
www.lymanproducts.com

PEDERSOLI
39-030-891-5000 (Italy)
www.davide-pedersoli.com

PIETTA
39-030-373-7098 (Italy)
www.pietta.us

REMINGTON
800-243-9700
www.remington.com

TENNESSEE VALLEY MUZZLELOADING
662-891-3000
www.tennesseevalleymanufacturing.com

TRADITIONS® FIREARMS
860-388-4656
www.traditionsfirearms.com

UMBERTI
www.uberti-usa.com

WOLF / CVA
855-236-5000
www.muzzle-loaders.com

WOODMAN ARMS
603-608-7218
www.woodmanarms.com

Appendix D

Optic Companies

(Scopes, Binoculars, Bases, Sights, Rails, and Ribs)

AIMPOINT®
703-263-9795
www.aimpoint.com

ATHLON OPTICS
855-913-5678
www.athlonoptics.com

ATN
650-989-5100
www.atncorp.com

BARSKA®
909-445-8168
www.barska.com

BENELLI®
800-264-4962
www.benelliusa.com

BRUNTON
307-857-4702
www.brunton.com

BSA® OPTICS
479-636-1200
www.bsaoptics.com

BURRIS® OPTICS
888-228-7747 / 888-440-0244
www.burrisoptics.com

CRIMSON TRACE CORP.
800-442-2406
www.crimstontrace.com

EOTECH®
888-368-4656 / 888-EOTHOLO
www.eotechinc.com

FIREFIELD®
817-790-9862
www.firefield.com

HOLOSUN®
909-594-2888
www.holosun.com

HUSKEMAW OPTICS
866-780-1072
www.huskemawoptics.com

KAHLES©
800-426-3089
www.kahles.at/us/

LEICA
570-368-3920
www.eurooptic.com

LEUPOLD & STEVENS
503-526-1455
www.leupold.com

MARCH SCOPES
81-266-75-5658
www.marchscopes.com

MEOPTA
420-581-241-111
www.meopta.com

NIGHTFORCE®
208-476-9814 Ext 3
www.nightforceoptics.com

NIKON
www.nikonsportoptics.com

N-VISION OPTICS
781-505-8360
www.nvisionoptics.com

RITON
855-39-RITON
www.ritonoptics.com

SIG SAUER®
603-610-3000
www.sigsauer.com

SIGHTMARK®
817-383-1163
www.sightmark.com

SPORTSMAN'S GUIDE
651-615-3006
www.sportsmansguide.com

STEINER OPTICS
888-550-6255
www.steiner-optics.com

SWAROVSKI/KAHLES
800-426-3089
www.swarovskioptik.com

TRACT OPTICS
631-662-7354
www.tractoptics.com

TRIJICON, INC.
248-960-7700
www.trijicon.com

U.S. OPTICS
828-874-2242
WWW.USOPTICS.COM

VORTEX® OPTICS
800-486-7839
WWW.VORTEXOPTICS.COM

ZEISS
800-441-3005
WWW.ZEISS.COM

Appendix E

Ammunition Manufacturers

AMERICAN EAGLE
800-831-8100
www.americaneagle.com

BARNES BULLETS
800-574-9200
www.barnesbullets.com

BLACK HILLS AMMUNITION
605-348-5150
www.black-hills.com

CHRISTENSEN ARMS®
888-517-8855
www.christensenarms.com

CUTTING EDGE BULLETS, LLC
208-609-4954
www.cuttingedgebullets.com

DAN WESSON FIREARMS
607-336-1174
www.danwessonfirearms.com

FEDERAL AMMUNITION
800-831-1732
www.federalpremium.com

FIERCE FIREARMS
435-462-0040
www.fiercearms.com

HORNADY
800-338-3220
www.hornady.com

ITHACA® GUN COMPANY
419-294-4113
www.ithacagun.com

NOSLER
800-285-3701
www.nosler.com

PPU
203-375-8544
www.ppu-usa.com

REMINGTON
800-243-9700
www.remington.com

SPEAR AMMO
877-426-7849
www.speer.com

SWIFT BULLET COMPANY
785-754-3959
www.swiftbullets.com

THOMPSON CENTER
866-730-1614
www.tcarms.com

WEATHERBY AMMUNITION
307-675-7840
www.weatherby.com

WINCHESTER
844-736-2767
www.winchester.com

Appendix F

Shooting Sticks Manufacturers

ALLEN COMPANY
www.byallen.com

BANKS OUTDOORS
800-262-4129
www.banksoutdoors.com

BLACKHAWK®
855-980-3157
www.blackhawkcom

BOG
833-250-6620
www.boghunt.com

B&T INDUSTRIES
316-721-3222
www.accu-shot.com

FIREFIELD
817-790-9862
www.fire-field.com

GOLDTIP®
800-551-0541
www.goldtip.com

HARRIS BIPODS
203-266-6906
www.harrisbipods.com

HIPSTICK / EBI INC.
www.hipstick.com

NATCHEZ
800-251-7839
www.natchezss.com

PRIMOS
800-423-3537
www.primos.com

SCHEELS®
701-356-8264
www.scheels.com

VANGUARD
800-875-3322
www.vanguardworld.com

Appendix G

Gun Cleaning Companies

BIRCHWOOD CASEY
877-269-8490
www.birchwoodcasey.com

BROWNELLS®
800-741-0015
www.brownells.com

GAMO®
479-636-1200
www.gamousa.com

HOPPE'S®
800-423-3537
www.hoppes.com

HORNADY®
800-338-3200
www.hornady.com

KLEENBORE®
800-477-7922
www.kleenbore.com

LYMAN®
800-225-9626
www.lymanproducts.com

OTIS™
800-684-7486
www.otistec.com

OUTERS
800-285-0689
www.outers-guncare.com

PROM M-PRO
800-423-3537
www.m-pro7.com

PRO SHOT
217-824-9133
www.proshotproducts.com

REMINGTON
844-736-2767
www.remington.com

SHOOTER'S CHOICE®
800-674-7847
www.shooter-choice.com

TIPTON
833-784-5521
www.tiptonclean.com

Appendix H

Rifles, Ammo, and Optics for 2025

When I completed writing this book in December 2024, it was before the 2025 Shooting, Hunting, Outdoor Trade Show (SHOT Show). SHOT Show is the largest firearms-focused trade show in the world, with the most recent event attracting over 54,000 attendees, as documented by multiple reliable sources. Held annually in Las Vegas, SHOT Show features countless firearms, ammunition, and optics companies, along with thousands of other exhibitors showcasing a variety of hunting and outdoor products.

I decided to include some of the most well-rated firearms, ammunition, and optics that I saw at the show in this appendix. Due to space limitations, I can only provide abbreviated product descriptions. However, I have also included website addresses for readers who want more details. To maintain impartiality, companies are listed alphabetically.

BIG GAME AMMO FOR 2025

FEDERAL

Federal Ammunition announced several new centerfire rifle options at SHOT Show. In addition to launching its all-new 7mm Backcountry hunting cartridge, Federal has expanded its Barnes LRX, Gold Medal Berger, and Terminal Ascent product lines. Terminal Ascent will now be available in 7mm Backcountry, 6.5 PRC, .300 RUM, and .300 Win. Mag. The bonded bullet construction of the Terminal Ascent ensures deep penetration at close range, while the patented Slipstream polymer tip initiates controlled expansion at extremely long distances.

Federal's all-new long-action 7mm Backcountry cartridge redefines what a non-magnum centerfire hunting load can accomplish. Utilizing a patented Peak Alloy one-piece, high-strength case, the 7mm BC achieves magnum-level performance while fitting a standard bolt-face rifle. With a 170-grain bullet reaching 3,000 feet per second from a 20-inch barrel, the 7mm BC delivers superior ballistics. The secret lies in its Peak Alloy steel cases, which safely handle higher pressures and outperform traditional brass ammunition. Find more details at www.federalpremium.com.

NOSLER

For 2025, Nosler brought back its famous Solid Base bullet for the Whitetail Country ammunition line. This cup-and-core boattail spitzer bullet has a bit of exposed lead at the tip and is designed for reliable expansion. Nosler offers Whitetail Country ammo in 6.5 Creedmoor (140 grains), .270 Winchester (130 grains), 7mm-08 Remington (140 grains), .30–30 Winchester (150 grains), .308 Winchester (165 grains), and .30–06 Springfield (165 grains).

In addition, Nosler has expanded its Straight-Wall line with two new cartridges: .350 Legend (180 grains) and .45–70 Government (300 grains). These flat-base semi-spitzer bullets feature a skived jacket for optimized performance in lower-velocity cartridges. For those hunting whitetails, mule deer, or similar-sized game at moderate ranges, the Solid Base bullets are more than capable of filling a freezer and putting a trophy on the wall. Whitetail Country ammo is priced at $34.95 for a box of 20, while .45–70 Government loads cost $39.95 per box. Learn more at www.nosler.com.

REMINGTON

For 2025, Remington has expanded its Core-Lokt line with the introduction of the "Core-Lokt Tipped Lever

Gun" and new calibers, including .400 Legend and .300 Hammer. The Core-Lokt Tipped bullet offers a more aerodynamic profile while remaining safe for use in tubular magazines. It is also available in .360 Buckhammer, .444 Marlin, and .45–70.

Additionally, Remington has added its own magnum cartridge to the lineup: the .300 Remington Ultra Magnum (300 RUM), now available with Core-Lokt Tipped bullets. With impressive velocity and grain weight, this round delivers top-tier performance on big game animals across North America. Learn more at www.remington.com.

WEATHERBY

Weatherby now offers premium ammunition in popular non-Weatherby cartridges, including .280 Ackley Improved, 28 Nosler, 6.5 PRC, and .300 PRC. The company has also introduced 7mm PRC ammo featuring 177-grain Hammer custom bullets. These bullets, turned on a CNC lathe, undergo meticulous quality control for precise weight and diameter consistency. Their high ballistic coefficient and aerodynamic design deliver outstanding long-range performance. Learn more at www.weatherby.com.

2025 RIFLES

BROWNING

Browning has continued to refine its X-Bolt 2 Western Hunter LR for 2025, incorporating key upgrades to enhance fit, recoil management, and overall performance for long-range shooters. One of the most significant improvements is the adjustable comb stock, allowing shooters to fine-tune their cheek weld for better alignment with optics. This translates to greater comfort and consistency when taking long-range shots. The new Recoil Hawg muzzle brake significantly reduces felt recoil compared to the original, making follow-up shots faster and more controlled. Browning also redesigned the bolt handle for a more ergonomic feel and easier manipulation. While both models retain the rugged reliability and Burnt Bronze Cerakote finish for weather resistance, the X-Bolt 2 now delivers an even more shooter-friendly experience. It is available in eight different calibers and two barrel lengths—24" and 26". Suggested MSRP: $1,470–$1,550. Learn more at www.browning.com.

CVA SCOUT

The CVA Scout is a no-nonsense, single-shot rifle built for hunters who value simplicity, accuracy, and reliability in the field. Available in a range of hard-hitting calibers, it features a stainless-steel barrel for durability in harsh conditions, while the lightweight synthetic stock makes it easy to carry on long hunts. The DuraSight scope rail allows for quick optic mounting, and the crisp single-shot action keeps things straightforward and dependable.

For hunters in states with caliber restrictions, the Scout is available in straight-wall cartridges like .350 Legend and .450 Bushmaster, offering legal and effective options for whitetail hunting. These calibers provide excellent stopping power while meeting state regulations, making the Scout an ideal choice for compliance without sacrificing performance. Available in 13 configurations for both straight-wall and bottleneck shooters, this rifle is perfect for those who appreciate the challenge of single-shot hunting. **Suggested MSRP:** $425–$495. Learn more at www.cvariflesusa.com.

STURM RUGER

Since its debut in 2015, the Ruger Precision Rifle has been a favorite in Precision Rifle Series and National Rifle League competitions. For 2025, Ruger has refreshed its lineup with an upgraded rear stock and the addition of popular competition calibers like 6mm Creedmoor. The Ruger Custom Shop variant now includes a barricade stop on the front of the magazine well, along with a gray Cerakote finish applied to the handguard and stock body. Suggested MSRP: $2,799. Learn more at www.ruger.com.

SMITH & WESSON

This year, Smith & Wesson introduced the Model 1854 Stealth Hunter, available in .44 Rem Mag, .45 Colt, and .357 Mag. Built on the Model 1854 platform, these lever-action rifles feature a flat trigger, large loop lever, removable magazine tube, and a fixed synthetic stock in black with textured grip panels. Additionally, a 10½-inch Picatinny rail allows for easy optic mounting, while the aluminum fore-end with 15 M-LOK-compatible slots enhances versatility. Lever-action rifles continue to surge in popularity among big game hunters, and the Stealth Hunter is a standout in this category. Suggested MSRP: $1,399. Learn more at www.smith-wesson.com.

2025 RIFLESCOPES

BUSHNELL MATCH PRO ED

The Bushnell Match Pro 6–24x50mm Riflescope delivers professional-level features at an entry-level price. Equipped with easy base-10 turrets for fast rev counting, this optic boosts shooter confidence. These turrets provide tactile and audible clicks and can be reset in seconds without tools. The 30mm main tube allows for 18 MIL of elevation adjustment for accurate shots out to 1,000 yards, while a 10-yard parallax adjustment ensures precise close-range targeting.

One of the Match Pro's standout features is the Deploy Reticle, which includes a precise, free-floating center dot and a lower pyramid structure of hash marks to accommodate bullet drop and wind drift at extended ranges. The precision-ground glass lenses with ultra-wide-band multicoatings reduce glare while enhancing light transmission. Additionally, the EXO Barrier protects against rain, mud, dust, and debris. This scope features 18 MIL of internal travel and 15 MIL of reticle holdover, making it an excellent choice for long-range shooting. **Suggested MSRP:** $449.99-$500.00. Learn more at www.bushnell.com.

LEUPOLD VX-6HD GEN 2

Leupold's VX-6HD riflescope utilizes the Twilight Max Light Management System to provide bright, high-definition images at dawn and dusk. Featuring a 6:1 zoom ratio and a fast-focus eyepiece, this scope allows for quick transitions from a wide field of view to pinpoint precision. The generous eye box ensures a full, clear sight picture effortlessly.

With the Custom Dial System Zero Lock 2 elevation dial, hunters can easily dial up two turns of elevation. On the second revolution, the button sinks in to indicate the adjustment level. The CDS-ZL2 elevation dial locks into place, preventing accidental shifts. Additionally, a free Custom Ballistic Dial is included with each purchase. The Guard-Ion lens coating repels rain, dirt, and fingerprints, while the 30mm aircraft-grade aluminum main tube is both waterproof and fog-proof. **Suggested MSRP:** $1,899.99–$1,999.99. Learn more at www.leupold.com.

SWAROVSKI Z5I+ SERIES

The Z5i+ 5–25x56 P BT riflescope is built for hunters demanding outstanding image quality at high magnifications, exceptional long-range visibility, and top-tier precision. Its 30mm main tube provides greater adjustment range, while the 56mm objective lens enhances light transmission. The newly designed Ballistic Turret and versatile reticle options make this scope an ideal choice for long-range precision shooting. Suggested MSRP: $2,269.00. Learn more at www.swarovskioptik.com.

TRACT OPTICS TORIC 34MM FFP

Because long-range shooting has become all the rage, TRACT Optic has introduced the TORIC 34mm FFP 4.5–30X56 MOA ELR. Featuring an advanced MOA ELR "Christmas Tree" style reticle and matching adjustments, this optic ensures precision at vast distances. The Ultra High Definition (UHD) optical system, utilizing SCHOTT HT glass and ED lenses, delivers exceptional clarity and light transmission.

A large eye box and quick-focus eyepiece provide 3.6–3.8 inches of eye relief, while the illuminated reticle offers 11 intensity settings for enhanced low-light performance. TRACT Optics sells directly to consumers. **Suggested MSRP:** $1,494. Learn more at www.tractoptic.com.

VORTEX VIPER HD 3–15X44

Rated as the best riflescope at SHOT, the Vortex Viper HD 3–15x44 combines rugged construction with outstanding optics. Featuring illuminated reticles with 10 settings, it can also be used without illumination. Capped turrets prevent accidental movement of the Dead-Hold BDC reticles, while fully multicoated lenses provide edge-to-edge clarity and distortion-free sharpness.

ArmorTek and argon gas purging ensure fog-proof, waterproof integrity. The scope includes a CR2032 battery, a neoprene cover, a sunshade, and a lens cloth. **Suggested MSRP:** $699.99. Learn more at www.vortexoptics.com.

Appendix I

Sixteen Dangerous Game Hunts That Could Kill You!

THE FACTS

The number of dangerous game hunters who are attacked while pursuing hazardous game is not officially tracked. However, anecdotal evidence suggests that hunting perilous game can be extremely dangerous. Historical references provide countless numbers of cases of hunters killed by big game throughout the nineteenth, twentieth, and twenty-first centuries.

When a hunter pursues life-threatening game animals, it is wise to keep this in mind; while you are a hunter, to a dangerous game animal you may be looked at as an all-you-can-eat buffet! The cold hard fact is humans are not *always* at the top of the food chain. Most hunters rarely come face-to-face in a life-and-death showdown with predators; however, that's not always the case. That in itself requires a hunter to know that there are numerous wild game animals that see hunters as prey—not predators. Here are 16 surprisingly deadly game animals of the world that hunters should pursue with extreme caution.

Last Word. When stalking perilous game, hunters should be meticulously thoughtful of the types of rifle calibers, cartridges, and even the type of terrain that will come into play. With that said, though, when a dangerous game hunt is bungled, even slightly, all the planning, skill, knowledge, and courage a hunter has amassed counts for exactly nothing!

1. **Alligator:** The southern alligator is smaller than a crocodile, but it too will devour a hunter without a shred of sympathy. Since gators are shot at relatively close ranges, a good choice is a .257 Magnum, which can be used for hunting them at reasonably close ranges. Other choices include a .22 LR, or a .22 WMR, which delivers better velocity and energy.
2. **Bison:** The iconic American bison is the largest North American land mammal. It is one tough animal to put down. A .338 Winchester Magnum offers substantial energy and penetration, particularly when using heavy bullets like 250-grain Barnes TSX or Swift A-Frame. Both are well suited to knock bison down for keeps.
3. **Black bear:** A North American black bear sow with cubs, or an old bear pose the most danger to hunters (Asian black bears are notorious for their volatile temperament). Good caliber choices include the .308 with 150, 168, or 175 grains bullets. Other good calibers include the .30-06 Springfield, .300 H&H Magnum, .300 Win Mag, 7mm-08 Remington, and the .338 Federal.
4. **Brown bear:** This bear poses a significant threat to hunters. Use extreme caution when hunting these temperamental bears. A .375 H&H Magnum is a classic brown bear cartridge. Calibers in the .30-06, .338, and .375 families are considered the bare minimum. Better choices are a .416 Remington Mag and .450 Marlin. Prioritize bullet weight and construction when hunting large bears.
5. **Cape buffalo:** As Robert Ruark so aptly stated, "the buff is so big and mean, and ugly, and hard to stop, and vindictive, and cruel, and surly and onery. He looks like you owe him money. He looks like he is hunting you." The top caliber choices include the venerable .375 H&H Magnum or a .416 Rigby or Reminton. In fact, any .400 bore or larger is considered suitable.

6. **Cougar:** Like the polar bear, mountain lions can view a hunter as a potential meal. Spot and stalk hunts are the most dangerous way to hunt puma. Cougars are considered thin-skinned game. Hence, they can be hunted with several types of calibers including the .30-30 Winchester, 6.5 Creedmoor, .270 Winchester, .280 Remington, and even up to a .300 Win Mag.
7. **Crocodile:** This semiaquatic reptile belongs to the family of Crocodylidae. They are known for their surprise attacks. A croc will eat a hunter without giving a second thought to it. It is highly recommended to use powerful calibers that deliver good penetration to hunt these large reptiles. A top choice is the .375 H&H Magnum; other good choices are .30-06 and .308.
8. **Elephant:** A bull elephant is the definition of dangerous game. Use calibers like the .416 Rigby, .458 Winchester Magnum, or .458 Lott for their increased all-important stopping power and heavier bullets. The old adage about calibers to hunt elephants is the bigger the better, as long as the hunter can tolerate the recoil and still shoot accurately. You don't want to wound a charging elephant.
9. **Grizzly bear:** This bear has instilled terror in the hearts of countless big game hunters. The .375 H&H Magnum is a top choice. Other calibers that could be used are the .30-06 Springfield, .300 Winchester Magnum, or a .338 Magnum.
10. **Hippopotamus:** No one should take hunting this animal lightly. It is quick in water and on land. Hippos are hell-bent on killing anything that enters its territory or even disturbs it. A minimum caliber is the .375 H&H Magnum. Better caliber choices that are more powerful and effective, especially at close range on land, include the .416 Rigby or .500 Nitro Express.
11. **Hyena:** Hyenas are most dangerous when hunted at dusk. They are formidable carnivores that can attack a human with chilling efficiency. When hunting hyena, a 7mm caliber is considered a minimum choice. Instead use heavier options like .308 or .30-06, which will be more effective.
12. **Leopard:** A leopard ranks among the most lethal of all the wildcats in Africa. In Asia, leopards are particularly known to stalk, kill, and devour humans, including hunters. The most recommended caliber to hunt these cats is a .375 H&H Magnum due to its robust stopping power and its ability to deliver a critical shot even at longer ranges. Other calibers include the .300 Magnum or .338.
13. **Lion:** Death by lion would be terrible. The savvy hunter will be well armed with a .375 H&H Magnum and be quick on the trigger. However, professional hunters and experienced big game lion hunters recommend calibers like .416 or .458, which deliver dependable stopping power.
14. **Polar bear:** This fearsome bear will intentionally stalk humans as a food item, so caution is paramount when hunting them. I will cut to the chase here. Use calibers that deliver powerful stopping power and excellent penetration. Choices include a .375 H&H Magnum, .300 Magnum, .338 Magnum, or a .44 Remington Magnum. Take no chances when hunting this bear.
15. **Wild boar:** Both sows and boars can be extremely aggressive and unpredictable. Feral hogs weigh 300 pounds or more and can charge at speeds of 30 mph. Their razor-sharp tusks can sever arteries in the blink of an eye. The giant forest hog is the most feared. Caliber choices with stopping power include the .308 Winchester, .30-06 Springfield, .300 Savage, .444 Marlin, and the .45-70.
16. **Yukon/Alaskan moose:** Veteran moose guides say they fear an enraged bull moose, because it is said to be more furious than a grizzly bear's ferocity! That alone should be warning enough not to take a charging bull moose lightly. Popular choices are the .308 Winchester, .300 Winchester Magnum, and 7mm Reminton Magnum. The .300 PRC (Precision Rifle Cartridge) offers flat shooting and energy.

Acknowledgments

Since embarking on my journey as a full-time outdoor communicator in 1984, I've been incredibly fortunate to encounter countless individuals in the industry whose generosity knows no bounds. Their unwavering support has been a cornerstone of my work, for which I am immensely grateful. Throughout the process of writing this tome, I've leaned on these remarkable individuals for everything from photo support and press releases to invaluable insights, quotes, and expertise. While I've expressed my gratitude to each of them personally, it's essential to acknowledge their contributions here as well. The acknowledgments section holds a special place in my mind, representing the culmination of countless hours of collaboration and support. So, from the depths of my heart, I extend my sincerest appreciation to all who have lent their generosity and expertise.

Abigail Gehring, associate publisher and editorial director, Skyhorse Publishing, Inc.
Allison Hall, Traditions® Firearms
Ashley Gall, Laura Burgess Marketing / Big Horn Armory
Beth Shimanski, director of marketing, Savage Arms Inc.
Caroline Russomanno, editor extraordinaire, Skyhorse Publishing, Inc.
Craig Boddington, book author, TV host, noted outdoor writer
Dabney Gray PhD, A long-overdue thank-you for the special Foreword written in *Rx For Deer Hunting Success*. It was genuinely appreciated.
Dr. George Dvorchak, book author, outdoor writer
Federal® Premium Ammunition Company
Heather Pleskach, Otis™ Products, Inc.
Hornaday
Irina Obrzhutovich, marketing, Pelican Products, Inc.
Jake Wallace, marketing brand and content coordinator, Winchester® Ammunition
Jason M. Gilbertson, director of marketing and licensing, Winchester Ammunition
Jay H. Cassell, emeritus editorial director, Skyhorse Publishing, Inc.
JJ Reich, senior media relations manager, Federal, HEVI-Shot, CCI and Speer Ammunition
Jon Allen, cofounder, TRACT Optics
Jon LaCorte, cofounder, TRACT Optics
Michael Schoby, noted book author, firearm authority, and magazine writer
Peter Cody Fiduccia PhD, pcfimages.
Plano
Randy Lehmann, marketing director, Brownell's, Inc.
Ron Spomer, noted book author/outdoor writer, ronspomeroutdoors.com
The Nerd Gang, Dr. Peter C. Fiduccia, Eric Schultz, Alex Brozdowski, Dr. Victor L. Schultz, Dr. Andrew M. Melchionna, William Schultz, Devin T. Martin, Daniel Valliere and Jay Cassell
Tony Lyons, president and publisher, Skyhorse Publishing , @tonylyonsisuncertain
Wayne Van Zwoll PhD

Notes

1 Mark Chesnut, "A Lever Action .30-30 Winchester Is Still One of the Best Deer Hunting Rifles (and Here's Why)," *Outdoor Life*, November 15, 2022, https://www.outdoorlife.com/lever-action-30-30-winchester-is-still-one-best-deer-hunting-rifles-and-heres-why/, Last accessed May 1, 2025.

2 Ron Spomer, "9 Tips for Becoming a Better Rifle Shot on Wild Game," *Outdoor Life*, September 3, 2020, https://www.outdoorlife.com/story/hunting/tips-for-becoming-a-better-rifle-shot-on-wild-game/, Last accessed May 1, 2025.

3 Jim Carmichel, "The Day I Shot the .700 Express," *Sporting Classics Daily*, May 13, 2016, https://sportingclassicsdaily.com/shooting-the-700-express/, Last accessed May 1, 2025.

4 Craig Boddington, *Shots at Big Game: How to Shoot a Rifle Accurately Under Hunting Conditions* (Stackpole Books, 1989).

5 Boone and Crockett Club, "B&C Position Statement - Long Range Shooting," First Adopted May 10, 2014 and Revised and Updated October 15, 2021, https://www.boone-crockett.org/bc-position-statement-long-range-shooting, Last accessed May 1, 2025.

6 Ben Greenfield, "The Science of Buck Fever (& 5 Ways to Get Rid of Target Panic Once & For All)," *Journal of Mountain Hunting*, https://journalofmountainhunting.com/the-science-of-buck-fever-5-ways-get-rid-of-target-panic-once-for-all-by-ben-greenfield/, Last accessed May 1, 2025.

7 Steven D. Verba, Brock T. Jensen, and Jeffrey S. Lynn, "Electrocardiographic Responses to Deer Hunting in Men and Women," *Wilderness and Environmental Medicine* 27, no. 3 (2016): https://journals.sagepub.com/doi/10.1016/j.wem.2016.03.005.

8 "A-hunting we will go – just be mindful of heart health risks," American Heart Association, November 25, 2024, https://newsroom.heart.org/news/a-hunting-we-will-go-just-be-mindful-of-heart-health-risks, Last accessed May 1, 2025.

9 Texas A&M University, "What is buck fever?" *ScienceDaily,* November 17, 2016, www.sciencedaily.com/releases/2016/11/161117115333.htm, Last accessed May 1, 2025.

10 Wayne Van Zwoll, *Deer Rifles and Cartridges* (Woods N Water Inc, 2006).

11 Wayne Van Zwoll, *Hunter's Guide to Long-Range Shooting* (Stackpole Books, August 15, 2006).

12 Michael Schoby, *The Hunter's Guide to Whitetail Rifles* (Stackpole Books, Jan. 31, 2007).

13 Boddington, *Shots at Big Game.*

14 John Barsness, *Optics for the Hunter* (Safari Press, November 8, 1999).

15 https://www.ronspomeroutdoors.com/.

16 www.chuckhawks.com.

17 PJ DelHomme, "How to Clean a Hunting Rifle: A Step-by-Step Guide," *Crazy Canyon Journal*, https://www.crazycanyonjournal.com/how-to-clean-a-hunting-rifle/, Last accessed May 1, 2025.

18 Tyler Freel, "Does Muzzle Tape Actually Affect Rifle Accuracy?" *Outdoor Life*, April 19, 2022, https://www.outdoorlife.com/guns/does-muzzle-tape-actually-affect-rifle-accuracy/, Last accessed May 1, 2025.

19 Tyler Freel, "How to Get Your Hunting Rifle Ready for Opening Day," *Outdoor Life*, June 26, 2022, https://www.outdoorlife.com/guns/how-to-get-your-hunting-rifle-ready/, Last accessed May 1, 2025.

20 Transportation Security Administration, "Transporting Firearms and Ammunition," accessed March 25, 2025, https://www.tsa.gov/travel/transporting-firearms-and-ammunition.

Other Bestselling Skyhorse Books by Peter J. Fiduccia

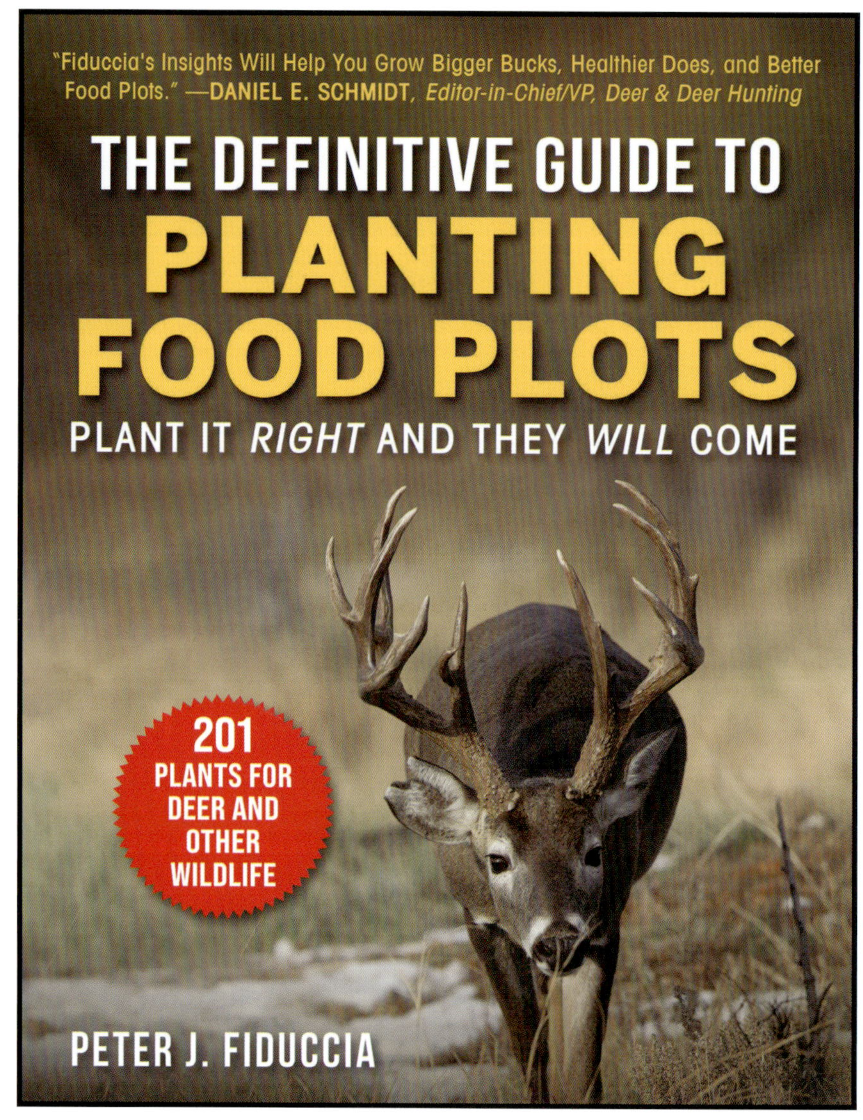

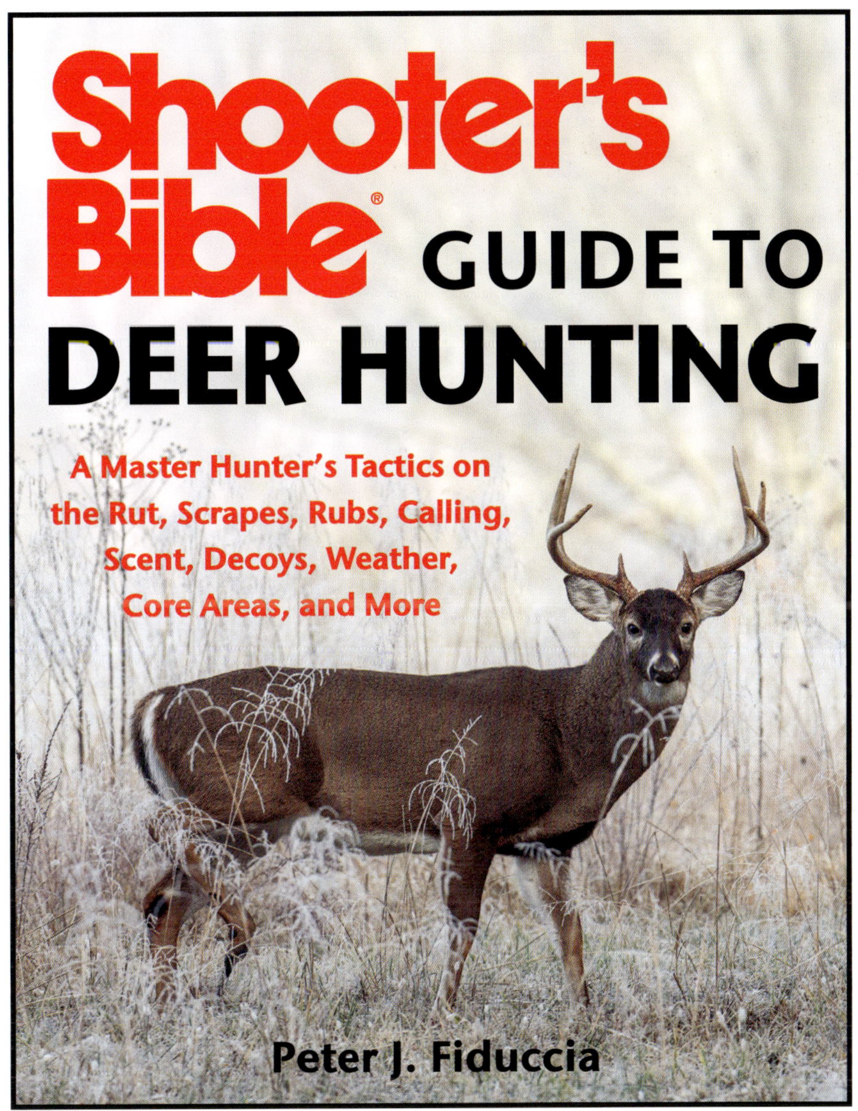
Shooter's Bible® GUIDE TO DEER HUNTING
A Master Hunter's Tactics on the Rut, Scrapes, Rubs, Calling, Scent, Decoys, Weather, Core Areas, and More
Peter J. Fiduccia

Rx for Deer
Hunting Success
Time-Tested Tactics from the Deer Doctor
PETER J.
FIDUCCIA

WHITETAIL
TACTICS
WINNER
EXCELLENCE IN
CRAFT AWARD
New York State
Outdoor Writer's
Association
Cutting-Edge Strategies That Work
PETER FIDUCCIA